The Wine Brats' Guide to
Living, with Wine

The
Wine Brats'
Guide to Living,
with Wine

Jeff Bundschu, Jon Sebastiani,

Mike Sangiacomo, and

the Wine Brats Coalition

St. Martin's Griffin ❧ New York

Book design by Leah Carlson-Stanisic

Library of Congress Cataloging-in-Publication Data

The wine brats' guide to living, with wine / Jeff Bundschu . . . [et
    al.]. — 1st ed.
        p.   cm.
    ISBN 0-312-20443-4
    1. Wine and wine making.   I. Bundschu, Jeff.   II. Title: Guide to
living, with wine.
TP548.W755   1999
641.2'2—dc21   99-24100
                                                              CIP

First St. Martin's Griffin Edition: June 1999

10   9   8   7   6   5   4   3   2   1

Contents

Part II: It's Party Time!

Acknowledgments

S pecial thanks goes out to all who made this bound collaboration possible. And because *Wine Brats* is far more than just a book, our organization's founders, Jon Sebastiani, Jeff Bundschu, and Mike Sangiacomo, found the list of acknowledgments to be wonderfully long. So here's their best shot at an orderly approach to delivering the kudos:

First, to our families and the vines that feed us.

To our special-projects book crew, Joel Quigley (Wine Brats), Darryl Roberts (*Wine X* magazine), Stewart Dorman (Adrian Fog Winery), and especially project manager Sarah Donnelly (Windsor Vineyards) for juggling the books *and* the writers. And to our agent, Dan Mandel, and editor, Joe Veltre, for putting up with our eccentricities.

To our fellow board members and staff Mimi Gatens, Dawn Dooley, Cailyn Quigley, Joe Naujokas, and Lisa Mancin for their support and contributions.

To our sustaining partners, Gallo of Sonoma, Lindemans/Penfolds, Sutter Home, Beringer Wine Estates, California Wine Institute, Korbel Champagne Cellars, and Kenwood Vineyards for their belief in us when others thought we were crazy.

To our regional chapter leaders, officers, and members for their hard work and commitment to the cause. We raise a glass to all of you.

And, of course, to the Wine Brats Coalition for their contributions and vision in bringing a collective new voice to wine. So just like in the movies, here they are in order of appearance: Kim Caffrey, Lora White, Brendan Eliason, Leslie Sbrocco, Tim Hanni, Tina Caputo, Bob Blumer (a.k.a. the Surreal Gourmet), Darryl Roberts, S. Duda, Joe Naujokas, Rosina Tinari Wilson, Gina Gallo, Stewart Dorman, Sophia Schweitzer, Steven Van

Yoder, Jeff Moriarty, and Amy Reiley. And because we can't thank them enough, we give yet another round of kudos to Darryl Roberts, Kim Caffrey, and Tina Caputo for the late hours and for meeting every screaming deadline. Though it be digital, E-mail has breathed new life into the written word. Cheers!

Foreword

by Joel Quigley

In just a few short years, the Wine Brats have blasted onto the national wine scene, chanting our mantra, "Wine for the People!" In our call for an end to institutional elitism, we have built a national network of members among both consumers and industry leaders, who are working to break down the cultural barriers that have surrounded wine for far too long. This book is a compilation of these ideals, expressed through the voices of our founders and cohorts, all representing a new generation in wine. Please join with us in our mission to bring the simple pleasure of wine back to the table, so that we may all sip the juice and break bread with our family, friends, and lovers in our celebration of life. Cheers!

Introduction

The Truth About the Juice, Its People, and Those Who Drink It

First of all, thanks for taking the time to crack the cover on this book. Secondly, we have a pretty good idea of what might have come to mind when you first saw the title *Wine Brats* burned across the top of said cover. How about, "Who are these guys and what's a Wine Brat?" If not, and we're lucky, you're already a member and know everything there is to know about the organization. However, if the previous scenario fits, the following history should enlighten and entertain as we explain the who, what, why, how, and when of our group and its philosophy. Now you ask, "Enlighten? Entertain?" Well, that's our goal, anyway.

To formally introduce ourselves, we are Jeff Bundschu, Jon Sebastiani, and Mike Sangiacomo, founders of the Wine Brats, a national educational organization. Our mission is to introduce a new generation (ours) to the wonders of life with wine. We simply want to share our passion for wine with our peers, though without the pretentious attitude so often perpetuated by the so-called "wine experts." In short, we want people to have fun while they learn and explore. The three of us grew up in Sonoma, California, where our families grow grapes and make wine. Among us, we represent Gundlach-Bundschu Winery (Jeff), Sangiacomo Vineyards (Mike), and Viansa Winery (Jon). Because of our family backgrounds, wine was always a part of everyday life. While growing up, wine was as much of a staple on our dinner tables as milk. When we jumped nest, however, and went away to our respective colleges, we found that our peers were totally unfamiliar with wine. We quickly discovered that drinking wine at college, instead of beer or tequila, meant you were some kind of elitist. Since we were all headed for careers in our respective family businesses, this was pretty disturbing to us.

When the three of us graduated and returned to Sonoma, we realized that we'd all had the same experiences with wine (or the lack of it) at college — and the same frustrations. Each time the three of us crossed paths in town or at an industry function, we ended up commiserating about wine's image problem. Inevitably, a camaraderie and philosophy developed among us, and we decided that we could do something about that image problem.

Not long after we began speaking up publicly as a team, a local newspaper reporter called us to set up an interview. We didn't even have a group name at that point but felt we had to come up with something for the article. So, literally two hours before the interview, we headed for Murphy's Irish Pub, the main spot where we did all of our thinking. There, over beers, we decided to go with the name our parents and some other people around town jokingly called us: the Wine Brats.

After the article came out, we suddenly had credibility, and expectation started to build. We then pulled off our first real educational publicity stunt at Restaurant Eleven in San Francisco's hip SOMA District. There, we lightheartedly accosted younger adult diners who didn't order wine at their dinner tables. Challenging them to taste their food, then sip their beverage of choice, a beer or cocktail, we then had them take another bite and taste an appropriate wine from our arsenal. The purpose? To demonstrate that wine is the best beverage on the planet at mealtime.

The press was on hand that evening to capture the feat, and the Wine Brat buzz really began to accelerate. People started tracking us down at work, by phone, and through letters, offering their support for our mission. It became time for us to sit down and ask ourselves if forming the Wine Brats on a larger scale was something we were really ready to do, and we decided that it was. How could we pass up the opportunity to educate people, have fun, and promote wine all at the same time?

Our next big step was sending out a fax to every winery in Sonoma and Napa to explain our mission and invite them to a meeting-of-the-minds mixer. We were absolutely stunned when eighty people showed up for this first gathering at Gaffney's Wine Bar in Santa Rosa, California. From that original meeting, the Wine Brats has grown into an organization with chapters around the country, while taking on a life of its own. Every year since has seen new developments and achievements. In 1998 we celebrated our five-year anniversary as Wine Brats. No one, including our parents, friends, and ourselves, ever thought we would get to this point.

Wine's Hoity-Toity Image: A History

Now that you know what we're all about, you may be wondering how wine's image got so overblown that an organization like the Wine Brats was necessary. Time for a little history on wine in America, especially that of California.

As recently as thirty years ago, the image of domestic wine could be summed up in two words: jug wines. Back then, the California wine industry was made up mainly of the children of European immigrants, who produced simple wines for the masses and viewed wine as a basic element of life. Then some mavericks during the sixties and seventies got *into* winemaking and began to reach beyond the Hearty Burgundy bulk-style, paying more attention to quality. And their wines really started getting good.

The big turning point for the industry came in 1976, when a California wine scored higher than those of the French at a now-famous comparative blind tasting in Paris. This was a momentous event because, all of a sudden, the world understood that California wines could be compared to the best in the world. An elite group of wine connoisseurs in the United States took notice, and immediately there was a market for premium wines from California.

When this happened, the wineries stopped focusing on the old Italian guys who drove up to the winery every week to have their gallon jugs filled, and went after the people who cared about what kind of soil the grapes were grown in and the "higher" cultural values associated with wine. In order to sell wine to the connoisseurs, the winery reps started talking about grape clones, fermentation, and all the technical aspects of wine that meant nothing to their old customers.

The same thing happened with people in the retail and restaurant businesses. As they learned more about wine, many began to view their wine knowledge as something that gave them a value and differentiated them from their competitors. Because the wine industry was now targeting these people, they learned to speak in very technical terms in order to compete and sell their product.

Needless to say, the language of wine completely changed in America, and nothing was done on the entry and middle levels to make wine accessible. In other words, when the audience base changed, a lot of people were left behind. There was no place for them to go learn about wine in a friendly way. So, in effect, wine became a victim of its own success. Promoting the simple, visceral joys of wine had been left behind in the intellectual dust of endless evaluation and self-importance.

However ironic, the Wine Brats' mission to deconstruct, or tear down, the walls that our forebears diligently built (no wonder they called us "brats") is by no means a form of disrespect. Every generation has its mission, and today's leaders have done an incredible job building quality and value into a great product, while also dealing with such important issues as health and the environment. They put their hearts and souls into educating the world that the flavors, microclimates, barrel aging, and fermentation that went into making California wine elevated it to world-class stature. The Wine Brats, by taking more of a reactive position than a radical one, seek to bring the enjoyment and education of wine back into balance.

So how does this uniquely American perspective on wine manifest itself through our generation? As illustrated above, we've grown up with the fact that world-class wines are not only produced in Europe but also in California and elsewhere, such as Oregon, Washington, Australia, South America, and so on. However, we also grew up with television and mass media, where the portrayal of wine has virtually always been as a *Lifestyles of the Rich and Famous* product. Thanks, Robin Leach. Now the industry is faced with a generation that may peripherally see wine as a quality product with great diversity, yet concurrently perceive it as an overwhelming, elitist beverage that requires a pedigree and diploma just to understand and enjoy.

TOP TEN PREDICTIONS FOR THE FUTURE OF WINE

10. *Wine advertisements during the Super Bowl (oops, already happened).*

9. *Screw caps will make a comeback—even on wines you'd actually want to drink!*

8. Genetically altered hybrid grapevines will be able to grow Cabernet, Chardonnay, and Riesling grapes all on the same plant.

7. Prohibition-era shipping laws will finally be updated, making it possible to send a bottle of California red to your Aunt Tillie in New York without fear of being thrown into the big house.

6. Decent wine will be available in bars.

5. Restaurants will only charge $30 for a $20 bottle of wine, rather than $60.

4. Wine marketers in the United States will realize that it's okay to translate French wine varietals into English, i.e., Sauvignon Blanc = Savage White.

3. Beer drinkers will finally realize there's no such thing as a wine gut, and switch!

2. Future astronauts will demand hydroponic vineyards on Mars!

1. Wine-flavored Powerbars!

—*Tina Caputo*

Wine Education, Brat-Style

Until recently, anyone who was looking for an entry-level way to learn about wine was pretty much out of luck. If you don't believe us, just pick up any issue of the top wine magazines and see how much of it you understand. The challenge with mainstream wine magazines is that they assume their readers are experts, which doesn't help those who are trying to learn. Reading these magazines first requires learning a whole new language. Again, television hasn't been much help. Most "wine shows" are complete snoozers with the same language and elitist barriers.

That's why we're reaching out to our peers to provide learning resources on a national and regional basis. Through special events and projects (like this book), the Internet, and our regional chapters, we hope to create more venues and outlets for novices, and those more experienced, to come together to enjoy and learn about wine. Peer-to-peer education, if you will. And unlike traditional wine tastings, our events integrate wine into venues and subjects where people of our generation are already comfortable. When was the last time you were able to have a glass of wine and see an alternative band at the same time? Or check out an exhibition of new-media art created by your peers while sipping a glass of Zinfandel? By bringing wine into the same arena as cutting-edge music, fashion, and art, we have a better opportunity of reaching those who haven't been given a chance to experience wine. Truth be told, this is where and how *we* prefer to drink our wine, anyway.

Knocking Wine Off Its Pedestal

To us, reaching the unconverted means knocking down those aforementioned barriers of elitism to make wine accessible to everyone, so that there is motivation through enjoyment to explore the history and language of wine. In places like France and Italy, people are exposed to wine their whole lives and it's no big deal. Many families in Italy make their own wine; grapes have more of a presence in their gardens than tomatoes have in ours. Our goal is to reverse the passé trend of placing "knowledge" in front of "pleasure" when sipping a glass of wine. Think of it this way, do you have to have a degree in filmmaking to know whether you enjoyed last night's movie on HBO? No!

The great thing about wine is that you can get into it at different levels. Wine is just as accessible and enjoyable for a complete novice as it is for the most knowledgeable connoisseur in the universe. It's a subjective thing, and that subjectivity allows anybody from any walk of life to judge whether or not a wine is good. Everyone's opinion is equally valid, whether you have four thousand three-by-five cards noting every wine you've tasted for the last ten years, like some people we know, or you're just cruising the wine aisle at the supermarket for something to drink with dinner.

As much as some wine "experts" out there would hate to admit, wine is a beverage just like beer. The important thing is to enjoy wine; once you do that, then we can talk about barrel fermentation and the differences between the various growing regions, which we offer within this book. The idea is to make it personal and fun, not a scientific dissertation that only a handful of humankind can decipher.

To reiterate, we *do not* want to break the walls down to the point where wine is synonymous with a Bud Lite. And sure, we want wine to be approachable and presented so that people can understand it, but we also want people to know the history behind the product and appreciate its heritage. Many of the wines out there have generations of blood, sweat, and tears behind them. That heritage makes wine a romantic beverage, and that's not something we want to lose. Believe it or not, it is possible to develop an appreciation for wine without treating it like a sacred elixir and boring the life out of your friends at dinner parties. We seek balance.

Living with Wine

One of the main motivations we had for doing this book is that we want to share the pleasure that wine brings to *our* lives. We can't imagine life without it, and not just in terms of our careers. What would mealtime be without wine? We don't want to know. Food is a pleasure in addition to a physical need, and wine makes the experience of a good meal even more enjoyable. Wine is like a spice in the way it adds another dimension to each meal. Each night it gives us something fun to think about, and each new bottle is like a surprise. Wine benefits us both mentally and spiritually. This is something we think a lot of people are missing.

So we've published this book not only for educational purposes, but to entice people to give wine a chance to enhance their daily lives. We'd love to see the day when wine evolves into a mainstream part of American life because it's a better life. That's what the Wine Brats are all about.

WHO ARE THE WINE BRATS?

The Wine Brats are an active group of adult wine enthusiasts who are mostly young in age but absolutely young at heart. We enjoy sharing our passion for wine with our peers and take pride in breaking down the cultural walls that for too long have mystified this beautiful beverage. Ultimately, the Wine Brats' purpose is to attract a whole new generation of adults to the wonders of life with wine.

Who Can Be a Wine Brat?
Anyone of legal drinking age who has an interest in learning more about wine is a welcome member of our organization. We do not discriminate against lack of previous wine experience. Anyone involved in the wine industry (wait staff, wine shop retailers, hoteliers, etc.) is encouraged to provide the leadership for each regional chapter. Your first step toward involvement would be to find the chapter closest to your neighborhood, then contact us. Currently, there are no membership fees.

Why "Wine Brats?" Why Not?
The Brats recognize the intimidation factor that wine can represent. The first-time or occasional buyer who wanders through the wine department of a store is faced with hundreds of brands, from a myriad of appellations and sub-appellations, with little or no explanation of what he or she is buying. Restaurant wine lists can be daunting as well, with harried waiters who may be less than hospitable toward the overwhelmed novice. As young representatives and enthusiasts of the wine industry, the Wine Brats are in a unique position to present wine to our peers in an accessible and unpretentious manner.

How Can I Contact the Wine Brats?
Call us toll-free, (877) 545-4699, or E-mail us at info@winebrats.org.
You can also check us out on the Web at http://www.winebrats.org.

The Players

If we haven't yet driven it home that this isn't going to be your usual wine book, just take a look at the list of names in the front of the book, of those we've recruited to help us in our mission. Recognize them? Probably not.

Rather than using the standard lineup of wine educators for the project, we're giving voice to a new generation of up-and-comers whom we've dubbed the "Wine Brats Coalition." We promise, they'll spare you the pretension by taking an entirely fresh approach to wine.

So there you have it, our little story. Now it's time to introduce the book itself. "Part I: Real People, Real Wine" will deal with the basics, like tasting versus drinking, shopping, ordering off the wine list, storage, and forgetting everything you know about pairing food and wine. "Part II: It's Party Time!" will help with tips on how to integrate wine into your life through dinner parties, blind tastings, party themes, wine cocktails, potluck strategies, and recipes. "Part III: Gettin' Dirty with the Winemakers" gets into the subject and lifestyle of winemaking, plus how to structure your own home winemaking club. Finally, "Part IV: The Eternal Search for Knowledge" wraps things up with reference guides dealing with wine regions, America's hot spots to sip wine, books and periodicals, finding wine on the Web, grape varietals, and, lastly, our glossary of wine terms and definitions.

Whew! We suggest you plop into your most comfortable reading chair, pour a glass of wine, and relax, because in the following pages we'll introduce each member of the Wine Brats Coalition and his or her given subject matter, plus any offhanded comments we felt inspired to make. In turn, the coalition members will not only offer up some of *their* true confessions about wine, but they will also take you through a chronological guide on learning to *live* with wine.

—j, j & m

Part I

Real People,
Real Wine

WINE, WOMEN, AND LAUGHS

*Kim Caffrey hails from Beringer Vineyards, where she handles tours
and education while generally stirring up trouble. We first met Kim in
a now-defunct bar, the Red Moon Saloon, on the square in our
hometown of Sonoma, California. This was back several years ago
when we were first organizing, when thirty to forty young upstarts in
the industry would gather for "planning meetings." Well, sure, we enjoyed our share of the vine at those meetings, but look what developed out of all those tasty bottles!*

*Anyway, we'll never forget the day back in '97 in San Francisco, as
we interviewed for public television's* Wine 101 *series, when Kim per-
formed her infamous "Taste Wine Like a Snob" bit for the cameras.
She brought down the house and ended up as the opening segment
for the three-part Cronkite/Ward series. In her following chapter,
"Tasting Versus Drinking" (which should jump-start your quest for
the juice), we begged her to include a sidebar on the subject just for
yucks (see page 5).*

—j, j & m

The Nose Knows, or Tasting Versus Drinking

by Kim Caffrey

I was new in town. One of my new friends had invited me to a party. High-class, uptown kinda party. The apartment was spacious and plush. The place was packed with people more beautiful and educated than me. Most were drinking wine. As my eyes circled each room nonchalantly, they came to rest on a table heavily laden with a variety of wines. I perused the labels, pretending to know something as I casually picked up a glass. I dared not look around to seek clues as to what to do. I filled my glass with something red, only two-thirds full, not wanting to appear gluttonous.

I took a small sip as I turned around and spotted a very debonair man eyeing me. He swirled his glass of wine, inhaled from it deeply, and drew a long, languorous sip, all so effortlessly that his eyes never left mine. I swirled my glass just enough to cause a minute stream of it to hit my skirt. I stuck my nose in to inhale slowly and instead snorted, causing myself to gag slightly, followed by a slight spurting of wine from my mouth and a brisk sweep of my hand to remove any wine from the end of my nose. When I regained consciousness and looked up, Mr. Suave was gone. I set down my glass, left the party, and mentally resigned from drinking wine, condemned forever to drink only suds. . . .

Has this ever happened to you? Funny thing is, I'm not the kind of person who is easily embarrassed (ask any of my friends, I am a stranger to shame), and I do recall being only slightly mortified, but some people would positively die if the same thing happened to them! The saddest part of this scenario is that it is so easily avoidable. Your mom and dad teach you how to ride a bike, swim, and make a wish when breaking a chicken's breastbone, but what the heck does that have to do with looking cool in social situations?

I, Wine Chick, am prepared to share my wine-tasting wisdom with you, lest you encounter a similar situation to the one above. Let me lay some ground rules before we get started, though.

Tasting Versus Drinking

One of the first subjects I plan to tackle here is the challenge of just getting the bottle open. Which means, once you do, you can basically drink the wine. Please, feel free to drink it as a cocktail, or with food of *any* kind, and in whatever vessel you deem appropriate. Kick back. You're just drinking it. I can't stress it enough: You don't have to evaluate every glass of wine you throw down the hatch! The only question you have to ask yourself is "Do I like it?" So there you have it. Drinking wine is simple. Pop the bottle. Pour the wine into a receptacle. Drink wine.

Of course, I could stop right here. But that wouldn't make much of a book, would it? So as long as you don't take me too seriously, let's talk *tasting* wine. Tasting wine can be a blast. In fact, later in the book we'll get into fun party themes and blind tastings, which can make the cocktail hour or even dinner into a playful game with friends. Now let's clarify: To *taste* is to experience wine or food in small amounts. Here, we hope to give you some inside tricks of the trade for tasting, not just drinking wine. But remember, at any time, I welcome your choice to break format and drink happily and freely from the glass in your hand. Also note, it is not necessary to extend your pinky finger during any of the following exercises.

TASTE LIKE A SNOB

While we try to simplify and demystify wine in this book, we also acknowledge that you may find yourself, from time to time, surrounded by severe wine snobs. Rather than bringing attention to yourself and risk being ridiculed, it's easier just to play along.

1. Pour a splash of wine in your glass and play along with me. . . . Hold the glass by the stem—hence the name "stemware." Holding it by the bowl points you out as a beer drinker. If you want to look extremely affected, find something you can lean against so that you may shift your

weight to one hip—and hold the glass by the base with your pinky extended.

2. Now begin swirling as you condescendingly look around the room. Swirl slowly, not frenetically. Hold the glass out at arm's length to observe its color. Bring the glass up to your nose for a deep whiff (be careful not to snort—that's painful), then look up . . . look pensive. . . .

3. Now take a long, languorous sip and chew, chew, chew your wine (like mouthwash), trill it if you will! (That backwards slurping kinda thing they do to draw aromas up to the olfactory nerve.)

4. After swallowing (or spitting!), if you liked the wine you're always safe with "Mmmm, it's very complex!" If you didn't like it, no Beavis and Butthead type comments like "Whoa, this *sucks!*" Say something snide like, "Hmmmm, interesting . . ." or "My, isn't *that* different?"

That's all there is to it! Now you're ready to go wine tasting with Biff and Muffy!

—Kim Caffrey

Getting the Sucker Open

If the wine comes with a screw top, it's pretty self-explanatory. Nothing wrong with this closure, by the way—it's great at avoiding getting a **corked** wine in beverages that are for immediate enjoyment. Don't agree? Think about this: $150 bottles of cognac come with screw tops! I know we'll be seeing more of them as well as synthetic corks in the future, in part due to a cork shortage. If the wine you've purchased has a cork (or corklike substance), you need a corkscrew of some kind. Below I've listed the top players in the field of cork removal.

> CORKED—When a wine has an odor of wet, rotten wood. The compound responsible for the foul smell comes from tainted corks (hence the term), although studies have shown that it may be generated by tainted BARRELS as well.

1. A *Waiter's Corkscrew* is most common and easy to use, once you've gotten the hang of it. Practice can be downright rewarding. The trick is to insert the worm at a forty-five-degree angle until the first turn is in, then straighten it up and finish screwing through. Then prop the boot on the lip of the neck and lift.

2. For a no-brainer, get one of the pocket *Screwpulls*. By simple leverage, it lifts the cork out of the bottle while you turn the screw.

3. The *Winglever* operates much like the screwpull; however, we find it can be pretty brutal on the poor cork.

4. *Ah-sos* (or butlers thiefs), which are the two-prong types, are easier for some (slipping down the sides of the cork, inside the neck of the bottle) but impossible for others. If you need practice, buy some crappy wine (chances are you may have some) and practice opening the bottles, reinserting the corks over and over, trying again until you have it. The Ah-so can also save you when the augers on corkscrews have shredded the cork, though it can take a delicate touch.

5. There are an endless list of new and old openers on the market that we haven't mentioned here, some costing a small fortune. Again, like the wine itself, it comes down to personal taste, and in the case of an opener, style. Experiment.

Other hints: Set the bottle down on a solid surface for leverage and never wear white. Next remove the foil, if present, from the bottle. If you're into aesthetics, trim the top of the foil. Now, it's a good idea to wipe the top of the bottle with a towel so that it's clean, then follow the appropriate instructions above. If the cork happens to disintegrate or push down into the bottle, take a butter knife and shove it deeper, then **decant** into any handy pitcher. This is best done at the sink. If all else fails, find a wine pro (biz or imbiber) who can give you personal instruction. **See REF.6: Wine Mumbo Jumbo.**

Check out www.winebrats.org for on-line video demos of corkscrews in action!

On to More Experimentation

There are some things that even I won't drink, but for the most part I keep a very open mind. How else can one discover new tastes and joys? I encourage everyone to try different wines outside the standard choices. Wine tasting is like dating—if you don't like it, dump it and go on to the next one. It's not gonna kill you.

Have the Guts to Form Your Own Opinion

Taste is subjective. No one can determine what is good for you except you. I don't give a damn if someone's appalled by what I'm drinking if I'm enjoying it!

Nasal Overload

When we say "wine tasting," we mean "wine smelling" almost equally. It is best to have as few competing **aromas** around as possible. No perfume, cigarette, or cigar clouds. No coffee, chocolate, or spicy food before we taste. No air freshener, either. Although mountain-fresh Sauvignon Blanc could work. . . .

AROMA—Individual smells in the wine like cherry, vanilla, cinnamon, earthy, and floral.

Chardonnay Slurpie Syndrome

Everyone knows the old adage "Red wines at room temperature and white wines chilled." Few people know that adage is over two hundred years old. Room temperature in northern Europe was about sixty-five degrees. Therefore, you do not drink Cabernet Sauvignon by the pool in August when it's 112! (If you do, and you still remain vertical, you may want to assess your drinking habits.)

"Chilled" meant bringing wine straight up from the cellar and drinking it, at about fifty-five degrees (equivalent to a half hour in the fridge from room temp, a half hour out from the fridge cold). It did not mean drinking Chardonnay in near-Slurpie form! If dry whites and reds are too cold, all you taste is **acid** and **alcohol**. If they are too warm, oak and alcohol. Either way, the fruit is lost and the wine is thrown off balance. A hard chill *is* recommended for wines with bubbles or any sweetness. But, of course, do whatever *you* want; these are only strong recommendations.

ACIDITY—One of wine's most crucial components. Necessity for aging wines. The combination of tartaric, malic, lactic, and citric acids in the wine give it its zing. Too little of it and the wine's flabby or flat. Too much of it pushes the wine beyond crisp into sour.

ALCOHOL—Result of yeast fermentation of natural sugars (in this case, grape juice). Largely responsible for the wine's body and mouthfeel. Helps to preserve the wine.

FERMENTATION—The process by which yeast converts sugars into alcohol. The formula is: yeast + sugar = alcohol + CO_2. If a wine ferments dry, its alcoholic strength is .55 percent of its BRIX. Fermentation can be stopped (arrested) by either chilling a tank to below freezing or adding alcohol to the fermenting juice, either technique leaving some of the grape's natural RESIDUAL SUGAR.

Glassware

Yes, it's true, the wine will taste different depending on the vessel you're drinking from. Whether or not it will taste better depends on your taste, however. The glasses I drink from most often are clear and tulip-shaped, to concentrate the aromas near the top of the glass. A jelly jar is better than Styrofoam, in my opinion. Plastic will often taste like plastic.

One of the best ways to get a collection of sturdy wineglasses is to ask your favorite watering hole if or when they plan to replace their glass. Many do so regularly because of scratches and/or haze from the industrial dishwasher. Offer to buy them cheap, then take them home, and give them a good wash and polish. If you're into spending tons of money on glassware, you can find a glass for virtually every style of wine. Personally, I'd rather have adequate glassware and spend the savings on good wine.

What Kind of Wine Should We Have?

What are you in the mood for? Something cold? Maybe a light, fruity off-dry Riesling, Chenin Blanc, or white Zinfandel, or, if you want more floral spiciness, a Muscat or Gewürztraminer. Perhaps a slightly cool, light dry white like Pinot Gris, Pinot Blanc, or Sauvignon Blanc would be nice. Then again, a nice rich Viognier or Chardonnay often does the trick. Lighter reds like Beaujolais and Pinot Noir are always so versatile. Zinfandels and Sangioveses are nice, zesty reds. Grenache and Syrah are lusty. Some won't settle for anything less than a big, rich Merlot, Syrah, or Cabernet Sauvignon. Then there're the blends . . . too many choices! **See REF.5: Variety Is the Spice of Life.**

Let's Taste, Already!

Basically, when you taste wine, you follow the five S's. See, swirl, sniff, sip, and swallow (or spit). Let's go through each, one at a time, as though a waitperson were pouring you a sample of something you had ordered from a restaurant. Open a bottle and get a glass and follow along. It's fun!

Look—See

Prior to evaluating the wine, you should look briefly at the cork. Don't smell it, it's only going to smell like cork. Waitpersons bet on whether you'll do that or not. "Table fifteen, think they'll smell the cork?" "Obviously, dude, look at 'em. . . ." It should be moist at one end (the wine end, duh) and dry at the other. If it's wet *or* dry all the way through, it just means to pay closer attention to the wine—it may have been stored improperly.

When a sample of wine is poured for you (go ahead and pour yourself one of those scant one-ounce portions), the first thing to check is the color and clarity of the wine. Hold the glass against a white background (by the stem or base, to keep fingerprints and the warmth of your hand away from the wine). The color should be appropriate for its type. If it's a white wine, it should be pale straw/yellow-green to gold in color. If it's a red, it should be ruby/garnet to deep black cherry/violet in color. The wine should be clear and brilliant (unless it's an unfiltered or old red, in which case a tad of purple haze is acceptable). If a white is amberish or a red is prematurely browning, it's a warning sign.

Swirl

We swirl all wine to release its aromas. Fill your glass less than half full to allow room for swirling, regardless of whether it's a tumbler or Austrian crystal that you're drinking from. If you're a beginning swirler, do it on the tabletop! Not too frenetic, just enough to mix things up. Some people swirl at breakneck speed. Either they are trying to soften/open up a big, chewy, **astringent,** tannic red, or it has just become a nervous tic over which they have little or no control.

> ASTRINGENT/ASTRINGENCY—Pucker perceived on the tongue, cheeks, and gums, most often from TANNINS in red wines. Severe astringency will cause you to look about the room nonchalantly for a butter knife to pry your tongue from the roof of your mouth. Softens with age, like most things.

Sniff

Most of what you taste is contrived by your sense of smell. The combination of different singular aromas possibly found in a Chardonnay, such as pineapple, vanilla, lemon, banana, pear, or butterscotch, together form what's known as the "nose" (or **bouquet**). Take a nice deep whiff of the wine. Don't worry about trying to smell all the aromas wine writers pontificate about. If you don't smell all that stuff, it's okay; it should just smell good to you. Chances are, if you like the way the wine smells, you'll like the way it tastes. You may not like the way the wine smells, but in order to send it back, there should be something wrong with it. When something is microbiologically wrong with the wine, it usually will have one of the following aromas: hard-boiled eggs, dead skunk, wet dog, sweaty horse blanket, vinegar, nail polish remover, and/or wet, rotten wood.

BOUQUET OR NOSE — The combination of aromas in the wine.

The bad aromas in wine are usually a result of problems during production. **Aerobic/anaerobic** bacteria, **oxidation,** too much sulfur/sulfites, etc., can all cause off odors. Good aromas are resulting from good fruit. It is against the law to add MOG — Material Other (than) Grapes. If a wine smells like cherries, it's because the aroma-bearing compound that makes cherries smell like cherries is also present in the wine. Why? Natural selection or divine intervention? Talk amongst yourselves. . . .

AEROBIC — In contact with air.

ANAEROBIC — Not in contact with air.

OXIDIZED — When the wine has been exposed to oxygen and has taken on a smell similar to sherry. It usually kills any fruit smells.

WHITE VARIETAL AROMAS

Chardonnay: Apples, citrus, pineapple, pear, tropical fruit, vanilla, nutty, toasty, buttery/butterscotch.

Chenin Blanc: Melons, peach, citrus, apples, floral.

Fumé Blanc: See *Sauvignon Blanc.*

Gewürztraminer: Floral (roses, violets, orange flower), spicy (clove, cardamom, nutmeg), grapefruit, lichee fruit.

Muscat: Perfumey, floral, melon, apple, peach, apricot, musk.

Pinot Blanc: Apple, melon, flinty, citrus.

Pinot Grigio or Gris: Citrus, green apple, spice, tart.

Riesling: Floral, apple, lemon, pineapple, peach, apricot.

Sauvignon Blanc: Citrus, tart pineapple, pear, fresh-cut grass, herbs, herbaceous, vegetal.

Semillon: Fig, citrus, herbs, light vanilla, banana.

Viognier: Flowery, tropical fruit (mango, papaya), peach, nectarine, perfumey.

—Leslie Sbrocco

WARNING: TRADITIONAL DESCRIPTORS HAVE THEIR LIMITS

Don't worry about applying the proper vocabulary to wine. If you like a wine, you like it—who says you need to have eight flavor descriptors to explain why? I think of this every time I do a consumer tasting or wine dinner. The phrases that people use when they like a wine are nearly always along the lines of "Oooh, that's yummy!" Not "I get cracked pepper and briery fruit in the nose, blackberries and tar in the mid-palate, and some of that French oak coming through on the finish." In fact, you may find yourself more inclined to describe wines not in terms of flavor, but rather personality, whether the wine is "bold" or "reserved" or "over the top."

—Gina Gallo

RED VARIETAL AROMAS

Barbera: Tart dark cherry, cinnamon, spice, hay.

Cabernet Franc: Plum, cherry, green floral, weedy, spice.

Cabernet Sauvignon: Black cherry or plum, jam, coffee, chocolate, tobacco, herbs, olives, bell pepper.

Charbono: Dried cherry, earthy, spice, smoky, wood.

Gamay: Raspberry, cranberry, strawberry, earthy, wood, stemmy.

Grenache: Spice, dark fruit, floral, bell pepper.

Grignolino: Tart cherry, spice, wood, citrus, stemmy.

Merlot: Black cherry or plum, jammy, chocolate, spice, tobacco.

Nebbiolo: Ripe or dried cherries, licorice, tar, rose petals, violets, raspberries, leather.

Petite Sirah: Dark plum, white pepper, raspberry, wood, earth.

Pinot Noir: Cherry, strawberry, violets, roses, chocolate, mushroom, earthy, cigar box.

Sangiovese: Cherries, licorice, tobacco, leather, pepper.

Syrah: Dark black fruit, pepper, cassis, tar, leather, licorice.

Zinfandel: Blackberry, briery, pepper, earthy, violet, vanilla spice.

See REF.5: Variety Is the Spice of Life.

—*Leslie Sbrocco*

Sip and Chew

No chugging! Take an ounce or so into your mouth and roll it around. The obtuse tongue can only discern sweet, sour, salt, and bitter, three of which can be found in wine. Most wine books you refer to will tell you that sweet is experienced on the tip of the tongue, sour on the sides, and bitter (and salt) on the top and back. Some say all taste buds perform equally. Regardless, it is important to get the wine to all surfaces of the tongue, even up into the cheeks and gums, to fully experience the wine's balance, **body**, and flavors. Sometimes a wine's nose will have great promise but will be disappointing once it reaches your mouth. **See REF.6: Wine Mumbo Jumbo and below.**

BODY—The mouthfeel/weight of the wine. The classic example is to think of light-bodied wines as nonfat milk, medium-bodied wines as regular milk, and full-bodied wines as half-and-half. The wine's body is a result of sugar, alcohol levels, and/or fermentation techniques. See REF.6 MALOLACTIC, LEES.

Balance: The mark of a truly great wine is balance. The harmonious blend of all the wine's components, fruit, acid, tannins, alcohol, and oak (if any was used), will announce its quality. Fruit is paramount. It is what wine is made from, yes? Its flavors should be allowed to shine through. Great wine is made from great fruit. Fruitiness is not to be confused with sweetness. If a wine is fermented dry, there is no palatable sweetness, even though the wine can be very fruity. Chardonnay is an excellent example. Sweetness would be in wines with actual residual sugar, like most Rieslings.

Fruit: Fruit is generally perceived on the top of the tongue, especially in the middle. If the wine feels "hollow" on the middle, as though there's nothing there, this indicates either a lack of fruit (due to not enough sugar in the grapes at harvest or to overhandling/oaking the wine) or a "closed" or "tight" wine (meaning the wine is young and needs bottle age—i.e., not fully ripe, like a green banana).

Sweetness: A wine's body is attributed to either sugar or alcohol. There are many world-class wines that are fairly light-bodied. Bigger isn't always better. What is appropriate for the type of wine is considered. You can't expect a full-bodied Beaujolais Nouveau. Likewise, you wouldn't expect a light-bodied Syrah.

Acidity: Acidity will generally zing (like lemon juice) the sides of the tongue, and if extremely high, will cause salivation.

Tannin: Acidity should not be confused with tannin, which dries the mouth out. Some wines grab the top/back part of your tongue in a game of uncle, requiring the aid of a butter knife to free it from your soft palate, indicating extreme astringency, a "Beat your chest, I am red wine, hear me roar" Tarzan wine. Hopefully, there will still be enough fruit there when the tannins soften in the wine over time.

Alcohol: When used in the context of winemaking, alcohol is very important to the body and flavor of the wine. Ever had a stiff drink and noticed the thickness of the liquid compared to water? Alcohol especially thickens when chilled. You've done the peppermint schnapps in the freezer trick, right? The stuff becomes almost gooey. So the higher the alcohol in the wine, the thicker its body. Of course, because alcohol is the result of yeast fermentation of the natural sugars, the higher the sugars are when the grapes are picked, the higher the wine's alcohol content. This is why you'll generally find that wines grown in warmer regions (California, southern France, Australia) can have alcohol levels reaching 13 to 15 percent versus those from a cooler climate such as Germany, where their white wines can have levels in the lower 8 percent range. It's basically a matter of degree of ripeness. This is also why sweet dessert wines are thick and higher in alcohol: They've been left on the vine to overripen to the point of becoming raisins.

Back to Balance: Too much oak and you can't taste the fruit. Alcohol in too-high amounts will make a wine **hot**. The winemakers' goal is to present you with a beverage that is balanced. Balance is everything in life, yes? And so it is with wine.

HOT—The wine is high in alcohol and warms the throat/nose. May cause the wine to be unbalanced, clumsy.

Chew and Gargle

If you want to turbo-taste, you can attempt trilling. Trilling is that backward kind of slurping thing that draws air across your tongue, bringing the wine's aromas back up to the olfactory nerve via the retro-nasal route. Try it at home with water first. Doing it for the first time while surrounded by a crowd (especially with a mouth full of red wine) can cause incalculable self-conscious distress. I once witnesses a man spew thousands of evenly dispersed Cabernet droplets onto his girlfriend's white linen jacket. The crowd gasped. The woman stomped. The man crawled out. The room roared. Practice at home.

Swallow/Spit

The **finish** of the wine is very important. Like in a piece of music or a story, if an ending simply fizzles, it doesn't leave you with a good impression, even if what came before it was pretty good. A short finish is common in lighter-styled or less distinctive wines, but for a wine to be of true quality, the flavor should linger. Also, the finish should be balanced.

FINISH—The taste of the wine in your mouth after you swallow/spit. Generally, wines of high quality will have lengthy, balanced finishes.

Whether or not you swallow, alcohol is absorbed through the tissues in your mouth. If you plan to be tasting several wines, it's best to spit everything until you've tasted what you want and, if you still have some sobriety left, go back and swallow a tad more of your favorites. Why get tanked on something you don't like?

That's It!

This whole process of evaluating/tasting a wine shouldn't take more than ten seconds or so. If you draw it out to impress, you risk the waitperson doing something really rude to your food that you don't know about. You should be able to surmise rather quickly if the wine is good or not. When having tastings at home, you can take as long as you want, but be wary of palate (and nose) fatigue. Your senses get burned out if you overwork them. Start a potluck wine-tasting club with your friends. Don't be a geek and sit alone at home trying to learn wine. It's a social thing! There aren't many other subjects you can have as much fun learning about as wine. **See Part II: It's Party Time!**

Wine Is Food!

Lastly, remember that wine should be thought of more as a condiment than a beverage. It is best consumed with food. If you are going to be attending a tasting, make sure you eat something first. Fatty foods coat your stomach and, along with lots of water, are your best defense against getting tipsy too fast. It doesn't have to be fancy fare. Remember, good wine makes cheap food so much more tolerable! Bon appetit!

GRAD SCHOOL LIT-SNOB RECLAIMS PUNK ROOTS

*Though we have never personally met Lora White, it seems that, be-
tween us, an intimate relationship of philosophy and language has
been made in the stars. All right, it's been her recent contributions to
Wine X magazine's "Rage" column that have made us fans of her fine
use of education-through-storytelling style. Her bio in the aforementioned magazine also furthered our respect for this new voice in
wine. It states that "she hopes they have South Park reruns in the af-
terlife." How wonderfully twisted, Lora. Now let's go shopping!*

—j, j & m

Adventures in the Wine Aisle, or A Taste of Wine Shopping Know-How

by Lora White

A Lesson from Italy

Twilight in Bologna. The wash of golden sun drains slowly from the fields, leaving behind an umber dusk that settles like a blanket over the ripe cherry trees in the orchard and the wooden ladders the pickers have left behind for the night. Paolo, a young worker from the main house, leads me down a well-worn path through the grass, the empty wine bottles in his arms and pockets clinking over the hum of the night's awakening insects.

Our feet are caked with soft summer mud when we emerge from the fields near Eduardo's farmhouse in the valley. The elderly Italian farmer sits on the fountain by his barn with a cigarette and espresso, waving in welcome as we skip through his rolling vineyard with the empty bottles held high. He leads us to the centuries-old barn and down into the cool musty earth of the wine cellar. Several large oak casks line the walls, and Eduardo taps one to fill a jam jar with his own special vintage. I sip the smooth potion slowly while he and Paolo fill our empty bottles. The rich red wine tastes of everything Eduardo has put into its creation: time, care, faith, and love. I don't know if it is Sangiovese, Barbera, or Nebbiolo, and I don't care. It's Eduardo's wine, delivered in plain bottles with a robust handshake and Italian jokes that make me giggle though my Italian is only crash-course Berlitz.

After kissing Eduardo's laugh-wrinkled cheeks, Paolo and I head back with a borrowed flashlight and as many bottles as we can carry. In the middle of the cherry orchard, Paolo stops to pull the cork from one of Eduardo's fine bottles. We pass it back and forth as we follow the bouncing flashlight beam through the Italian countryside, gazing up now and then at the heavy harvest moon and stars unfiltered by the dull halo of city lights.

An hour later we're back in the bustling kitchen and the remainder of the bottles are gone, enjoyed by hungry, chattering cherry pickers who unwind at the long wooden table over steaming bowls of pasta and roasted lamb. All save for one that I've stashed in my knapsack to carry back home to California, a reminder of Eduardo's vineyard, the robust living of these summer days, and of what the pleasure of wine is really about.

Crushing the Myth

Shopping for wine in America is seldom as simple as paying a visit to the cellar of a fifteenth-century farmhouse. Novice drinkers in search of a good wine are often intimidated by the reputation wine has in this country, the presumption that it should be enjoyed only by those dripping in diamonds and real estate who have personally collected soil samples of every wine-growing region on the planet. The tendency of those in the wine business to look down on the viticulturally uneducated doesn't help matters; for many of us, all it takes is a condescending look from a wine clerk and the utterance of terminology in a foreign language to send us running for craft beer in the refrigerated section of the supermarket.

In almost every other country, wine is as ubiquitous as milk and water, an enjoyment for pope and peasant alike. Contrary to the myth that wine is the privilege of the rich and famous, it is in fact an equal-opportunity pleasure for the underpaid, the collegiate, and the chronically broke. With a little knowledge and cultivated irreverence for stodgy tradition, you can confidently buy and enjoy wine by following a few basic guidelines.

Know What You Like

Wine is not a symbol of a flush bank account or blue-blood lineage. It is not a status accessory to acquire like a downtown loft or a Range Rover. Don't buy it to impress your friends, your boss, or your in-laws. The only worthwhile impression wine should make is on your taste buds. The key to shopping for a satisfying wine is refusing to equate the beverage with a class-o-meter and simply purchase what you like. Forget about wineries. Forget about regions and the Pouilly Fuissé and Châteauneuf-du-Pape of the world. Even forget about the woeful, seventies-divorcée reputation of blush wines. Figure out what you enjoy drinking.

If you don't have a lot of experience with wine, the least expensive and most noncommittal way to determine what makes your mouth sigh, what is too heavy, even what gives you a headache, is to order wine by the glass at restaurants or find local wine merchants who sponsor tastings for a few bucks. Ask for suggestions from your server, or simply go with the first choice that strikes you. Try to be adventurous. If you've enjoyed Cabernet in the past, give a Syrah or Merlot a try. If Chardonnay suits you, what about a Gewürztraminer or Riesling?

Take notes about each glass for future reference. Having a "cheat sheet" that lists varieties you've sampled will save you time and energy when shopping for a bottle, and you won't risk ending up with a wine that could double for cough syrup.

Boutique Versus Barn

Thirty years ago, it wasn't easy to find good wine in America. Thanks to an ever-growing appreciation for the pleasure of wine, it's now possible to find a vast number of American and international wines at establishments from gourmet shops to wholesale beverage outlets.

No matter where you shop, there will be benefits and drawbacks. While "boutique" wine shops boast a wide, quality selection of wines, their products may be more expensive and their staff more inclined to the "wine snootiness" that many novices find so intimidating. Wholesale "beverage barns," supermarkets, and import stores are usually cheaper, but their selection is more limited and there may not be knowledgeable staff to assist with purchases.

Some wine experts believe that the few extra cents or dollars you might pay at a wine shop are worth the opportunity to consult knowledgeable sales staff before making a purchase. Others think a reasonably well-informed consumer should do without the hypereducated help and pocket the savings at a chain store or wholesaler. As in all matters related to wine, it's up to you to weigh the pros and the cons, decide whether the service at a wine shop is worth the cost and potential exposure to snobbiness, and then shop where you very well please. The good news is that there seems to be a convergence trend happening, creating a best-of-both-retail-worlds scenario, where boutiques are lowering prices while chains are offering educated help in the aisles.

Consult Your Wallet

Whether you choose to buy wine from a swanky local shop or a chain outlet in a highway megamall, decide how much money you want to spend before you walk in the door. If you prefer wine that comes in a bottle (as opposed to a box or a baggy), it's possible to drop anywhere from $4 to $400 on a single bottle. A wise shopper will decide on a budget before entering the store, lest they be seduced by a beautifully artistic label or the shop's rarefied atmosphere into spending next month's student loan payment on three glasses of Merlot. Setting financial parameters will also immediately narrow the selection of wines from which you have to choose, thus relieving the sometimes compulsive urge to pore over every bottle in the shop before buying.

If you find your wine budget is closer to $4 than $400, don't assume that you'd be better off picking up a jug-and-screw-top affair. In today's market, it's possible to enjoy a high-quality wine for less than the price of a movie ticket, provided you know what to shop for.

The best-known and priciest wines hail from California, Australia, and Europe, but good wines also come from regions all over the world. Because some excellent wine regions are yet to become trendy, the prices on wines from these areas remains low. This is true of wines from Chile, Argentina, South Africa, the Languedoc-Roussillon region of southern France, and, to some extent, the French regions of Alsace and Loire. In the current market, experts emphasize that you needn't spend more than ten bucks to partake of a quality bottle of wine. It's not being cheap to explore wines from lesser-known regions; it's being hip to the twenty-first-century global village.

Red, White, or Other?

Having determined your spending limit, you can further narrow your wine search by considering the occasion for which you are shopping. If the wine is for your own pleasure or to share at a party where food will be limited to hors d'oeuvres, you need go no farther than your own taste. If the wine will accompany food, however, you'll want to select a type that will complement the textures and flavors of the meal. For the scoop on pairing food and wine, **see Tim Hanni's EDU.5: Forget Everything You Know About Food and Wine Pairing.**

If you haven't got a clue what's on the menu or aren't sure what kind of wine your host prefers, consider bringing a dessert wine or Port. Though these rarely show up on dinner party tables, they are a satisfying note on which to close almost any meal.

Seek Advice (Human)

Having made your preliminary wine-buying decisions, you can either peruse the aisles on your own or, if you'd prefer some enlightened suggestions, seek the help of a salesperson. With wine more popular in America than ever before, it's possible to find knowledgeable salespeople everywhere from the corner market to chain import stores. If you prefer to avoid even the possibility of boutique wine shop humiliation, you can still find good advice about wine in a more laid-back environment.

Wherever you end up shopping, don't be afraid to ask the staff for help. Armed with your tasting notes, tell the salesperson your preferences (dry versus sweet wine, light versus heavy), the occasion for which you're buying, whether the wine will accompany food, and how much you are looking to spend. You'll know in the first ten seconds of interaction whether or not you are dealing with someone who is well-trained and can truly be helpful, or whether he or she is simply part of the shop's interior design. Remember, you are never, ever, under obligation to purchase a bottle of wine. If you feel pressured, if your requirements are ignored, or if you simply don't like the vibe you're getting, by all means, take your business to another juice joint.

Seek Advice (Written)

If you prefer to shop solo or can't find reliable sales assistance, there are still a number of clues and resources in a wine aisle that can help you select a good bottle. In a wine shop (and even some supermarkets and wholesalers), you will probably find some wines that are flagged with handwritten notes of recommendation from the owner or buyer. Generally, these notes are trustworthy. By making a public recommendation of a particular wine, the buyer is putting his or her reputation at stake and isn't likely to be misleading. These notes can prove very helpful if you're on the fence about trying a new wine or can't decide between two bottles.

Another mode of evaluation intended to help consumers is scoring systems. The two most well known are the twenty-point University of California at Davis system and the hundred-point system used by such organizations as the *Wine Spectator*, American Wine Competition, *Wine and Spirits*, and wine critics like Robert M. Parker, Jr. It's up to the individual buyer to decide how much credence to pay the scoring systems; if you don't buy wine regularly, they can simply seem confusing and of little value. In general, a wine rated between 13 and 20 on the UC Davis scale is considered to be of average to outstanding quality. On the hundred-point scales, a rating of 75 and up indicates a wine whose quality is somewhere between "recommended" and "superlative." **See EDU.3: Finding the Tastiest Grapes.**

You may also want to consider medals that are awarded to wines by competitions, the most notable of which is the American Wine Competition. They rank wines with Platinum (superlative), Gold (exceptional), Silver (highly recommended), and Bronze (recommended) medals. Of course, one wine lover's "exceptional" is another's "recommended," so don't assume either these medals or any ratings to be the Rosetta stone of wine buying. As always, let your own taste be the ultimate judge.

Decipher the Label

After you've gotten past the notes and the taste scoring system and the awards, consider the wine's label. In these days of eye candy, many labels now double as fine art, but all still bear important information about the vino contained within.

The most obvious information on the label is the name of the winery and the name of the wine. Wines can be named for the grapes they're made from, the region where they were made, or dubbed with "fantasy" names (usually called after the vintner's wife, horse, or child). New World wines from the United States, Australia, South Africa, New Zealand, Chile, and Argentina are usually named for grapes, as in Syrah or Chardonnay. European or Old World wines are generally named after the regions where they were made (Bordeaux, Chianti, etc.). **See REF.1: Around the World in Eighty Bottles.**

Some labels also highlight the exact origin of the grapes, or the specific area of a region in which they were grown. For example, a label that indicates a wine hails from California means it could come from any vineyard in the state. A Central Coast wine originated somewhere between San Francisco and Los Angeles. A Napa or Sonoma wine comes from that specific area, while a wine from the Stag's Leap District comes from a particular region within the Napa Valley. As you come to know and enjoy wines from certain regions, being able to pinpoint where a wine was born can be an important part of the selection process.

Next, take note of the wine's alcohol content, which is an important indicator of the wine's taste and body. Grape juice becomes wine when its sugar ferments into alcohol. If all the sugar is fermented, the result is a dry wine of about 12 to 14 percent alcohol.

The **vintage,** or year the wine was produced, will be prominently displayed on most labels. Vintage is often touted as the most crucial factor in choosing a good wine. While vintage is important with top wines from France, Italy, and Germany, where cold can keep grapes from ripening and impact the crops of a certain year, it is less of an issue with wines that come from the warmer regions of California, Australia, and South America. If you want to be cautious to buy wine that's a "good year," wine shops and vintage charts can guide you. If, however, you're purchasing within a modest budget and are thus inclined toward warm-climate wines, don't lose a lot of sleep over whether that bottle is circa 1956 or 1996.

European wines state a "quality level" on their label. The basic level is table wine. The French have a good value midlevel rank called *Vins de Pays*, or country wines, which are widely available in the U.S. for around $6 to $8 a bottle. The top level is "named of controlled origin" wines, called Appellation d'Origin Controllée (AOC) in France, Denominazione di Origine Controllata (DOC) in Italy, Denominacion de Origen Calificada (DOC) in Spain, and Qualitatswein mit Pradikat (QmP) in Germany. These wines are considered the highest quality and cost between $10 and $400 or more. In the United States, if a grape "varietal" (Merlot, Cabernet Sauvignon, Zinfandel, Chardonnay, etc.) is declared on the label, the wine must contain at least 75 percent of that varietal. This percentage goes up the more focused the grape source becomes—meaning, if the producer lists the "Russian River Valley" appellation, it must be 85 percent. If it lists the actual vineyard, such as "Scherrer Vineyards," it must be 95 percent.

APPELLATION—A geographic area for growing grapes. Examples would be Napa Valley, Beaujolais, Carneros, Sancerre, North Coast, and Vosne-Romanee. See REF.1: Around the World in Eighty Bottles.

Some wineries may also denote certain wines as *reserve*. The Spanish *reserva* and Italian *riserva* mean that the wine had extra months or years of aging in oak barrels. France and Germany don't use the reserve category. If it is noted on a bottle of California wine, it usually just means that the winery is hyping that particular wine as one of its best and indicates no specific augmentation of quality.

A HELPFUL LOOK AT A DOMESTIC WINE LABEL

Every label of every wine sold in the United States has been scrutinized by the infamous Bureau of Alcohol, Tobacco and Firearms (BATF), the agency that interprets and enforces the rules enacted by Congress that regulate the sale of alcoholic beverages. There are myriad rules that govern what is printed on a label; wineries expend enormous efforts to comply with these rules (and horror stories abound). Let's look closely at a sample wine label to understand what is listed there and why.

The Brand Name
Could also be the actual producer, could be a "virtual winery," or could be a restaurant or grocery store chain that contracted with a winery for a "special label" purchase.

Vintage (optional)
The year in which the wine grapes themselves were harvested. By law, if a "vintage" is "declared," 95 percent of the wine must be made from grapes harvested in the declared vintage.

Produced and Bottled By
The actual "Bonded Winery," which may be producing and bottling the wine under special contract for a third party (a restaurant or grocery chain, for instance).

Estate Bottled
The producer owns or directly controls the vineyards from whose grapes this wine was produced. The winery itself also must be physically located on the specified vineyards.

Declaration of Sulfites
If the sulfite content of the wine exceeds ten parts per million, by law the phrase "Contains Sulfites" must be printed on the label. See REF.6: Wine Mumbo Jumbo.

Government Health Warning
A law taking effect after the 1988 vintage specifies that this message must be prominently displayed on the label. Wineries have become quite creative in how they blend this message with the rest of the label.

Varietal
By law, if a "varietal" (Merlot, Cabernet Sauvignon, Zinfandel, Chardonnay, etc.) is declared on the label, the wine must contain at least 75 percent of that varietal. Some wineries use nearly 100 percent of the same varietal. Some wineries blend a major varietal with similar varietals for better flavor balance. Others blend in "filler" varietals to get the most of their Merlot wine supply. Still others don't declare a varietal at all and simply identify the wine by a proprietary name, such as "Hearty Burgundy" (Gallo) or "Le Cigare Volante" (Bonny Doon) or "Conundrum" (Caymus).

Appellation of Origin
The region where the grapes were grown. If a political boundary is named (e.g., Sonoma County, California), then 75 percent of the grapes must have been grown within that boundary. If a "Viticul-

tural Area" is named (Napa Valley, Sonoma Valley), 85 percent of the grapes must have come from the specified area. And if a specific vineyard is named (Martha's Vineyard, Scherrer Vineyard), 95 percent of the grapes must have been grown in that particular vineyard.

—Amy Reiley

A LOOK AT A FOREIGN LABEL

Wine labels written in a foreign language can seem pretty intimidating at a glance. However, because the United States so carefully regulates what appears on the labels of all alcohol sold in this country, you'll find foreign labels pretty straightforward once you understand a few key concepts

THE FRENCH LABEL

All wines from countries in the European Community are designated by quality. This means that when you examine a European wine label, you can get a good idea of the quality level of the wine in the bottle. The French take their winemaking traditions more seriously than most; as a result, the quality controls indicated on the label are extremely stringent.

Status
French wines are regulated by the laws of Appellation d'Origine Controlée (AOC or AC). Status designation is important on European wines not only for prestige, but also because it is more than a place name; it also defines quality, variety, growing method, and winemaking method. Only 35 percent of French wines are worthy of AC status. The status level below AC is Appellation d'Origine Vins Delimites de Qualite Superieure (AOVDQS) Below this designation are Vins de Pays (table wines from a specific geographic region) and Vins

de Table *(table wines). One of these status levels will appear on every bottle of French wine, indicating the quality of the wine and level of adherence to a set of strict production rules followed by the winemaker. A status of* Vins de Table *does not necessarily indicate a bad wine. It may mean that the winemaker chose to use experimental blends or grow grapes not designated in his region.*

Varietal
The type of wine is usually pretty obvious when looking at a French label. Sometimes, along with the varietal, there will be a denotation of vieilles vignes *(old vines). Winemakers print this on the label for prestige, but it is a deregulated term and is often meaningless.*

Chateau Bottled/Domaine Bottled
The terms Mis en Bouteille *au* Chateau and Mis en Bouteille au Domaine *mean estate bottled. Watch out for labeling* Mis dans nos Caves, Mis par le Proprietaire, *and* Mis en Bouteille a la Propriete. *These terms are not regulated and can be misleading. On some French wines, the estate name will be embossed on the bottle rather than appear on the label.*

Classified Growths
Another indication of a wine's quality and prestige is classified growths. The word cru *appearing on a French wine label identifies villages with exceptional wines. For example, if the term* Premier Cru Classes *appears on a Bordeaux label it indicates a wine of the rarest quality, such as a Margaux.* Cru Classe *is Bordeaux's second-highest classed growth. Wines that are judged to be of a quality just below classified growths are labeled* Cru Bourgeois. *In Burgundy, the indication of the highest classed vineyard is* Grand Cru. *(A good rule of thumb is that any French wine with the word* cru *appearing on the label is bound to be of excellent quality.)*

Importer
The name and address of the company that imports wine to the United States will also appear on every foreign bottle of wine.

*Other foreign expressions that may appear on a French wine la-
bel include: the name of the producer, the village name, and the
vineyard name.*

THE ITALIAN LABEL

*The Italians also take their winemaking very seriously and as a re-
sult have a great deal of meaningful information regarding quality
on their labels.*

Status
*As in France, quality wines come from regulated zones that essen-
tially define what is in the bottle, from quality to grape-growing
method. These zones are dictated by the Denominazione di Origine
Controllata (DOC). There are more than two hundred zones re-
stricted by stringent DOC rules. Wines with the DOC demarca-
tion are those of extremely high quality. Of an even higher
quality are wines that bear the stamp* Denominazione di Origine
Controllata e Garantita *(DOCG). Wines with the label* vino da
tavola *are table wines. (Like the French, Italian table wines are
often far better than ordinary.)* Vino da tavola *with a geographic
name attached are table wines from grapes of a specific growing
region.*

Estate Bottling
Terms that indicate a wine has been estate-bottled include: Imbottigliato all'origine, Imbottigliato del Produttore, *and* Meso in Bot-
tiglia all'origine.

VIDE
*Vintivinicoltori Italiani d'Eccellenza is an organization of estate bot-
tling winemakers who have a system of quality controls even more
stringent than the DOC or DOCG. Only wines that pass specific
chemical and taste tests may bear the VIDE stamp on their neck label.*

Barrel Aging

The term riserva *indicates that a wine was aged in wood for an amount of time specified by law.* Riserva Speciale *means the wine was aged in wood for one year longer than a riserva.* Stravecchio *means that the wine has been barrel-aged for an extremely long time and is very rare.*

Italian Varietals

Spumanti *is a sparkling Italian wine.* Frizzante *is semisparkling. If the secondary fermentation of either style of sparkling wine is completed in the bottle, the label may bear the phrase* Metodo Tradizionale *or* Metodo Classico. Passito *is both a term for making sweet wines and for the wines made in the passito style using semi-dried grapes.*

Other mysterious phrases that may appear on an Italian bottle include:

Superiore—*usually an indication that the wine is of a higher alcohol content than the varietal would typically possess.*

Classico—*appears on DOC labels where the grapes have come from the heart of the growing region.*

Secco—*indicates a dry wine.*

Liquoroso—*a fortified dessert wine.*

—*Amy Reiley*

Take Note of Storage Conditions

Regardless of whether you shop for wine at a "bottle barn" or a hip boutique, if the proprietors don't observe proper conditions for wine storage, you might as well be buying vinegar. When you go into a shop, be aware of how the merchandise is stored. Extreme temperature fluctuations and direct sunlight cause corks to expand and contract, letting air get to the wine. Pass on any bottles that have been kept near heaters, air conditioners, or freezers. That window display of wine bottles may look pretty, but if it's been there for a while, chances are the sun has already caused a good deal of damage to the wine inside.

If the storage atmosphere appears stable, examine the bottle of wine itself. A good bottle will be filled up to the neck. The cork should not be pushing out of the bottle, and there should be no signs of leakage. If you're buying for a collection, you'll also want to check the condition of the label. While this is unimportant on "ready to drink" wines, the label is a factor in the value of certain collectable wines.

Shopping in Space

For the frantically busy, geographically compromised, or agoraphobic buyer, Internet wine shopping is the greatest thing since obtaining legal drinking age. The World Wide Web now boasts numerous on-line wine shops that offer recommendations, advice on food pairings, occasional sale prices, and front-door delivery all for a few mouse clicks and the secure on-line submission of a credit card number.

While on-line shops are a good place to find "limited edition" collectors' wines, most also offer a good array of low- to medium-priced bottles. You'll pay a bit more for shipping, but the convenience can be well worth the bucks if you're pushed for time or suddenly have the urge to order wine at four A.M. Also, be aware, many states do not allow direct shipping of alcoholic beverages. **See REF.3: Finding Wine on the Web.**

BOTTLE SIZES

A standard *size bottle is 750 ml. A* magnum *is 1500 ml, equal to two bottles. On that, we all agree. For some crazy reason, bottle names and sizes differ in the Bordeaux and Burgundy regions of France. In this country you will find the following terms used for most wines: A* jeroboam *is 3 l, equal to four bottles. A salmanazar is 9 l, equal to twelve bottles, a full case. Other party bottles include* rehoboam *(six bottles),* imperiale or methuselah *(eight bottles),* balthazar *(sixteen bottles), and* nebuchadnezzar *(twenty bottles), rarely seen anymore. Word is, big bottles age slower than standard ones.*

—Kim Caffrey

Bulking Up

You've tasted, you've experimented, maybe you've made a few mistakes. But with your growing knowledge and awareness of your own wine style, you've hit upon some varieties that are perennially guaranteed to please. You've surpassed the single bottle stage; now it's time to step up to buying in bulk.

Purchasing wine by the case is not like taking on a pallet of toilet paper or a ten-gallon jar of mayonnaise. A case is twelve bottles. If the case contains wine you've chosen carefully and with consideration for your personal taste, having bottles stashed away can feel as luxurious and comforting as a naughty little sin. Buy in bulk, and your wine will always be there for impromptu picnics, gift giving, late-night guests, or rainy afternoons with a good book (or computer game). An added benefit of purchasing en masse is the 10 to 15 percent discount most retailers offer on a case. Of course, now you have to consider the issue of storage. **See EDU.6: Home Wine Cellars for the Rest of Us.**

A GUY WHO DOESN'T BELIEVE IN SCORING?

Some of us work our whole lives just to achieve the lofty goal of speaking in complete sentences. Brendan Eliason, whom we first met in '96 while he was working as an intern for Gallo of Sonoma, already speaks in complete book. And very fast. (Watch out for Brendan at cocktail parties after a couple of sips!) Brendan now splits his time between studying enology (the scientific study of wine) at Cal Poly and getting his hands dirty as an assistant winemaker at Caffaro Winery in Sonoma's Dry Creek Valley. Once you read his piece on how to decipher wine scores, you'll understand our gutless disclaimer stating, "The opinions of Brendan Eliason are not necessarily those of the Wine Brats or Caffaro Vineyards." Then again, maybe they are. It's all subjective.

—j, j & m

Finding the Tastiest Grapes, or Deciphering and Using Wine Scores

by Brendan Eliason

Be happy! Never in history has there ever been so much great wine available in so many places. Although there is still a wide range of quality levels, it is getting progressively harder to find a truly bad bottle of wine. Unfortunately, this ever-expanding selection has made it progressively harder to narrow your choices down to a single selection. Luckily, there are lots of basic steps that people can learn in order to help make their decisions easier.

The most obvious of these is to read wine reviews. These can be found anywhere from popular wine magazines, to your local newspaper, to a wide variety of Web pages. Unfortunately, most wine reviews are best enjoyed while wearing a pair of waders and carrying a shovel. Reviews can be somewhat helpful as long as you don't take them too seriously. Reviews come in a wide array of shapes and sizes that run from hundred-point scales, stars, Xs, general recommendations and, my favorite, the prestigious Stooges rating system (there is nothing better than a triple Larry with two Moes and a touch of Shemp). These reviews can contain a lot of valuable advice; just remember, "they're only opinions."

The first lesson is to be very skeptical of any system that relies on a 100-scale. People who use such scales want you to believe that there is a real and measurable difference between one wine they score as an 89 and another they score as a 90. This is bunk. My favorite issue of the *Wine Spectator* was the November 15, 1997, issue, titled "The Chardonnay Challenge."

In this issue, two of *Wine Spectator*'s most preeminent editors (James "Mr. California Chardonnay" Laube and Per-Henrik "The Burgundian Baron" Mansson) sat down to do a side-by-side tasting of ten of the best California Chardonnays versus ten of the best French white Burgundies (a.k.a. Chardonnay) from two different vintages. Both of these men are longtime, professional wine judges, and both are among the world's foremost experts on the Chardonnay varietal.

What happened when they sat and judged the same wines back-to-back? They weren't even close. Laube scored the 1995 Gainey Chard at a whopping 98 (out of a possible 100 points on *Wine Spectator*'s very exacting scoring system). Per-Henrik, however, scored the wine as merely an 89. That's nine points' difference! This held true across the board as the two tasters flip-flopped around and only agreed on the score for two wines. Now ask yourself, "If two of the world's most highly experienced experts can't even stay within nine points of each other, and disagree on the exact score of thirty-eight out of forty wines, then should I be concerned about the difference between an 88 score versus a 93 score? Probably not."

The next most popular technique for reviewing wines is the "fruit salad" approach. A standard review reads, "Tight and well-oaked, with a complex array of cedar, plum, currant, anise, cherry, and spice. Finishes with tight, chewy tannins, a dash of mineral, and richness." There is nothing in general wrong with this approach except it can be somewhat intimidating for a beginner. I think that sometimes wine writers forget how many years of constant practice it took before they could really dissect all of these flavors from the wines they drink. The average wine drinker is left thinking, "Cedar? Anise? Chewy tannins? All I taste is wine!" Many also get the intimidating feeling that if they don't get the same flavors as the reviews, they are somehow not able to enjoy the wine they are drinking. My advice: Relax; have another glass of wine.

The truth is that wine is full of organic compounds that mimic the flavors found in a wide variety of fruits, vegetables, etc., and, with a lot of practice and years of experience, you really can start to pick individual flavors out of the wines you drink. This is, however, hardly a necessary task for the enjoyment of wines. In fact, it can occasionally be detrimental to appreciating wine because people can get too caught up in what they're tasting and simply forget to enjoy the wine. Bottom line: You don't need to know how a plane flies in order to enjoy the flight, and the only decision you need to make is whether you like what you're drinking.

Luckily, I think there are some very good general guidelines along with scoring that will help in tracking down some good juice:

1. Wine is good.

2. Ask yourself, "What is Pinot Grigio?" Try new things. Don't get stuck in a rut. Remember, there are over five thousand varieties of grapes grown for wine in the world today and most of them are pretty darn good. Choose to be excited by this fact and not scared or overwhelmed. Although Chardonnay, Cabernet Sauvignon, and Merlot are great varieties, they are only a fraction of the great wines you can find if you look and ask questions. In white wines look for more Sauvignon Blanc, Pinot Blanc, Pinot Grigio, Viognier, Roussanne, Dry Gewürztraminer and Riesling, Chenin Blanc, Semillon, and others. For red try Zinfandel, Syrah, Pinot Noir, Cabernet Franc, Grenache, Barbera, Sangiovese, Nebbiolo, Mourvedre, and many others. Remember Rule #1: Wine is good.

3. Talk to friends. Other people, especially your friends, are the best information network for wine. The number of wines that can be tried increases exponentially with each new friend you can network with. Even better is to just get together with a bunch of friends and have them each bring a favorite bottle of wine. This may lead to parties and frolicking. (A small legal warning: Frolicking of any nature is prohibited in many states. Please check local laws and ordinances before having too much fun.) **See Part II: It's Party Time!**

4. Try a local wineshop. Wineshops will most often be slightly more expensive than a big discount chain or a supermarket, but this small price increase is almost always made up for by a unique selection of wines and knowledgeable service. There are very few things that will make your life easier than finding a good local wineshop. You'll know when you've found one if they make you feel comfortable about asking questions and consistently help you find wine that you like and that is within your price range.

5. The U.S. government (a.k.a. BATF) requires that every wine label tell consumers how much control the winery that bottled the wine had in making it. At the top of this standard is "Grown, Produced, and Bottled By." These words can appear on a wine label and tell you who ac-

tually made the wine in the bottle. Although not a guarantee one way
or the other, these words can be a general indication of a quality wine
because they show that the same winery grew the grapes, fermented
the wine, blended the wine, and bottled it. This generally points to a
level of control and quality from the beginning to the end of the winemaking process. The downside is that this extra attention to detail also
makes many of the wines more expensive, so it pays to shop around.

6. There is no such thing as a "dumb" question. Remember, everyone
you talk to has been where you are. The best way to learn is to talk
with a wide range of people and get a variety of opinions. If you ever
meet anyone who makes you feel stupid or intimidated about trying to
learn more about wine, just remember: The Wine Brats are a powerful
international organization with thousands of members and resources
that span the globe. Not even the CIA has the unique level of covert
operatives that the Wine Brats have at their disposal. People who hin-
der others in their enjoyment of wine shall be hunted down and "reed-
ucated."

7. Read the rest of this book.

8. Remember, wine is good.

PERSONALITY FILLED TO THE RIM

Leslie. That's Leslie Sbrocco. You see, here in California Wine Country, Leslie can be referred to simply by her first name. Since we initially met her while planning the first-ever WineRave back in '97—and she was writing and developing the wine pages for Microsoft's SF Side-walk—Leslie quickly made a personality for herself. Her ability to write, sip, eat, sing, and schmooze simultaneously has made her a new voice to reckon with in the biz. She is currently managing editor at WineToday.com and a married mother with one beautiful baby girl. Even so, she still manages to be the queen of the restaurant and wine scene, which is why she's dishing up the inside scoop on surviving the challenge of ordering a bottle from the wine list.

—j, j & m

Unraveling the Mystery of Wining and Dining, or Ordering Wine Off the List

by Leslie Sbrocco

The performance anxiety builds as you discreetly wipe your moist brow. Deciding between the deep, voluptuous one with great legs or the racy one with a firm body is strenuous. You breathe a sigh of relief when it's finished, yet you question your decision.

It's exhausting to order wine. Dealing with wine in a restaurant can be a challenge, but it doesn't need to instill fear (or make any body parts perspire). I admit it—today I qualify as a wine geek and can manage with the quagmire of Rhône or Rhine, Syrah or Shiraz, and Burgundy or Bordeaux, but it wasn't always so easy.

The Crime

Growing up in the Midwest, I had little appreciation for the virtues of the vine. Beer was plentiful and it wasn't a question of what kind, just how much. When it came to wine, however, I was clueless. If I was handed the wine list, I'd casually leaf through the pages and randomly pick a bottle. It felt like I was reading a French dictionary.

But after moving to San Francisco, within one hour of the vineyards of Napa and Sonoma, I began a quest to understand wine. Like Charles Atlas, the ninety-eight-pound weakling who transformed himself into a muscle man, I changed from wine rookie to wine geek.

What I discovered along the way is that, armed with the right information, unraveling the mysteries of a wine list need not raise your blood pressure. These days, the only times I feel my heart race and palms sweat during dinner are when my date is playing footsie.

Finding the Clues

When it's your turn to peruse the wine list, look for clues. Start with how the wine list is organized. Most traditional lists begin by separating wines according to categories such as regions or grape varieties. For example, all the red Bordeaux is listed together, and the Chardonnay comprises one grouping. The wines within a category are organized alphabetically or by price, making it simple to scan for a well-priced bottle or for a producer you recognize.

In many innovative restaurants you may notice a newfangled list that organizes bottles according to the way each wine tastes. It starts with wines that are mild and a little sweet, progressing to those that are drier and stronger tasting. "The idea is to organize the list so that you can find a wine that's delicious without having to jump through hoops," says Tim Hanni, a Master of Wine from Beringer Vineyards in California's Napa Valley, who pioneered the new concept. "The wine industry and 'experts' are pretty bad when it comes to simple things, like helping you find the wine you'll like the most." **(See Tim's food and wine pairing theories in EDU.5.)**

Dubbed a "progressive" wine list, the format separates bottles into categories from relatively light to full-body, from mild to strong tasting, and from sweet to dry. You don't need to know Alsatian Riesling from California Chenin Blanc—if the wine is situated at the top of the list, it will be lighter and a little sweet. Pick a bottle from the bottom of the list and it will be a fuller-bodied, drier example. With this it's easier to target a wine with flavors you like and not simply guess what's in the bottle.

Other eateries, such as the Old Tavern in Grafton, Vermont, organize bottles by variety and further break down each category by body and style of wine. "We've laid out our list so that the big, fat, lush Chardonnays are at the top and the most austere and acidic ones are on the bottom," noted vice president and wine buyer Kevin O'Donnell. He said it helps customers find what they're looking for easily by knowing in what order the wines are listed.

The Pricing Puzzle

On your journey to get through an often-unintelligible wine list, the next clue is price. This is usually the top priority when choosing vino at dinner, but how do you know if you're getting reamed or getting respect?

Restaurants charge wildly varying prices, yet most double or triple the wholesale price. For example, a retail store or restaurant buys wine from a wholesaler for $10. The retailer will raise the price 50 percent to $15 while the traditional restaurant markup would escalate to between $20 and $30.

The markup reflects a number of factors including overhead for decor, staffing, and glassware. Fancy establishments—the impress-your-date kind of places—usually charge more for everything. (I've always found that the dimmer the lights, the higher the markup.) Other hangouts might have lower margins, but on the average you should anticipate paying twice what you would in the store.

Just to make it more difficult to understand a wine list, markups are all over the map. Don't always go for the cheapest wines as they're usually the ones with the highest markup. Conversely, wines pushing the three-digit price range tend to sport the lowest margins. Restaurants are hesitant to double or triple their already high prices because very few people will drop more than a monthly car payment for a bottle of fermented grape juice.

Luckily, restaurateurs across the country are getting hip to the value of a reasonable wine-pricing strategy. "You take money to the bank, not margins," said Debbie Zachareas, wine director for EOS Restaurant and Wine Bar in San Francisco. She's structured the five-hundred-bottle list at EOS to make buying wine easier by selecting high-quality wines and keeping prices low. According to Zachareas, "My goal is to have fun developing the wine list and to make it exciting for our customers. I want people to experiment with the wines, and to do that they have to be able to afford them."

O'Donnell of the Old Tavern Inn echoes Zachareas's philosophy. "We simply price our wines six to ten dollars above our cost. It encourages guests to choose wines at higher prices because the value is directly related to the price of the wine."

Watson to the Rescue

Even Sherlock Holmes needed help on rare occasion. So if you've scoured the list and still want a recommendation, ask your server. But how much wine knowledge do most servers possess?

According to Darryl Beeson, **sommelier** and cellar master of the Mansion on Turtle Creek in Dallas, Texas, "It used to be that the wine knowledge of the server was inversely proportional to the number of body piercings and tattoos they had. That person may now be the owner of the trendy eatery where you're dining." So don't make assumptions, positive or negative, about a server's wine-savvy quotient. In many restaurants wait staff is trained in wine, but it's not a universal practice.

Debbie Zachareas of EOS recommends that you ask them a question about a wine you know. If they give you an answer you agree with, then fire away with questions. If not, you might want to flag down the sommelier.

> **SOMMELIER** (pronounced "som-el-yay")—A French term for a wine specialist. Usually associated with restaurants. A sommelier's job is to advise patrons on wine selections and to be able to describe certain characteristics of every wine on the establishment's list. Then they should be able to present the wine and serve it properly. Other job responsibilities include buying wines for the establishment and keeping the cellar stocked.

Don't think of the sommelier as a condescending wine snob. It's his or her job to compile the list and assist customers. I often ask for sommeliers when I'm dining out because they know where the hidden gems are on the wine list. If you're excited about tracking down an unknown label or unique varietal, have them help. In most cases, they'll be as excited as you are. (This wine list thing is a sexy subject.)

If price is a factor in your decision—as it is to most of us—tell the server or sommelier how much you anticipate spending. Are you on a hot date or with a client and want to be discreet? Point to a bottle in the price range you want and indicate that you'd like a comparable wine.

Servers and sommeliers can help even more if you give them direction and focus. Note that you prefer oaky Chardonnay or fruity Sauvignon

Blanc. "Be prepared to name a couple of your favorite wines to establish your taste preference," said Beeson. "It's fine to say 'I enjoy Kendall-Jackson Chardonnay' so they can find a similar wine."

Uncovering the Bargains

A good wine list should give you "the big O" (which stands for options). They include alternative grape varieties and regions, unique producers, a wide range of price points, and a way to order nice wine one glass at a time.

A strong wine-by-the-glass program is a sure sign that the restaurant respects its wine-loving clientele. Most eateries serve decent but fairly generic wines by the glass and charge a pretty penny for them. The policy doesn't encourage imbibers to explore, sample, and enjoy unfamiliar wines if all they're offered is standard fare. But wine bars and savvy restaurants are beginning to treat wines served by the glass with the credibility they deserve.

EOS Restaurant and Wine Bar serves more than one hundred regularly rotating wines by the glass. It's a mecca for wine lovers in the San Francisco Bay Area who flock to the sleekly decorated spot for **enological** adventure. Check around your area for restaurants or bars that have committed to a solid program of serving wines by the glass. It's the best opportunity to taste wines you might not otherwise have a chance to try.

ENOLOGY—The scientific study of wine.

Other options to search for on any wine list are within categories of grape varieties or regions that may be unfamiliar to you. If you have a handle on Chardonnay and Merlot, try Viognier and Syrah. If you like red Burgundy but can't stomach the price tags, head for the Pinot Noir section and look for wines from California or Oregon. **See REF.5: Variety Is the Spice of Life.**

Keep in mind that it's often very expensive to explore new wines at a restaurant. You might not like them and feel disappointed that you dropped $40. Consider trying unfamiliar wines at home and discover the ones you enjoy. Then feel confident as you get adventurous with Alicante Bouschet, or sample supple Sangiovese when dining out. **See Part II: It's Party Time!**

I'm not one to complain about the success of Cabernet and Chardonnay, but there are a couple of wines in particular that I think deserve more attention. Zinfandel, for one, is a versatile variety that goes with a lot of different foods. With lots of up-front fruit, it can be very appealing, though not necessarily complex. And Barbera, which grows in the shadow of Nebbiolo and Sangiovese in Italy, is another quiet champion in my wine experience. Barbera has a lot of powerful fruit and good acid but hardly a trace of tannin. These qualities make it a cinch for lots of different foods. We've now started to grow it in Sonoma and are excited with the results. Stay tuned!

—Gina Gallo

Good Cork, Bad Cork

The decision has been made and the mystery of choosing a wine for dinner solved. Just when you thought you could breathe a sigh of relief, however, the bottle arrives and is presented like a diamond on a platter. Now what do you do? Forget the pomp and circumstance surrounding opening a bottle of wine, but consider these few suggestions:

Do

Look at the label to make sure it's the right wine and the correct vintage you ordered. Then, eye the cork to make sure it isn't crumbling and dried out. If a bottle has been stored properly, on its side, the cork should be moist. Next, swirl, smell, and taste the splash of wine in your glass to determine if it tastes good or is flawed. If the wine smells like rubber, sherry, vinegar, wet cardboard, or a barnyard, have the server or sommelier smell and taste it. It's rare and sometimes hard to detect, but when you smell or taste flaws, don't be afraid to send the bottle back.

Don't

There's no need to pick up the cork and smell it. Smelling it won't tell you anything except that it's cork. When you sample the vino, forget swishing it around in your mouth and making rude sucking noises—just drink it. If the wine isn't flawed, but you don't like it, do not send it back. The only reason to send a bottle back is if it's flawed. As a move to impress your date, this tactic will fail. Though most restaurants should take back wine if you're unhappy with it, it's best to just drink the wine and chalk it up to a learning experience.

After you've motioned to the server to pour wine for everyone, make sure they don't pour the glasses too full. It's hard to swirl the wine and it makes it easy to spill the wine all over your new shirt. Another common mistake is that wine is served too cold or too warm. Don't get hung up on the perfect cellar temperatures and carry a thermometer around, but keep in mind that red wines taste better when they're a bit cooler than room temperature and whites, especially full-bodied ones, shouldn't be served ice-cold, as it masks the aromas and flavors.

Closing the Case

What about bringing your own wine to a restaurant? It's not like college days when BYOB was the norm. There are rules to bringing wine into a restaurant, and in many states it's simply illegal. Corkage fee varies, with some restaurants utilizing a sliding scale of around 10 percent of the price that the wine would sell for on the restaurant's list. Most of the time, though, a standard corkage fee of around $10 to $15 per bottle applies.

The main rule of thumb is to only bring special bottles that are either old or unique. Do not bring a wine that would appear on the establishment's wine list. Tacky, tacky. If you still want to bring in a bottle, heed this advice from cellar master Darryl Beeson: "Know the policy of the restaurant. Call ahead and see if they have a corkage fee and ask about bringing in a bottle. Tell them what it is to make sure it's not on their list. When you arrive at the restaurant, try to be discreet. Don't parade in with a bottle in a paper sack looking like Otis from *The Andy Griffith Show*."

Remember, wine is not something to fear or revere—it's to enjoy. Cheers.

NAMING WINES BY REGION VERSUS VARIETAL

Remember that wines are named according to either regions or grape variety. In the New World (United States, Australia, Chile, etc.) wines are mainly named after the grape variety they are made from: Chardonnay, Merlot, and Cabernet Sauvignon are types of grapes. On the other hand, wines from the Old World (France, Italy, Spain, etc.) are named for the region they are made in: Bordeaux is a region in France, Rioja is a region in Spain.

Here's a brief guide to a few major varieties and some of their equivalent regions:

Chardonnay (shar-do-*nay*) = white Burgundy
Chardonnay can be made in many styles from full-bodied with heavy oak to light and fruity. Top chards from California and France's Burgundy region can be very costly, so look to wines from Chile and the New World countries.

Pinot noir (*pee*-know *nwar*) = red Burgundy
If Cabernet is the king of red wine, then Pinot is the queen. The noble grape produces elegant and earthy wines that might qualify as the best all-around dinner vino. Wines from France's Burgundy region can be the costliest on Earth, but **quaffable** *bottles named Bourgogne are usually well priced. Top California and Oregon Pinots are rivaling Burgundy's best, but price tags reflect that.*

QUAFF—A dignified way of saying gulp or guzzle. Quaffing wines are those you throw back easily poolside on a hot day, usually with no oak and lower alcohol.

Cabernet Sauvignon (cab-er-*nay sew*-vin-*yawn*) and Merlot (mare-low) = red Bordeaux (bore-*doe*)
Red wines from Bordeaux are the yardsticks against which most cabs are measured. Bottles can include blends of five grape varieties, including: Cabernet Sauvignon, Merlot, Cabernet Franc, Petite Ver-

dot, and Malbec. Cabernet Sauvignon is the dominant variety in most regions, but wines from Pomerol and Saint-Emilion are Merlot-based. Most expensive Bordeaux and California Cabernets are big wines and you should look for older vintages. Young ones can have pronounced tannins, so be prepared.

Sauvignon Blanc (sew-vin-*yawn* blahnk) and Semillon (sem-ee-*yawn*) = white Bordeaux (bore-*doe*)
Sauvignon Blanc is made in many styles, from grassy and steely to fresh and fruity. Semillon is usually a blending grape known for its honeyed quality, but some producers (especially from Australia) bottle it separately. SB, as it's affectionately dubbed, is another good choice for dinner, and it's usually more affordable than Chardonnay. Look for bottlings from California, Australia, and New Zealand.

Syrah (si-rah) = northern red Rhône and Australian Shiraz (shear-ahz)
France's Rhône region produces some of the heartiest red wine in the world from Syrah. Big, chewy, rustic wines such as Hermitage, Saint-Joseph, and Cornas can be better deals than an expensive Cabernet or Bordeaux. For value, look to Australian Shiraz (the Aussie's name for Syrah), easy-to-drink blends called Côtes-du-Rhône, and Syrah from California.

Viognier (vee-ohn-*yay*) = white Rhône
In the wine lovers' quest for alternatives to Chardonnay, many have turned to Viognier. This floral, delicate grape variety has been a staple in the Condrieu region of France's northern Rhône region for centuries. French versions are pricey, but California produces slightly more reasonably priced bottlings.

Sangiovese (san-geeo-vay-*zay*) = Chianti
A grape variety that's very food-friendly due to high acidity and bright, fruity flavors, Sangiovese is the staple of wines from Italy's Chianti region. Many producers worldwide are experimenting with

this grape, so keep your eyes open. In any case, Chianti tends to of-fer good value and makes an ideal complement to Italian fare. NOTE: In a few regions in Europe, such as Alsace, they sell their wines by varietal.

—Leslie Sbrocco

DAMN REBEL, ANYWAY!

Not only has Tim Hanni—yet another Beringer crony—broken through the wall of stereotypical food and wine pairings with a completely new approach, he's also done the same with what many might perceive as who or what a wine "expert" is personally. Let's just say Tim isn't the over-serious wine geek who's forgotten to pull his nose out of the glass for several decades. You know the type, so insulated from the real world that they believe all life centers around their opinion of wine. This ain't Tim. In fact, dare we say, Tim's a bit wacky? Sure. And in a good way. We'd even bet a top-shelf harvest that Tim is probably the most entertaining, down-to-earth Master of Wine walking the planet today. All right, rumor has it he's a blast to party with. It must be his rock-and-roll roots. Anyway, let's cut to the chase and see what revelations Tim has concerning the ancient art of washing back some good grub with a tasty glass of wine.

—j, j & m

Forget Everything You Know About Food and Wine Pairing (Self-Explanatory)

by Tim Hanni, M.W.

Have you ever dreamt that you're a senior, about to take the critical final exam that will allow you to graduate, and you realize you've never been to class, much less opened the book? It's a huge relief to wake up from that dream. My problem was that I couldn't wake up because I was living my dream. As a self-proclaimed "expert" at food and wine pairing, I was sitting with professional chefs who had come to Napa Valley to learn my food and wine pairing philosophy, and I was about to admit that I didn't know what the hell I was talking about.

I should have been full of confidence, if not arrogance (an attitude not unknown to me or to the wine and food world). I grew up in a family that held Burgundy tastings for friends, and I always volunteered to empty the glasses and take them out to the kitchen for washing (note the order in which I did these tasks). By the time I turned seventeen, I had devoured every wine book in the library. Reading about wine sparked my interest in cooking, and my parents once gave me an omelet pan for Christmas (gee, thanks, Mom). Eventually, I became a professional chef, always with wine as a major adjunct to my work, and I then switched to the retail wine business, importing rare wines and designing elaborate wine and food pairing occasions for my best customers. Finally, I went for broke: I decided to take the prestigious Master of Wine exam in London.

No American had ever passed this grueling exam, which required a dissertation just to apply and progressed to a four-day marathon in London, writing about 125 pages of essays and completing three blind tastings, with twelve wines in each flight. It took me a couple of tries, but in 1990 I passed, and I got to put those initials after my name that qualified me as one of the 235 or so wine experts who have passed this exam since its debut forty-five years ago. **See PARTY.2: Flying Blind.**

That's how I ended up as the wine and food pairing instructor at Beringer Vineyards' School for American Chefs, a kind of graduate program for working chefs directed by the great teacher/author/culinarian Madeleine Kamman. I had one day to impart my infinite wisdom on pairing wine and food to these chefs. And I was suffering big time from what I later learned to call "cognitive dissonance," or to use a simpler term, barefaced lying. I was about to teach them a set of principles that I neither believed in nor operated under myself. I might have told them, for instance, that plain grilled beef and a big, tannic red wine was a marriage made in heaven because the "heavy" beef required an equally "weighty" wine. I might even have said something like "This combination works because the colloidally suspended polyphenolics in the red wine, which normally denature the proteins in your mouth, combine with the residual proteins from the beef, and the fat from the steak replaces the lost lubricity, lessening the astringent sensation, and . . ." Hey, who's going to argue with a line like that?

Instead, I told them the truth. I didn't really know what happened when we tasted wine and food together. I couldn't even precisely define "taste." As it turns out, neither could those chefs. Admitting that proved to be a catharsis for all of us. We had a clean slate and the beginnings of an investigation of wine and food that I've been engaged in ever since.

Food in Balance

You should drink the wine that tastes best to you. And you should drink it with the food you prefer. Does that sound weird or illogical or even revolutionary? You wouldn't think so. But the subject of wine and food pairing has been shrouded in mystery, confusion, and, alas, more than a little intimidation. In this section, I'll identify two basic principles that will help you make sure you get what you want when you enjoy wine and food together.

Forget the Conventional Approaches to Wine and Food Pairing

Wine and food pairing "rules" come in many shapes and forms. But they have one thing in common. They don't always work, and they don't take into account what you expect from a glass of wine. Here's why.

Forget Color Coding!

You've probably heard the old advice to serve white wine with white meats (fish, poultry, or pastas with cream sauce) and red wine with red meats (lamb, beef, venison, and so on). We refer to this as "color coding" of wine and food. But if you prefer a mild-tasting wine like a Riesling or a white Zinfandel, you should drink that wine with any dish, even a big, rare hunk o' meat. Conversely, you might enjoy a big bruiser of a red wine even more with a delicate piece of fish than with red meat. If people insist on having red wine with red meat, I respect their preference. What I promote is an "equal opportunity" approach to the subject.

Forget Flavor Matching

Here's an approach that at first glance seems more logical: Mirror the flavors in the wine with the flavors in the dish. So if you want to drink Sauvignon Blanc, which often has an herbal aroma, pair it with a dish containing lots of herbs and garlic, like tarragon-sautéed chicken, say. Or if a Zinfandel has blackberry and spicy pepper aromas, serve it with steak coated with peppercorns and a blackberry/Port sauce. Better yet, if you're eating a spicy Chinese pork dish, drink Gewürztraminer (*Gewürz* means spice in German). Sound good? Unfortunately, we've found that in certain combinations the Gewürztraminer or Sauvignon Blanc you loved at the start of this meal can end up tasting as bitter as a farewell note from a departed lover. And what if you simply don't like the taste of that wine to begin with?

Forget "Classic" Combinations

Well, you may be thinking, the food and wine combinations we've copied from traditional winegrowing regions must be unassailable. After all, the

French and the Italians know everything there is to know about food and wine, right? Maybe, but somewhere along the way we've made assumptions about the historical basis of wine and food pairings that may not be true. Is pasta with a tomato-based sauce traditionally served with an Italian red wine? Perhaps now, but tomatoes were considered to be poisonous in Italy until about 150 years ago. Does venison with black cherry sauce "work" with a Cabernet Sauvignon from Bordeaux because the dish was created to reflect the cherry aroma in the wine? A little research showed us that this dish originated in Germany's Black Forest, where it was served with Riesling, not Cabernet.

In fact, serving red meat with red wine is not an essential part of any regional cuisine in France. Red meat was a special-occasion dish, not an everyday staple. And people in winegrowing regions traditionally drank only one type of wine, red or white, whichever they produced from the barrel in their basement, with no thought of changing wines according to the dish they were serving that day, much less the different courses of a meal.

Other Theories and a New Direction

I could go on. "Weight" matching, for example: the idea that there are "little wines" that go with "little foods," or that something as "heavy" as a steak deserves a "heavy" wine like Cabernet Sauvignon or Syrah. Here's a party trick for you: If you pour some dry red wine very gently into a glass of sweet white or blush wine, like a white Zinfandel, the Cabernet will float to the top. So which is the "heavier" wine?

"But wait," you're saying. "You're using two different definitions of 'heavy.' One refers to density, and the other refers to flavor, richness, or, well, what does it refer to?"

What are we referring to? About the time of my wake-up call with the chefs, I realized I had memorized a lot of conventional wisdom about wine and food pairing without really testing it for myself. I had been seduced by the very evocative writings of "experts" describing their personal, emotional experiences with wine and food, and I had swallowed (often literally!) the notion that experts could identify "good" and "bad" pairings of wine and food. But I had never questioned the most basic definitions and assumptions used to talk about wine and food pairing. I was about to start.

What Is the Taste of Wine?

I quickly realized that there were as many definitions of two key terms, flavor and taste, as there were reference books. How can we communicate about wine and food if we don't use words in the same way? So our first step was to agree on the definitions you see here, which I'm glad to say are gaining wider acceptance.

Two Key Terms

Taste: One of five basic sensations in the mouth: sweet, sour, salty, bitter, and savory (*umami,* to use the Japanese term).

Flavor: A sensation in the mouth and nose arising from a combination of taste, smell, and touch sensations. Our psychological disposition, including our physical or emotional state, the environment, and our past experiences and expectations, greatly affects how we perceive flavors.

Focusing on Taste

Taste comes first. I believe it is the strongest determinant of our individual preferences for certain wines or wine and food combinations. So we're not going to talk here about how the aroma of wild strawberries in your Pinot Noir reminds you of spring walks in the woods, how the flavors in a rosé evoke that special August evening on the beach at Antibes. All that comes later.

Instead, we'll focus on the five taste sensations that you are programmed to recognize from birth: sweet, sour, salty, bitter, and savory (*umami*). Because you've been eating all your life, you can easily identify these tastes and give examples: sweet honey, sour lemon, salty soy sauce, bitter endive, and . . . huh? What's *umami?* you're wondering.

Umami is the Japanese term for the taste we refer to in English as "savory." It's the delicious taste, neither sweet, nor sour, nor salty, nor bitter, in foods like crab, aged beef, mushrooms (especially dried mushrooms), baked potatoes, chocolate, and stocks and broths. To get technical for a moment, the savory taste comes from an amino acid (glutamic acid) that occurs naturally in foods. Japanese food researchers were the first to identify and extract this taste, which is very common in the Japanese diet. It's no more important for you to know its chemical makeup than it is for you to understand the chemistry that makes sugar sweet. But it's a taste you are very familiar with, even if you've never named it. Without this savory *(umami)* taste, food does not taste satisfying.

Some Tastes Come Naturally

Are all five tastes equally good? Not to babies, as I discovered when I started feeding pureed foods to my infant son, Landon, a human taste-o-meter. He likes two tastes, sweet and savory. Applesauce? Smack, smack! Mashed potatoes? Yum, yum. But if I give him foods high in bitter, sour, or salty tastes, it's "Blah!" and back on the spoon, or worse.

Some anthropologists theorize that our innate attraction to sweet and savory (umami) tastes and our repulsion for bitter, sour, and salty tastes developed to help us humans separate wholesome, nutritious foods from foods that could be poisonous or otherwise damaging. Whether that's true or not, we all seem to start out like baby Landon. Later, as adults, we learn to tolerate quite high levels of sour, salty, and bitter tastes. But we also have our own ideas about how much of each of these basic tastes is too much.

Tastes in Wine

The basic tastes in wine are sweet, sour, and bitter. (Astringency, some-times confused with bitterness, is a sensation of touch, not taste; it's that puckered, dry feeling you get in your cheeks from an underripe persim-mon, or a tannic wine. Tannins in wine, which come from the seeds and skin, can result in both bitter taste and astringency.)

I love all three of these tastes, even quite high levels of sourness and bit-terness. In fact, I sometimes refer to myself and other wine lovers who have acquired a taste for sour or bitter wines as "taste mutants." This is because we crave the tastes we are genetically programmed to reject. But I respect the right of others to prefer sweeter wines. It's merely a matter of taste, and we all know what we like, or what we prefer on certain occasions. Let's face it: Some people like coffee with cream and sugar, some like it black. Or you may like café latte in the morning and espresso after dinner. The same is true with wines, and you'll easily recognize which ones are more or less sweet, sour, or bitter, without any "expert" advice.

How Tastes in Wine and Food Interact

Once you have decided the taste you prefer in wine, or the taste you want on a specific occasion, you don't want someone fooling around with that taste. And certainly the winemaker wants you to experience the wine as he or she intended it to taste. But the taste of a wine can change in reaction to the foods you eat with it. Fortunately, we've found that the way the wine changes is pre-dictable, and tied directly to those five basic tastes, all of which occur in food.

Two Key Reactions

Foods that are sweet (from sugar, fruit or fruit juice, hoisin sauce, honey, or the like) or savory (well-aged beef, ripe tomatoes, mushrooms, caviar, and even ketchup) in taste make any wine taste stronger. By "stronger," I mean drier (less sweet), more acidic (sour), and more tannic (bitter and astringent).

You can demonstrate this for yourself. Take a sip of your favorite full-bodied red wine, a Cabernet Sauvignon, for example. Now take a bite of a sweet apple or mango, then another sip of the wine. I'm willing to bet that the wine tasted more bitter—the sweetness of the apple making the wine taste "stronger." Now think about the combination we mentioned earlier, steak with blackberry/Port sauce served with Zinfandel. For most of us, the savory taste in the meat and the sweetness of the berries and Port sauce will make the wine taste stronger, just as the sweet apple did. If you appreciate that strong taste, fine. But other folks want the wine to remain unchanged.

In contrast, sour tastes in food (vinegars, citrus, dry wine reductions) or salty tastes (including table or sea salt, soy sauce, olives in brine, and Asian fish sauce) make wines taste "milder," that is, less dry (sweeter), less acidic (sour), and not so tannic (less bitter and astringent). But wait a minute. Haven't we always been told that vinegar and lemon in foods are enemies of wine?

See for yourself: Taste your favorite Chardonnay or Cabernet, then lick a wedge of lemon, and try the wine again. The wine's fruit, acid, and tannins are balanced just as the winemaker intended. Now try one more experiment. Taste the wine again, sprinkle a little salt on an apple slice, then take another sip of wine. The wine tastes milder, mellower. You may like this, or you may have preferred the stronger taste resulting from the sweet apple. Again, it's a matter of taste.

The Beringer Balance (see below) summarizes these two simple cause-and-effect reactions: Salty and sour tastes in food make wine seem milder; sweet and savory tastes in food make wine seem stronger. These same reactions will occur with all wines, but will be even more pronounced if the wine is aged in oak, like many Chardonnays, Cabernets, and Merlots. It's just that simple.

Salty Taste in Food

Salt, soy sauce, fish sauce, olives, olive brine.

Sour Taste in Food

Vinegars, lime, lemon, dry wine reductions.

Sweet Taste in Food

Sugar, most fruit and fruit juices, hoisin sauce, honey.

Savory (*umami*) Taste in Food

Meats, seafood, poultry, tomatoes, onions, green vegetables, ham, bacon, sauces and stocks.

Wine and Food in Balance

Working for a winery as I do, I'm prejudiced. I don't want you to drink wine that doesn't taste like the winemaker intended it to taste. So, jointly with Beringer executive chef Jerry Comfort, I've learned to use my understanding of these two reactions to balance the basic tastes in foods so that the wine stays the same.

Balancing Act

Revisit the experiments you just did. When the sweet apple made the wine taste stronger, you sprinkled on some salt and brought the wine back into balance. A lick of lemon had the same effect. We've found that the two groups we've identified, salt and sour tastes on the one hand and sweet and savory tastes on the other, balance each other out, leaving the wine alone. And you can follow these principles whether you are cooking or eating out.

Here's another experiment to show you how. Taste a wine you've chosen, maybe a Chianti this time, then a spoonful of your favorite commercial tomato-based pasta sauce (admit it, you buy it in a jar rather than stand over a hot stove all evening!), then taste the wine again. I'm willing to bet that the savory and sweet tastes in the sauce make the wine less yummy, to use the technical term.

Now mix a spoon of that same pasta sauce with a few drops of balsamic vinegar and a little salt, and take another sip of wine. See what I mean? The tastes in the food are balanced, and the wine tastes great.

Here are some ingredients that will increase the sour or salty tastes in a dish, whether you are cooking or reading a menu description:

Sour

Vinegars (cider, balsamic, or wine, including rice wine)
Lemon, lime or other citrus juice, or zest
Mustard
Verjus (juice of unripened grapes)
Reductions of dry wine (for sauces)
Dry fortified wines (dry Sherry, Madeira, or Vermouth)

Salty

Salt (table or sea salt)
Soy sauce
Olives or olive brine
Asian fish sauce
Fermented black beans
Parmesan cheese

Not too hard, right? Think of pizza with salt-cured olives, pasta well sprinkled with Parmesan, or a beef and broccoli stir-fry with garlic and black-bean garlic sauce. In a restaurant, if you find the food is out of balance with the wine, sprinkle on a judicious amount of salt or soy sauce, or ask for wedges of lemon or lime or a little balsamic or rice wine vinegar, depending on the cuisine. None of these adjustments make the dish "unauthentic" or "culturally incorrect." They just make it taste better with wine.

It's unlikely that the sour and salty tastes in a dish will make the wine you've chosen taste too mild. But if they do, use these tools from the sweet and savory side of the balance to adjust the food:

Sweet

Sugar or honey
Fruit or fruit juices
Hoisin sauce

Off-dry wines (Riesling, Chenin Blanc, Gewürztraminer, white Zinfandel)
Sweet wines (Port, Madeira, Mirin)

Savory

Worcestershire sauce
Asian oyster sauce
Asian fish sauce (also salty in taste)
Reduced stocks or demi-glace
Ketchup

As you adjust your food, remember that balance is key. Paying attention to this balance may actually improve your cooking, because the result is usually a flavorful, delicious food. And you will always have the perfect measuring tool: your tongue, which will immediately tell you how the basic taste in the wine changes in combination with the food.

Just one word about spicy seasonings: Chilies, black or white peppercorns, raw garlic, and other hot, spicy ingredients sensitize your mouth (a tactile sensation called chemesthesis). This sensitivity increases your perception of bitterness (and astringency) in wine. And this sensation can persist and even increase as the seconds and minutes pass. Salty and sour tastes in food tend to soften this effect.

The Wisdom of Traditions

Earlier, I was pretty hard on what we called "classic" pairings of food and wine. Now I'd like to give our predecessors in traditional winegrowing regions their due. In Tuscany, where Chianti is king, *bistecca alla fiorentina* (grilled Florentine steak) is served with a wedge of lemon and a generous sprinkling of salt. Savory plus sour and salt equals a mellow wine. In Burgundy, red wine is served with rabbit (savory) in a sauce that incorporates vinegar, verjus, or mustard (sour again). And in the area of France that produces Muscadet, they know that an acidic wine tastes much more delicious if the savory oyster served alongside is dipped in a mignonette sauce made with vinegar (sour) and shallots. The cooks in these regions, without consciously analyzing the principles of reactivity and balance discussed here, instinctively created dishes that showed the local wines at their best.

In the United States, we don't have centuries of winemaking history behind us, although we're getting there. More important, our taste in food has "gone global," and we want to enjoy wine with foods from around the world, even those areas where wine was not traditionally a part of the meal. By understanding basic tastes and the principles of reactivity and balance I've shown you here, we can enjoy delicious food and wine combinations regardless of the cuisine we choose.

From Taste to Flavor: The Emotional Side of Food and Wine Pairing

Have I told you all there is to understand about wine and food pairing? Of course not. Wine offers a lifetime of learning, of new experiences and new pleasures to discover. Once you are confident about your taste preferences and your ability to enjoy those tastes with the food you choose to eat, you can start to create your own wine history.

Flavor Is Subjective

Look again at the two definitions we mentioned earlier. Taste is simple (well, almost) and fairly objective. We can all identify sweet, sour, salty, bitter, and savory (although some of us genetic "super-tasters" are more sensitive to lower levels of these tastes than others). And we've seen how important the reactions between these tastes are in pairing wine and food. Flavor is complex, comprising sensations of taste, smell, and touch, and is very subjective. Our culture, our environment, our experiences, and our expectations all influence how we react to different flavors. We can also choose to amend our reactions to flavors, to "acquire" certain tastes. The first time I drank coffee, at about age fourteen, I was totally repulsed. But grown-ups drank coffee, and my need to identify with the grown-ups gradually overcame what my intuition was telling me.

The emotional component is huge. The writers who seduced me with their descriptions of their favorite wine and food pairings weren't giving a neutral, sensory analysis of wine and food. They were writing about their experience, what the flavors evoked for them. That crisp rosé and the black olive tapenade and the sun on the hills of Provence and the pleasure of lunching with friends all ganged up together to make one experience perfect.

And that's not bad. As long as it's not prescriptive: "My expert opinion is right; if you don't share my vision, you're wrong." Personally, I want to create my own perfect wine and food experiences. And so should you. What I've tried to do here is give you the tools to create these experiences more frequently and predictably. If you do so, I guarantee you'll significantly reduce the "suckosity" of your wine and food experiences.

THE BOLD, THE BEAUTIFUL, THE PROLIFIC

What can the Wine Brats say about our longtime associate and friend Tina Caputo? Well, she's a freelance writer who has penned for such cutting-edge rags as Bikini *and* Might, *and interviewed the likes of American pop icon Bob Barker (*The Price Is Right*). But writing credits don't make a person, so let's do the cheesy and obvious stunt of comparing her to a fine wine. Maybe a California Rhône–style blend of Syrah and Grenache: dark, brooding, and progressive, yet fun and spicy, an up-and-coming star who can't be stopped. Oh, yeah, we like that!*

By the way, we first met Tina when she worked at the California Wine Institute, where she and a compatriot produced an in-the-street video titled Hard to Swallow. *No, not porn, but a no-flinch look at the next generation's attitude toward wine. All right, indifference. The video certainly opened industry eyes to its failure to reach Tina's peers. Now here comes the segue: Tina recently experienced her own eye-opening ordeal when she read an article in a major newspaper about building home wine cellars, which presented an array of lovely choices ranging from $7,000 to $60,000 a pop. Yeah, right. The following is her rebuttal to the day-to-day reality of storing wine, which in these United States mainly occurs on the front seat of the car as we drive home from the local grocery store. Go get 'em, Tina!*

—j, j & m

Home Wine Cellars for the Rest of Us, or Storing Wine Safely on a Budget

by Tina Caputo

M y wine cellar had its humble beginnings about six years ago, after an unexpected phone call. The destiny caller was my wine-shipper friend, Susie, offering to score me a case of white wine for the low-low price of $24. For all I knew, the stuff tasted like lighter fluid, but for $24 I was pretty sure I could live with that. Can you say, "Two bucks a bottle"?

When Susie dropped the wine off at my apartment, I was then faced with the challenge of finding a place to put the stuff. I mean, aside from my gullet. After sticking a couple bottles in the refrigerator, I still had ten left to deal with. Because I live in a two-room studio, my available closet space was not exactly overwhelming. As it was, I had to donate clothing to the Salvation Army to make room every time I bought a new outfit.

Then I remembered the Kelvinator. The Kelvinator was one of those ancient built-in icebox thingys people had in their kitchens before refrigerators were invented; sort of like a wall safe with a latch instead of a combination lock.

Anyway, the one in my oh-so-modern kitchen wasn't getting much use anymore, due to the fact that my landlord have finally given in to my demands for a fridge that ran on electricity rather than twenty-pound blocks of ice. It was the perfect spot for my wine! I stacked the remaining ten bottles in the Kelvinator and latched the door. Ta-da! A wine cellar.

Six years and two apartments later, my wine cellar isn't much more sophisticated. Sure, the wines have gotten better (I don't mean to brag, but these days I have been known to pay up to ten bucks for a bottle of wine!), but I still keep them humbly stored in a dark, cool closet, next to that ironing board I never use.

Of course, some people believe that something more elaborate is required, like a custom-made, redwood wine cellar with a built-in cooling unit. It always drives me crazy when I see those articles in hoity-toity wine magazines, implying that your average Joe can spare thousands of dollars to have a state-of-the-art wine cellar built in the spare room next to the servants' quarters. In my world, that's about as realistic as telling me I can build my own space shuttle out of pipe cleaners, blast off into outer space, and pick up some Martian wine to stock my $20,000 cellar.

Welcome back to Earth. Most people I know don't have that kind of scratch, let alone an extra room to build a cellar. Well, the good news is you don't need wads of cash, an east wing, or even a vehicle for space travel to start a wine cellar. All you need is a little imagination and the ability to interpret the word *cellar* loosely.

Why Would I Want a Wine Cellar?

Wine cellars aren't just showpieces for the rich and pretentious—there are actually very good reasons to have one. Probably the best reason is to have a few bottles of your favorite wines handy so you don't have to run out to the corner store every time you want a red to go with your pizza. I like to keep a variety of red, white, and sparkling wines on hand so I'll be prepared for anything. Steaks for dinner? I'm ready with a bottle of Cabernet. Chinese food? Bring on the Riesling. The neighbor upstairs with the yapping dog is moving out? Time to open the bubbly!

Don't worry about filling your wine cellar all at once. Stocking up on the stuff you like when it goes on sale is a great way to get started, and unless you plan to drink your wine right away, it's a good idea to have a special place to keep it.

This is because wine can be damaged if it's not stored correctly. Wine has many enemies, and I don't mean neo-Prohibitionists. I'm talking about excessive light, heat, and vibration. For example, if a wine is exposed to extreme heat, or bright sunlight, it can end up having a "cooked" taste. Vibration can cause a wine to age too quickly. And a combination of these storage "no-nos" can cause your wine to start "bleeding" up through the cork like a vino stigmata!

It's important to remember that, unlike you, wine doesn't like change.

That's why you should store it someplace where temperatures are fairly constant (about fifty to sixty degrees Fahrenheit is ideal) and avoid moving it from one place to another. Humidity is also good for wine because it keeps the corks from drying out and letting oxygen in. (Once oxygen gets inside your bottle, it's good-bye tasty wine and helloooooo salad dressing!)

When stored properly, your surplus wine will retain its quality—and will often taste even better if you hang onto it for a few years. Many harsh, "tannic" reds that grow hair on your tongue will soften and improve with a little time in storage.

Before we move on, let's review. In terms of wine storage, these places are BAD:

- Inside the oven
- On top of the refrigerator
- The trunk of your car
- In your pants (a bad place to store most anything, if you ask me)
- A sunny windowsill

So Where Do I Put My Cellar, Smarty Pants?

Even if you live in a one-room apartment with sixteen of your brothers and sisters, you can still find room for a wine cellar. Basements are a great place to store wine, but if you don't have one at your disposal, be creative! Building a cellar can be as simple as asking for an empty wine box at the grocery store, sticking a few bottles in it (be sure to lay it on its side to keep the corks moist), and shoving it in the closet next to those old Rick Springfield albums you're so ashamed of.

(Disclaimer: Although I've never had a problem with this, some experts say that cardboard boxes are not suitable for long-term storage because they're manufactured with chemicals that can affect the wine. If you plan on leaving your vino in the same box for years, you might want to ask your local wine merchant to sell you a couple of wooden wine crates.)

Still need home cellar inspiration? Take a look at these innovative real-life cellars!

Doug's Super Combination Wine- and Water-Closet

Doug learned to love wine while working as a bartender at, of all places, Hooters. Formerly a strict beer drinker, Doug was converted to wine when one of his coworkers introduced him to the joys of Cabernet. From there he moved on to Pinot Noirs and Zinfandels. Now he says he can't imagine life without wine, and has about twenty bottles in his home collection.

Doug stores his wine in the bathroom because it's unheated (i.e., cold) and damp. "People must think I'm pretty weird when they come in here to do their business and see all that wine stacked up next to the shower," Doug said, "but after the initial surprise, they think it's pretty cool."

Card Catalog Reincarnated as Wine Cellar

While working as a college librarian several years ago, Craig "acquired" some old wooden card catalog drawers. Meanwhile, his new career as a chef was drawing him into the world of wine. Perfect timing! As his wine collection grew, Craig realized that the card catalog drawers from his former life were the perfect size to store individual wine bottles (in alphabetical order, of course). And with the limited space in his studio apartment, Craig found the card catalogs could double as coffee tables when he cut the legs off them!

The Vino Files

Habib was introduced to wine at a young age by his parents, who made wine in his grandfather's basement. Today he runs a graphic design company out of his San Francisco apartment, leaving little to no space for a wine cellar. But instead of giving up his wine habit, Habib devoted one of the file drawers in his "office" to keeping his liquid assets healthy. "My landlord refuses to have the heater fixed in that room, so it's always about sixty degrees in there," said Habib. "I freeze my butt off, but the wine is happy."

Of Penny Loafers, Pumps, and Pinot

Jill was only an occasional wine drinker until she became friends with a woman who worked for a winery. (Translation: free samples!) Through her friend, Jill began to learn more about wine, and to love it enough to start keeping extra bottles around the house.

Jill was the only one in our survey group with a rack for her wine—a shoe rack, that is! The dark, cool closet that houses her shoe collection also makes a handy perch for her wine collection. "The only thing that's likely to damage my wine in here is the smell of my stinky old shoes," Jill laughed.

See, kids? Making your own wine cellar is easy! All you need is an interest in wine, a few bucks, and some creativity. The hard part is actually leaving a few bottles in your makeshift cellar to drink later.

TEN WAYS TO FILL UP YOUR WINE CELLAR QUICKLY AND CHEAPLY

1. Have a stock-the-cellar party. Invite your friends over for a party, asking each guest to bring a bottle of wine they enjoy that costs $10 or less. Open a few of them up to drink that night and tuck the leftovers into your cellar when the festivities are over. Hey, if you close the deal on one bottle, you're off and running.

2. Keep your eyes peeled for wine sales. Warehouse stores are great sources for discount vino. When you find something you enjoy at a good price, pick up a case. Buying by the case will usually score you between 5 and 10 percent additional savings.

3. Getting married? Why not register for gifts at a wine shop? You may end up with some amazing bottles of wine—and fewer fondue sets that you will never use.

4. Don't forget about Christmas and birthdays! When your loved ones

inevitably ask for clues on what to give you, drop a few not-so-subtle hints about the gift of vino.

5. Befriend someone who works in the wine industry and hope they'll take pity on poor, wineless you and hand over a few surplus bottles.

6. Get a part-time job in a wine shop. Can you say "employee discount"?

7. Join a wine-of-the-month club. Before you know it, your cellar will be brimming with new and interesting wines; no shopping necessary!

8. One day each week, take the money you would have spent on lattes, beer, bagels, new socks, etc., and buy a bottle of wine instead.

9. Take up a home winemaking hobby. (Not enough space you say? Who needs that bathtub anyway?) See BREW.3: Home Winemaking Comes Out of the Closet.

10. Stock your very small cellar with very large bottles (think magnums!).

—Tina Caputo

BREAKING THE WINE STORAGE RULES: HEALTHY REBELLION OR RECKLESS WINE ABUSE?

After reading through my wine-storage tips, some of you may be wondering if all that coddling is really necessary. Not a bad question to ask.

Previously, I'd blindly taken the advice of wine experts and kept my vino in a dark, cool place. But what if I did the opposite for a couple of weeks? Would my wine be rendered undrinkable by the ravages of heat, light, and motion? In the name of Journalistic Integrity and Good Drinkin', I had to find out.

At the risk of proving the information in my own wine storage article wrong and making myself look like an idiot, I decided to engage in a little "wine abuse." What would happen if I took two perfectly innocent bottles of Bordeaux from the same case and subjected one of them to rigorous torture, while leaving the other to rest in a cool, dark closet?

To get the experiment off to a sadistic start, I stuck the unlucky Bordeaux in my freezer—a major wine storage "no-no." After an hour of this torment, I moved the bottle to the refrigerator to contend with rotting vegetable odors and constant vibration.

The next morning, I put the bottle in the trunk of my car, where it rolled around freely for a week, breaking the "no movement" rule. I then passed the baton over to a friend, who left the battered bottle in his sweltering, sun-drenched office for a couple of days (in flagrant violation of the "avoid excessive light and drastic temperature changes" rule) before popping it into his oven to let the pilot light take over. On day four, he announced that the wine was leaking out of the bottle and bleeding down the label.

At last, the wine was ready for testing.

To avoid any bias on my part, I put both the coddled and abused bottles in paper bags and tasted them side by side. There was a definite difference: One of the wines had a decidedly vinegary aroma and tasted less fruity than its twin. But which wine would it be? What if I ripped off the paper bag to reveal that the wine I preferred was the bleeding oven-roasted wine?

Much to my relief (hey, I'm not an idiot after all!), the mistreated bottle was the inferior one.

See . . . I was right all along! Never doubted it for a minute.

—Tina Caputo

Part II

It's Party Time!

ENTER THE UNIVERSE OF THE SURREAL AT YOUR OWN RISK

If you haven't skipped ahead, and you have even the slightest ability to retain tidbits of information, you'll remember our introduction to Tina Caputo and our reference to her writing and interview credits. It was through one of these interviews, and Tina's subsequent intro-duction, that we met the Surreal Gourmet, a.k.a. Bob Blumer. She'd explained to us that his take on food closely matched our philosophy about wine: Make it fun and entertaining. Not long after we'd con-tacted Bob at his home in Hollywood, we were all gathered together in Napa at the home of Brat board members Dawn Dooley and Mimi Gatens for an unforgettable Surreal Meal.

Now on that night, back in early '97, Bob set the tone for some fifteen guests, all original members of the Wine Brats, by poaching salmon in the dishwasher. He proceeded to dazzle and entertain throughout the evening with his Salvador Daliesque Culinary Spin right up to dessert, which was ice cream served in frying pans, made to resemble sunny-side-up eggs (pick up one of his eye-popping cookbooks for details). Needless to say, the Surreal Gourmet and the Wine Brats have become coconspirators many times over the past few years in our parallel missions to bring good wine and fine food to the people. So we ask, who better to set the table than Bob Blumer for "Part II: It's Party Time!," which is our best effort at help-ing you integrate wine and food into your busy lives.

—j, j & m

The Surreal Circus, or My Favorite Dinner Party

by Bob Blumer (a.k.a. the Surreal Gourmet)

O nce a year I make a pilgrimage to Vancouver, Canada, to visit friends and eat French fries with garlic aioli at a bar called the Wazubee. Ever since I accidentally wrote a cookbook, my visits have become synonymous with dinner parties. I play ringleader, and everybody joins the circus in the kitchen. By now, the clowns who masquerade as sous chefs have all cultivated their own areas of expertise. Jow peels garlic, Ange and Johnny pit olives, Erin grates Parmesan, Aynsley hovers about making sure my wineglass is topped, and whoever is new to the group inherits the unenviable task of destemming endless bunches of fresh herbs. When we finish the prep work, I assemble the meal and usually blow up the kitchen in the process. Around eleven o'clock, I emerge from a cloud of smoke with the plated entrees, and we proceed to eat, drink, and have way too much fun. Each party ups the ante, and every time I return, we try to outdo ourselves.

On my last trip, the circus traveled to a cottage on Gambier Island, a tiny spit in the Georgia Straight, thirty miles from the nearest food processor. There were no matching plates or cloth napkins, no electricity, and no place to run to for last-minute ingredients. But these minor shortcomings were no challenge for the harmonic convergence of fresh-caught Coho salmon, four bags of groceries, an assortment of inexpensive wine, a case of Prosecco (a light Italian sparkling wine), and a bottle of Lagavulan (most of these friends were starving artists, but they never compromised on their single-malt Scotch). As usual, the kitchen was a cacophony of slicing, dicing, and laughter, accompanied by *The Best of Abba* on the boom box. Our sense of accomplishment and appreciation for our bounty of fresh produce was heightened by the twinkling Canadian sky. As we sat down to eat, the stars aligned—both literally and figuratively. It was a magical evening that no dining establishment could rival, at any price. Of course, on my next visit, we'll be putting more gunpowder in the cannon.

Doable Dinner Parties

As the aspiring patron saint of dysfunctional kitchens, short attention spans, and mismatched cutlery (most of my pieces have airplane logos stamped in them), I am here to champion the dinner party anchored by joie de vivre, a few memorable dishes, and a bounty of freely flowing wine. Whether you have been planning a party for weeks, or you're simply throwing a last-minute potluck, focus on the spirit, not the faux bourgeois etiquette promoted by TV's home decorating gurus and glossy catalogs. As they say at Burger King, "Sometimes you've just gotta break the rules." Here are a few tips to help you have it your way.

Take the Leap

No kitchen or dining room is inadequate. Dinner parties that are forced to battle the limitations of micro–cooking spaces, cramped eating quarters, insufficient furniture, or [your excuse here] tend to generate a special sense of communal accomplishment as the host and guests bond while surmounting the obvious challenges.

Invite Trouble

In addition to the mix of usual suspects, invite one outspoken, controversial "ringer" whom you can count on to invigorate the conversation. I trade numbers with these types when I meet them at other events, and I lure them to my parties with the promise of fine wine and food. Do the same, or bait your own hook.

Make Memorable Food, Not Memorable Portions

Great food fuels the party spirit. But that doesn't mean one needs to spend the entire day cooking, or break the bank to finance the groceries. I use one fundamental rule when determining what to serve: Make a minimal number of dishes, but make each one memorable. A finger food, a salad, and an entree should be enough to satiate any guest's hunger, as well as their palate. A crusty Italian or French baguette, served hot from your oven, will improve the taste of almost anything it accompanies. At about two bucks a loaf, it's the ultimate affordable luxury (if your bread is a day old, baptize it with a sprinkling of water and toss it, uncovered, in the oven for about six to eight minutes at 300 degrees, or until it's hot and crispy).

Even the most culinarily challenged novice can throw together impressive meals with minimal appliances, a few fresh ingredients, and a heavy-handed infusion of fresh herbs and spices. Pastas, risottos, roasted chickens, and gumbos are a few examples of simple, affordable dishes that you can find foolproof recipes for, then enhance with your own signature twist. (If this prospect still seems daunting—have I got a book for you!) When time or finances are an issue, never hesitate to ask every guest to bring a bottle of wine, and delegate the appetizers and dessert to those who call offering to bring something special—if they didn't mean it, they shouldn't have asked. **See PARTY.7: The Art of Culinary Delegation**

Be Accommodating

These days it's virtually impossible to randomly select a dozen people who will eat everything placed in front of them. You can count on dietary quirks such as allergies, ancient religious traditions, politics, diets, and bad childhood experiences to create a menu minefield. To play it safe: Steer clear of the most obvious offenders (i.e., Iraqi veal cheeks sautéed in whale blubber); add ingredients from the allergy quirk list (i.e., nuts and dairy products) at the last minute so that some portions can be dished out before it's necessary to dial 911; prepare extra salad and vegetables so that there will be enough to create meal-sized portions for anyone unable, or unwilling, to eat the main course; and if you suspect in advance that your dinner party may turn into a quirkfest, serve up a trusty tomato-based pasta, or a Build-Your-Own burrito dinner featuring an assortment of ingredients. Everybody loves to assemble their own dinner, and the interaction B.Y.O. meals create acts as a great icebreaker. Other simple B.Y.O.'s include shish-kebabs, fondues, pizza, and ice cream sundaes.

Energize

It's exciting to walk into a room and feel that a great dinner party is about to take place. This highly sought-after sensation is triggered by a mysterious "energy" that emanates from a combination of smells, lighting, music, and decor, as well as the "vibe" of the crowd, and, most important, the host (remember, guests feed off your energy as much as your food). If a little attention is focused on each of these details, they will project an overall impression that becomes contagious.

Wing It

Although something is always bound to go wrong at a party, with the exception of mass food poisoning and/or choking, no catastrophe merits spoiling the evening. Be prepared. But if that doesn't work, be prepared to wing it. If you run out of food, call a restaurant, pizza joint, or store that delivers. If that's not an option, try borrowing from an accommodating neighbor (knock on their door with a glass of wine or piece of dessert in hand). If neither the store nor your neighbor delivers, order the goods with a credit card and call a taxi to pick them up.

If only half the invited guests show up, reconfigure everything to suit the number of people in attendance. Remove excess settings and chairs, fold up the table flaps, and reduce the volume of food accordingly. If nearly no one shows up, look out the window for signs of imminent natural disasters. If none are in sight, check the date in your daybook. If it's the correct day, ask yourself, "Am I a bad person?" If the answer is no, divide the dinner up into single portions, freeze them, and pour yourself a glass of wine.

If twice the number of invited guests show up, consider yourself a social and culinary god and pour yourself a glass of champagne to celebrate. Then divide the portions in two, double the amount of garnish, pretend you are Wolfgang Puck, and rechristen the meal "California cuisine." The freeloaders will be so grateful to be welcomed at such a popular event that they will never notice the lean cuisine.

Enlighten

The soft glow of candles can transform the simplest meal into an occasion. If you are feeling extravagant, light the entire space in which you are entertaining with candles. Ikea specials and inexpensive paraffin utility candles work beautifully—and produce the exact same light as the infinitely more expensive hand-dipped variety.

Be Territorial

Avoid the party-in-the-kitchen phenomenon by making all of the other rooms as inviting as possible. Keep the lighting flattering, the temperature comfortable, and the stereo volume below the level of conversation. If your guests still don't take the bait, lure them out of the kitchen by moving the wine bottles and finger foods into the desired areas. When all else fails, do as I do and section off your cooking space with yellow DO NOT CROSS POLICE LINE tape.

Stuff Your Chest

A well-stocked party treasure chest will help you rise to the occasion of a spontaneous party or rescue a dull one on a moment's notice. Add the following tried-and-true crowd pleasers to your own personal arsenal: noisemakers, serpentine streamers, party hats (you know the party is going well when someone puts one of these on), birthday candles, penny candy (Tootsie Pops, licorice twists, jawbreakers, red hots, Pez dispensers, etc.), and a camera (35 mm, disposable, Polaroid, or video) for those "Kodak moments."

Set the Pace

My own exhaustive morning-after research has determined that toward the end of the evening, people tend to continue drinking as a reflex action rather than from a desire to consume more alcohol. Present a second option by putting out bottles of sparkling mineral water.

Dish It

After the party has wound down and the guests have departed, one of the evening's most pleasurable moments still awaits the host and his or her chosen confidant. It's the party "postmortem." Pull a stool up by the sink, sit your coconspirator down beside you, and let fly while you do the dishes. Even the worst culinary crises, political gaffes, and social faux pas can be laughed at when scrutinized under the postmortem microscope. Bad hair, bad dress, bad manners, and bad dates are all fair game once the guests are out of earshot. If this seems uncharitable, don't fret: They're sure to be critiquing you and your party on the drive home. By the time the gossiping has reached a feverish pitch, you will have plowed through all of the dishes and the party will be officially wrapped. Then you can drift off into dreamland, satisfied and sanctified.

HOW TO KEEP INEBRIATED GUESTS FROM DRIVING HOME

Above all, at every step, make your guests feel good about their decision not to drive.

- Collect keys at the door as guests enter.
- Create a cab fee insurance fund (i.e., everyone contributes two dollars as they enter).
- Provide a comfortable sleeping space and promise an enticing breakfast and lots of aspirin.
- Post the number of a safe-ride service or a friendly taxi company.
- Ride share: Match those who need rides with those who can drive.
- Body tackle.

—Surreal Gourmet

Bob Blumer is the author/illustrator of *The Surreal Gourmet Entertains: High-Fun, Low-Stress Dinner Parties for 6 to 12 People* and *The Surreal Gourmet: Real Food for Pretend Chefs*. His forthcoming book is entitled *Off The Eaten Path: Inspired Recipes and Culinary Adventures*. Bob only owns three plates that match. Visit him at www.surrealgourmet.com or order his books directly at 1-800-FAUX PAS.

TROUBLEMAKER OR EDUCATOR? YOU MAKE THE CALL

Yes, here's real trouble: Darryl Roberts, publisher and editor of Wine
X *magazine, the guy who has single-handedly (and with the help of
an incredibly talented young staff) deconstructed the concept of
wine publication and built it back up into an editorially irreverent,
take-no-prisoners, graphic feast for the eyes. We've said on more
than one occasion, "Darryl makes the Wine Brats look conservative."
Thanks, bud. Nothing like a fully charged cattle prod to wake the
sleeping herd.*

*Let's flip the coin: Since '93, Darryl's vision, and that of our crew,
have been on parallel tracks, rumbling toward a future when wine is
an American staple. And through the Wine Brats' network of regional
chapters, events, and special projects like this book, and* Wine X's
*full-color bound portrait of a new wine scene, have come these new
industry voices, now represented as the coalition within these pages.
So the truth is, Darryl is much less of a rebel and more of an educa-
tor to the masses. He has entertained, enraged, and enlightened. Just
our kind of people. So thanks, Darryl, for all your contributions to the
industry and especially this book. Now, in return for such high praise
and groveling, how about giving us some insight into conducting a
visually challenged tasting. Please?*

—j, j & m

Flying Blind, or How to Conduct a Visually Challenged Wine Tasting

by Darryl Roberts

I played a practical joke on some friends. I added red food coloring to a bottle of Chardonnay and asked them to name the varietal. Guesses ranged from Pinot Noir to Syrah. Only one person didn't suggest a red varietal. (No, they weren't blind.) They didn't guess Chardonnay, either. They merely pointed out that the nose (the smell) of the wine reminded them of tropical fruits and apples, two characteristics indigenous to Chardonnay. Of course, it was the color that had them confused.

The point of this exercise was to judge a wine on its smell and taste, not sight. Too many times wine tasters—from novice to expert—get so caught up in a wine's appearance that they forget about the senses that matter the most when it comes to wine's enjoyment—smell and taste. So, with that in mind, let's explore one of the best methods for evaluating and learning about wine: a blind tasting.

Now, I know what you're thinking: Why would I want to conduct a blind wine tasting? I have enough trouble choosing wines when I can see them. Well, not only will you learn more about your senses of smell and taste, but you'll have fun doing it. Uh-oh, there's that word the old wine school doesn't want to associate with wine, fun. Yes, wine tasting can be, and should be, fun. And by adding another dimension to it, like tasting blind, you not only raise the entertainment meter level, but you also learn a great deal about what you like and don't like in wine.

Conducting a blind tasting, or, in this PC world, a "visually challenged" wine tasting, is really rather simple. I know your first instincts may be to blindfold your guests. From personal experience, that's probably not a good idea. (I tried that once. We're still trying to get the red wine stains off the ceiling.) So the next best thing is to blindfold the wines, meaning, place the bottles in paper bags or wrap them in tin foil so you can't see the labels. Yes, you can tell what color they are, but you'll be surprised, just as my friends were, by how the color doesn't tell you as much as you think it does.

Now, before we get into the different types of blind tastings, we first need to discuss who brings or buys the wines. I've tried it both ways—the host purchases the wine, or each guest brings (or is assigned) a bottle. And to tell you the truth, it really doesn't matter unless you're looking for something specific, such as specific wineries and/or regions. (I once had a party and told each person to bring a food item. We ended up with ten boxes of Ritz crackers.) If you're looking for specific wineries and/or wines and each guest is to bring a bottle, have one person assign the wines to bring. This way you're assured the wines you want to show up do and the ones you don't, won't. If guests are bringing random selections, it's a good idea to set a price range so no one feels "over-generous" or vice versa. And regardless of the type of blind tasting you're conducting, it's always best to make one person responsible for coordinating the materials needed.

Legally Blind

There are several levels of blind tastings. The first is called "single-blind," or as I like to call it, tasting "legally blind." This method involves covering the bottles but knowing what the wines are. Meaning, you provide a list with the names of the wines but you don't know which one is which. Again, from experience, you don't want to have six different types of wines, such as one Chardonnay, one Cabernet, one Merlot, etc. This tasting usually proves to be short but pointless. The idea is to have a selection of "like" wines—all Chardonnay or all Cabernet or whatever—then try to guess their identity. It doesn't matter who purchases the wines, but to achieve the maximum benefit from this kind of tasting it's best to vary the styles. For example, if you're tasting Chardonnays, try to have a selection from light and fruity to rich and oaky. This way you and your guests will learn what flavors, qualities, and characteristics you appreciate most in Chardonnay.

Okay, everyone's bringing a bottle. They don't need to be covered when they arrive since there'll be a list with their names on it. One person should take the wines into the kitchen (or any secluded location) and place them in paper lunch bags or wrap them in foil. It's best to secure the top of the paper bag (around the neck of the bottle) with either tape or a rubber band.

(I prefer a rubber band. Makes it easier to remove the bottle at the end of the tasting.) Then the same person should pop the corks, leaving them out and randomly placed. Then everyone should leave the room. Another person should go in and randomly number the bags. If you're moving the wines to another location and are afraid of spilling, you can put the corks back in the bottles. But do it after numbering the bags. This way the corks won't go back into their respective bottles and give the whole tasting away. Again, from experience.

At this point you're ready to taste. If you have more than six wines, I recommend that you break the tasting into one or more "flights" (*flight* is a wine-geek term for stages). In other words, if you have twelve wines, break the tasting into three flights of four wines each. It's easier to keep track of the wines and requires fewer glasses. Speaking of which, the best-case scenario is for each person to have one glass for each wine per flight. This is achieved simply by asking each guest to bring his or her own set of glasses. By having a glass for each wine, you're able to go back and forth between them in order to distinguish their subtle yet distinctive differences. If one glass per wine isn't possible, don't fret. It's not absolutely necessary. Just more convenient.

Okay. You have the bottles, the glasses, you've handed out the tasting sheets with the list of wines; it's time to turn everyone loose. Make sure to allow plenty of time for the actual tasting. Don't hurry through it. Like good sex, it should be comfortable and memorable, and not leave anyone unfulfilled.

After you've tasted all the wines, it's time to reveal their identity. It's always fun to tally the guesses to see who and how many thought what was which. Did that make sense? Anyway, you get the idea. It's also neat to offer a prize to the person(s) who guessed the most correctly. (It's not a good idea to reward the person with the least correct. Unless it's the resident wine geek. Then by all means throw a parade!) Regardless of who wins, remember, it's supposed to be fun and educational.

WHEN ENOUGH'S ENOUGH

I know the urge is to go nuts and try to taste a hundred wines, but it's better to stick with ten to twelve. Despite what you hear about how the "professionals" do it—hundreds of wines at a time—I'll guarantee you that after the first dozen or so their palates are use less. Anyway, if the idea is to have fun and learn at the same time, it's important that your palate doesn't OD from exhaustion. And, for most people, that means keeping the number of wines reasonable.

Single-Blind Tasting Sheets
It's a good idea to have two columns. In the left column, simply list "1" through however many wines you're tasting. In the right column, list the names of the wines. That's it.

Taking Notes
I highly recommend taking notes whenever you taste wine. There're too many choices and too few brain cells to remember which one you liked or, more important, didn't like. And, despite what wine geeks may want you to think, taking notes doesn't have to mean scripting a novel about each wine. A simple "liked it" or "didn't like it" does just fine. Or, if you want to get a bit more detailed, noting the flavors that you experience works well, too, especially if you plan on matching the wine with food. Personally, I note the simple flavors and then what the wine reminds me of. For example, if a wine is crisp, well-balanced, and exciting, I might note it's like Katerina Witt or Elvis Stojko. Whatever.

Check List of Tasting Items
Wine
Paper lunch bags or foil
Rubber bands or tape to secure bags/foil
Glasses (any kind will do)
Tasting sheets with pens or pencils
Black felt pen for marking bags or foil
Door prizes for "Best Guesser"

—Daryl Roberts

Totally in the Dark

The second method of tasting blind is called "double-blind," or tasting totally in the dark. This is similar to single-blind, except the names of the wines are withheld, meaning you have absolutely no clue as to what's in front of you. Not only do you have to guess the varietal or type of wine, you also have to guess who produced it. (There are actually people who cannot only name the varietal and producer, but also the year and sometimes even the section of vineyard the wine was produced from. Of course, these people also have an affinity for pocket protectors.)

Anyway. If your guests are bringing a wine, remember to have them cover the bottle and remove the cork (replacing it with another producer's) before they arrive. If you haven't before, note that many producers print their names on the cork. I know the "cork" thing seems like a no-brainer, but you'd be surprised at how many people forget.

With a double-blind tasting it's not necessary to do a specific varietal or type of wine, although you can if you want. But I always find it more mysterious knowing nothing about the wine—that it could be anything from anyone from anywhere in the world.

Now, I know what you're thinking: What if two people bring the same wine? Well, it's a long shot, but it can happen. Think of it this way: It'll add another dimension to the fun—to see if anyone guesses two bottles are the same. And I'll bet you very few, if any, will guess correctly. Course, last time I made that bet . . . let's just say I now drive a 1968 Dodge Dart and leave it at that.

Well, that's it. Blind, double-blind, it doesn't matter unless you and your guests have fun. Please remember to drink in moderation. And if there's a wine geek who's ruinin' the whole party? Do what I do. Roll up one of my magazines and whop 'em upside the head.

WE SAID SHE WAS PROLIFIC

In Tina's last introduction, we headlined "Bold, Beautiful, and Prolific." We truly believe her writing style validates the Bold. You'll have to take our word on the Beautiful. However, on Prolific, again her writing says it all. When Tina's given an assignment, it's always on time and dead on the mark, even though she always seems to be working on multiple jobs within a given week. (Have we mentioned she also works full-time as an importer with Maisons, Marques & Domaine? How's the dating life, Tina?) She also surprised us by throwing in a few extra sidebars for the book for good measure. And now that we've read through Tina's next piece, we should have included Very Creative and Damned Fun to her title.

—j, j & m

It's My Party and I'll Wine if I Want To, or Party Theme Ideas

by Tina Caputo

My first wine-related theme party happened accidentally, when I was writing an article about wines with weird labels. I had about eight different samples to taste and review, so I thought: Why not make a party of it? Naturally, my wine-swilling friends were more than happy to join me for some tasty (and free) vino, and I was more than happy to turn a "work" activity into a festive soiree. So we sampled the wines, I took notes for my article, and best of all, we had a swell time. So swell, in fact, that "wines-under-five-bucks" and "wines-with-Jesus-on-the-label" parties were soon to follow. Now I find myself trying to come up with creative wine theme party ideas, even when I don't have an article to write. My friends have even volunteered to chip in for the wine!

At this point, you may be asking yourself: What's the difference between a wine party and a keg party? Good question. Although both types of parties can be a rollicking good time, wine parties are usually devoid of things like chugalug contests, vomit, and regret. Of course, that doesn't mean that wine parties have to be lame cork-sniffing, note-taking, ultraserious geek-fests, either. Your friends wouldn't stand for anything that dorky, would they? Just have fun, drink the wine, and, if you're so inclined, learn something.

To host a successful wine theme party, you'll need three things: (1) friends, (2) wine, and (3) an idea for a theme. Just follow these guidelines and you'll soon be on your way to a swingin' juice bash of your own.

How Much Wine?

Under normal party circumstances, one bottle of wine for every two guests should be sufficient. (A 750 ml bottle contains about four or five glasses of wine.) However, since the point of a wine-tasting theme party is to sample an array of wines, you may want to consider having more bottles on hand than people. Don't worry if you end up with leftover bottles; you can always send them home with your guests! Hint: locked safely in the trunk and only if they're sober.

BYOW?

Wanna try some great new wines without spending loads of cash? Instead of buying all the party wines yourself, invite your friends over for a wine "potluck" and ask each guest to bring a bottle that fits in with your theme. Cheap for you; cheap for them. Chances are your friends will bring some interesting wines you never would have thought to buy yourself.

To help you get started, here are some ideas for wine-related theme parties. Just add friends.

Wines of the World

Choose a location on the globe, whether it's a state, country, or appellation, and serve various food and wines from that region. Some obvious choices include France, California, Italy, and Spain. If you want to do something more adventurous, try having a Southern Hemisphere, New York, or Eastern Europe party. As a variation on the theme, have an Around the World wine party, assigning each guest a different region and asking them to bring a bottle of wine from that part of the world.

Varietal Is the Spice of Life

Serve several wines made from the same grape variety, such as Cabernet Sauvignon, Zinfandel, Sauvignon Blanc, or Chardonnay. (If you really want to be wacky, go for lesser-known grapes like Sangiovese, Viognier, Sylvaner, or Gewürztraminer.) This will give you the opportunity to discover how dissimilar wine made from the same grape variety can taste in the hands of individual winemakers in different wine regions. An interesting (and tasty) experiment! Beware: You may actually learn something.

Red Wine and Chocolate Party

This is a good party to have around Valentine's Day. Rich red wines, such as Cabernet Sauvignon and Port, are amazingly good with chocolate. So let decadence rule! Simply put together a spread of luscious chocolate treats (for variety, use dark, milk, and white chocolate), set out several bottles of red wine, and watch your friends start drooling as soon as they come in the door.

Wines Under $10 Party

How many times do I have to say this? Good wine doesn't have to be expensive! Find out for yourself by hosting a wine party where nothing over $10 is allowed near your palate. Once you start perusing your local wine shop, you'll be surprised at how many wines fall into this affordable category, and I don't mean jug wine! Be sure to check out the international wine sections for bargains; countries like Chile and South Africa have been making great value wines for years!

Champagne and Trailer Park Vittles Party

Prove to your friends, once and for all, that champagne goes with everything, not just oysters and caviar. Serve the finest bubbly you can afford with trashy favorites like pigs-in-a-blanket, Twinkies, Spam, and cocktail weenies. Impose a dress code of "trailer chic" and award a bottle of wine to the best (worst) dressed in the bunch. For added entertainment, rent *Deliverance* and continue the party with the strains of "Dueling Banjos" in the background. Yee-haw!

Lobster and Chardonnay Party

A couple of years ago, my friend Julie had a party where each guest chipped in $10 for a live lobster of their very own. After the ritual lobster boil, about twenty people sat on the floor of her living room, tearing lobsters apart with their hands and dipping the succulent chunks in giant Tupperware bowls full of melted butter. The only thing that would have made this pagan feast even more heavenly? Copious amounts of rich, buttery Chardonnay to wash it down. No dining room necessary; just set out a few nutcrackers, plenty of newspaper (the funnies), and several varieties of Chardonnay. Picnic blankets aren't a bad idea, either. Trust me, your friends will worship you forever.

The All-Wine Dinner Party

Wine and food are natural companions, so why not take that combination a step further with the All-Wine Dinner Party? The idea is to prepare a dinner where every course of the meal includes wine as an ingredient. Some tasty examples include salad with red-wine vinaigrette, champagne risotto, coq au vin, and pears poached in red wine. Each course should be paired with a different wine. Hint: The Internet is a great source for recipes. A keyword search for "cooking with wine" will provide you with enough options for a week of all-wine dinners! See REF.3: Finding Wine on the Web.

The Label Game Scavenger Hunt

Ask each of your guests to bring a bottle of wine with a picture of something specific on the label, such as an animal, plant, woman, mode of transportation, mythological figure, or musical instrument. More abstract label designations could include concepts like love, nature, passion, or fun. With all the amazing label art out there, your friends should be able to come up with just about anything you ask for!

The Grapeless Wine Party

You may have to do a little searching, but nongrape wines are more common than you might think. Look for varieties like Dandelion, Garlic, Ginseng, Tomato, and Strawberry. Even if the idea of such wines makes your hair stand on end, you're certain to have a memorable party!

Whether you use one of these suggestions, or come up with an idea of your own, wine theme parties let you exercise not only your imagination, but your brain and palate, too. So gather your friends together and get ready to party. The best part is, you don't even need an occasion.

A TASTE OF THE GROOVE

Have you read this guy's work in Wine X *magazine? You know, he handles the "Sex, Wine & Rock 'n' Roll" department where he reviews and pairs music and wine. Or maybe on Amazon.com, where he's the managing editor for their music Web site. Or maybe* Rolling Stone. *Or* SOMA. *It's strange, how through some sort of eclectic, trip-hop voice that sets both a hypnotic and seductive groove, S. Duda takes the reader on a literal pop-culture ride. And just about the time you begin to feel his language envelop you in a righteous buzz of semi-incoherence, you reach the end of a paragraph, and the truth within his words rises up from the page like . . .*

All right, so we can't write like S. "Groovin'" Duda. And his style is probably something that can't be taught, only gained through a series of questionable life experiences. Hey, questionable life experiences can be good. Actually, we're jealous. Another element to S. Duda's intellectual makeup is his ability to be genuinely opinionated. So we suppose we shouldn't have been surprised when we received his submission on the tricks of pairing wine and music. We've been doing the like in off-beat, fun ways for a while now. Well, that wasn't enough for Mr. Duda. He basically used the premise to step up on his soapbox, where he takes on the issues of corporate consolidation and redefining the meaning of "snob." We had two immediate responses: (1) Don't publish it or (2) put it at the front of the book. Once we regained our composure, we put it right where we'd planned here. We'd be hypocrites if we didn't. Now our question is, Is this prose, debate, or slam poetry?

—j, j & m

The Groove, the Juice, and Consolidation, or Pairing Music and Wine

by S. Duda

"This (Wine) Is Our Music"
— *bastardization of album title by Ornette Coleman, circa 1960*

D o you have trouble trying to mate wine with music? Have you ever felt embarrassment creep red and steamy across your face at a cocktail party because you can't find that perfect beat and your guests are turning up their perfect noses at your chards and zins? Do you torch hours searching for that perfect combination of tunes and juice that makes as much sense as a pairing the likes of Aussie Shiraz and grilled lamb? Here's some simple advice. Stop. Please. Before you embarrass yourself, blow all that stock option cash, and fry valuable bandwidth searching for a secret code that doesn't exist.

It is a temptation to try to pair individual wines with certain musical genres (Indonesian Gamelan with Sauternes) or with an individual artist (Louis Prima with, say . . . Grappa). And the more the thought is sloshed around the brainpan, the more sense it seems to make. If foodies can run themselves in circles matching cuisine with reds and whites, why can't we, the (serious) winos, do the same with music?

The reason why it's so difficult to understand is because, perhaps, it is so obvious: Attempting to tie one whisper sip of wine into one fragile, fleeting sliver of music is—to be generous—akin to chasing dragonflies.

While it's an elementary thought to sketch the meat = red and fish = white algebra (which is also passing into extinction), the equation somehow doesn't hold up when one tries to make the analogy to the marriage of wine and music. Jazz = red? Rock = white? Sadly, there's no science to this abstract art.

We want the fast and easy combinations to work; we want for there to be some chart or spreadsheet to tell us that while avant-garde jazz goes swell with a flinty New Zealand Sauvignon Blanc, you're somehow a yutz if you cue the jazz accompanied by the likes of a young and springy Oregon Pinot. Life might be easier if it worked this way, but it wouldn't be as interesting. Nature makes us think, again.

Still, the temptation to pair wine and music, regardless of this fatal flaw, is irresistible. Many writers and pro-wine geeks have tried; all have failed. It's understandable: Music and wine *do* belong together. Like music, a glass of good wine is nothing if not a collection of notes composing a profound and literal truth. The many into the one. A living, breathing organism fired by the spark and genius of the artist. Wine. Music. Both true and beautiful things. After all, wine is truth. In *vino veritas*, as the man said. And music, also sayeth the man, is the art to which all others aspire. Wine and music, a marriage true and whole. Two separate elements—unique creations touched by the fickle hand of creativity, amplified by each other's presence. The great god Pan, conducting the delicate negotiations between the two stormy, passionate lovers. The perfect metaphor.

Pushing the metaphor: Wine and music are both, at their very essence, blends. A unanimous statement drawn from many voices. Even if you only drink single-vineyard, reserve bottles, you are still drinking a blend. Likewise, a performance such as Bach's legendary pieces for solo cello—work that is as austere as anything in the history of music—is a blend of tempo, melody, and tone. Everything is a variable and everything affects the blend. If you break it down, sooner or later you'll be analyzing the effects of every single grape blended into the infinity of one single bottle. Ever try to break down the effect a single note can have on a symphony? What does one note in a solo by Hendrix or Coltrane mean? The mind reels; thus, our problem: Ascribing a "right" piece of music to a bottle of wine is lunacy. It will make you crazy.

No matter. Booze and music, in forms rough and refined—barroom to boardroom—belong together. But frankly, no one really cares what boring, flavorless CD some writer/reviewer yutz slaps in the player when s/he pops the cork on a bottle of too expensive cab. That's where the problem exists. While it's hard to resist the heavy breathing of a bottle of big Cali zin, it's darn easy to hate someone else's music. The combination of lamb and Aussie Shiraz will always be welcome. The combination of your brother-in-law's jug Chablis and Journey bootlegs may not be anyone's cup of chai. People care about their own wine and their own music—not mine, not yours—theirs.

And that's the *real* problem. Where to get the oh-so-important wine/music fix in an age when our relationship to both music and wine has been slowly and inexorably defiled by nitwits, goons, and MBAs. These are the villains and enemies of good taste who have traded art for commerce, and appreciation and meaning for "moving units." This is the trade-off that has made the delicate witchcraft/abstraction/guessing game of music/wine pairing much more difficult than nature intended.

Wine's '90s–'00s renaissance roughly parallels what's been happening in the music industry during the same years. In a word, the trend has been consolidation. Small wineries are bought up by corporate farms or international concerns with ties to the "spirits industry" to reap the usual, numbing benefits—economies of scale, better distribution, more money to pour into staff and equipment and, of course, the aid and comfort of the marketing geniuses and their diabolical spreadsheets that show, hey, maybe it's time to start pushing wine coolers again. And if that don't work, we'll just redesign the label.

On the music side of the ledger, the trend toward consolidation and record company mergers has proven even more disastrous. As the record companies merged—supposedly to be more efficient—somehow the money dried up. In jazz, rock, and even classical divisions of major labels the world over, bands and artists stopped being signed in hopes of cultivating a long and prosperous creative career. Instead, artists became expected to produce an instant hit. No hit? See ya. Meanwhile, scores of independent record labels were purchased by majors and became part of the machine. Once-singular, thriving sources for new music became stagnant, stale—sold out. All the while, the marketing weasels plot a presentation to prove that there is still room to launch a new version of the Spice Girls. Oh, you wanted innovation, creativity? Sorry.

In an attempt to globalize both the music and wine industries, marketers have made an unacceptable deal with the devil. In essence, both music and wine have moved from artist-produced craft products to global commodities. The result is a diluted product divorced from the magic conjured by the artist. Mass production, as even the novice social critic/grouser knows, is the enemy. After all, if you're going to McDonald's for fine food, why not go to McWine for the grog to wash it all down? And while you're at it, turn up McHit radio for ambiance. Wine for the whole world? Sorry, not into crowds. Music for the masses? They can have it.

While the disconnect between what marketers want us to consume and what we *actually* want to consume is both wide and deep, there are solutions. This solution, however, is not new, innovative, or necessarily foreign to either wine or music aficionados. The answer is to be a snob—an unapologetic, aware, and opinionated music and wine brat, if you will.

The word *snob* may have a few unfortunate connotations, but it's nothing that can't be worked around. When one thinks of a wine snob, the trailer that flashes across the movie screen of the mind is a cartoon. A tubby, pompous man with a handlebar mustache blowing dust off bottles of something French and sniffing and swirling like a maniac. The music snob, poking through musty towers of vinyl, pulling some obscure record from the stack and then reciting the band's entire bio as the record twirls and crackles on the player. While these images are common, and may have been more or less true at one time, contempo music and wine snobbism is an entirely different animal.

To be a wine or music snob means simply to be discriminating, open to discovery and, just as important, to have the resources and wits to procure the good stuff. Wine and music snobs take their pleasure seriously. They are willing to put time into the avocation. They have opinions and are usually more than willing to voice them loudly. Most important, they are fearless explorers, searching out the obscure, the little-known diamonds of pure art unsullied by the clumsily clueless hands of commerce.

Snobbism, of course, must be separated from elitism. Remember: Wine and any number of musical genres (jazz, contemporary classical composition, electronics, traditional acoustic folk forms, and virtually every avant-garde form) have been banished by our consumerist culture's clueless elite. Instead, there is a steady diet of overhyped superstars with great personalities and even better haircuts. Sometimes these people actually make records and play live. More often, however, it's magazine covers and talk shows.

Talking about wine—as opposed to actually drinking it—is in ready abundance. Everyone, it seems, likes "a red, a nice, kinda dry red." Everybody says it, but everybody drinks beer. What we are is a generation of fakers, impostors, and closeted art conservatives. We fake being down with new music and instead slip it over to the alt-rock station on the drive home.

We make in-the-know chatski about Cali zin but line up for pints on Friday night.

Why? The simplest of those theories is this: The masses are indifferent to music and wine because most of it sucks—that is, it's not the good stuff. There is the more complex sociopolitical stream of thought that claims wine and adventurous music are not popular because, philistines that we are, we simply cannot appreciate the sublime and singular form. And, finally, there is the economic theory: Nobody likes wine and jazz because marketers haven't figured out how to sell them to us yet. Of the three theories, I favor the first but have the creepy feeling that the third may have more to do with the problem than we care to admit.

Both problems have the same solution: information.

Previously, buying wine—and actually ending up with something great, artistic, even—was a speculative market, a fishing expedition. And while it may be generally true that you get what you pay for, you never really know what's in the bottle till you pop the cork. Not that there's a lot of help. Wine reviews are 99 percent hot air and 1 percent bullshit. Wine marketing often seems a strange, leftover relic from the Soviet era. We walk into the vino store armed only with hunches, mix-and-match bits of random knowledge, and a vague belief that somehow a cool label portends a groovy wine. We might as well have been buying scratch lottery tickets.

Likewise, finding music to consume with joy and true hunger was once next to impossible. A handful of radio stations with a few formats offered few choices. Cable music video stations served as free advertising for the major-label Top 40 hit machine. Things were bleak.

Somehow, as though we were waking from a Soma hangover, we awoke, squinting into the beautiful light of the information age. Digital network communications, unbridled search and organizational capability, and, best of all, the Internet!

Today there is no limit to the information we have at our disposal. The gates have been flung open, distance doesn't matter, excuses are shriveling like worms on hot asphalt. Every piece of music can be sampled before purchase, every small label releasing futurist drum and bass, sci-fi dub, and lazy acid jazz can be contacted directly. Any bottle of wine can be had over the Internet. Futures can be purchased from dinky but amazing wineries (usually allowing the snob super-primo wine at a bargain-basement price).

There are few wineries, or, for that matter, winemakers—who are not available via E-mail.

Subverting the dominant wine and music industry paradigms is not only fun, it's now the law for informed snobs the world over. The good news is that both industries are changing—fast. You can help shape them by making the industry pay attention to you. Make them give you the good stuff—on your terms. Join a small winery's reserve club. Buy your wine on the Internet. Go to the local shop's tasting night and ask some young, musty-smelling winemaker with a bad haircut about their wine. You'll be amazed at how eccentric they are (way more spaced-out than musicians; think inferior genetic bonding between a painter and a sugar-beet farmer), and you'll also begin to see the failure of elitist/ageist/classist marketing that cannot see the truth laid bare before it. Smart, knowledgeable people make our favorite arts. The same type of folks drink it.

PHILOSOPHICALSPINDOCTOR.COM

Can you say "Ground Zero"? Well, that's where Joe Naujokas (pro-nounced nie-yo-kas) comes into the Wine Brats' equation. Back in '93, when we called the first public gathering to see if interest in our mission went beyond our own personal vision, Joe showed his face at Gaffney's Wine Bar in Santa Rosa, California. (Along with eighty others who felt there was a need to rethink how the industry presented wine's place on the American table.) Though many of those original activists have moved on to other places and careers, and we are deeply grateful for every idea and moment of time they gave to us, Joe relentlessly pursued his desire to be involved.

So many years later, and Joe heads up his own company, Grapevine Studios (www.gvstudios.com), while also managing to hold down the position of Director of Online Media and Development for Wine Brats. Not only has he been the leading force in fully developing our place in cyberspace, he's influenced many policy decisions concerning membership directives by asking one simple question: "How can we better serve our members, while achieving our mission?" It is exactly this kind of "think tank" mentality and philosophical review, and the fact that Joe delivers solutions, that make him such a critical member of our team. Of course, wouldn't you know it, when we asked him to put together a list of "wine cocktail" recipes, we got the following peek inside Joe's deliberative yet playful brain.

—j, j & m

PART.5

Joe's Place: An Eclectic, Philosophical Mix of Conversation and Wine Drinks

by Joe Naujokas

"What'll it be?" the bartender asks, gently furrowing his peppery eyebrows. With both hands and a white bar towel he polishes a rocks glass, crisply, professionally, without looking at me except for a brief glance to acknowledge my presence. Behind him a colorful, and specific, arrangement of liquors and spirits waits for his measured hands.

What will it be? Always the same question at five-thirty on a Wednesday night. Whatever drink I choose, I'm confident that my guardian angel behind the counter knows exactly how to prepare it. And I know exactly how it will taste. That's why I come to this bar. It's predictable. It's safe. No surprises. No sudden corporate takeover leaving me jobless, no username and password to forget, no fickle E-mail addresses. I wonder if this guy's even heard of E-mail.

Ahh. Simplicity. Consistency. I settle into one of the worn leather bar stools. My eyes wander past the familiar elixirs—bottles of gold, bronze, red, and sometimes green liquids. Classic liquors, classic flavors. Yes, this is exactly what I had in mind.

But tonight my eyes linger on a section of dark glass bottles at the far end of the familiar lineup. "What are those?" I ask the bartender, pointing to the strange characters. "I don't think I've ever seen them before."

"That's wine, my friend. Always been here, you've just never noticed." The furrow on his brow seems etched in stone. His hands look like they've been polishing the same glass for a thousand years—and probably will be doing so a thousand years from now. "Wine?" I think to myself, still mildly entranced by the endless burnishing. Now, that's a thought. Maybe I should practice with it so I don't look like a fool the next time I get the wine list at a restaurant. . . . In the corner of my mind, a spark of curiosity lights up, but fades quickly from general fatigue. Look, let's be realistic: It's been a long day. I'm tired. I don't have the energy for exploring. It's cocktail time, and everyone knows you can't make a cocktail with wine.

Almost as if he were waiting for me to finish my thought, the bartender says, "You look like you could use a Martini Grigio."

What the . . . ?

Still holding the towel, he sets down the now-crystal-clean glass and, for the first time, looks up to survey the bar. It's late in the afternoon, and the few lurking customers are either quietly nursing their drinks or absorbing themselves in quiet conversation. The neon sign in the window bathes the front of the bar in a soft red glow and the fragrant notes of an Italian opera drift lazily in the air. The bartender turns his face back to me, but his eyes are focused elsewhere.

"A measure of Pinot Grigio, a dash of vermouth, shaken with ice, with a twist of lemon and an olive. Yes?"

"I, uh, well . . ." I'm a little intimidated by his clairvoyance, but something tells me I shouldn't say no. "Sure, whatever you say."

He withdraws a clear glass bottle of pale, lemon-tinted wine from the refrigerator, uncorks it, and splashes a glassful into a shaker. Next he takes a bottle of vermouth from the lineup of liquor bottles and passes it ceremoniously over the shaker. I can't tell whether anything actually falls out of the bottle—his ethereal motion is too fuzzy to see clearly. He covers it, shakes, rubs a lemon rind around the rim of a martini glass, drops it in, and sets the glass down in front of me on a fresh coaster, and pours the contents of the shaker into the glass. Tiny crystals of ice float gently in the mixture, which comes up just short of the rim.

Wait, how could this be? I begin to doubt his skill, until he drops a toothpick-impaled olive into the glass. An olive! In wine! The garnish displaces just enough liquid that the surface tension barely contains the elixir from spilling out over the side.

"There you are. A Pinot Grigio martini. A Sauvignon Blanc will do as a substitute, just don't bother using a Chardonnay. It's usually way too oaky and buttery. That'll be five bucks . . . start a tab?"

I nod. Disconcerted a bit by the olive, I hazard a sip of his wine martini. Jeez, it's not half bad. Certainly doesn't have the powerhouse alcoholic punch of a real martini. I could put a few of these down and be none the worse for wear. And its bright fruitiness has the unexpected effect of cheering me up, unlike the juniper flavor of a gin martini, which always seems to evoke a feeling of northern European midwinter melancholy. "I have to admit. I like it. A lot."

A smile of satisfaction flickers across the bartender's face. "Thought you would. When you're ready, I'll make you a wine margarita. I call it a Margaret."

This must be a serious passion for this guy . . . or he has a lot of time on his hands. Either way it never hurts to stroke your bartender's ego. "Okay, I'm curious. How the heck do you make a . . . what did you call it? A Margaret?" I ask, courageously digging the olive out of the glass.

"You start with two parts Gewürztraminer. No substitutes."

Geh-what? I ask myself.

"Gewürztraminer."

Hey! He did it again! Oh, maybe he noticed me trying to mouth the word after he said it. No, couldn't be—I was busy munching the olive. Which, by the way, was an unexpectedly perfect touch. Hmm.

"I know, it's a humdinger to pronounce. Geh-verts-trah-mee-ner. It's a German wine that's usually a little sweet. It's also a bit spicy, like tequila. Mix it with one part margarita mix and a dash of orange liqueur. Grand Marnier, if you have it. It's best on the rocks, and I always salt the glass."

Two hours ago, the combination of salt and wine would have sickened me, but I'm starting to become oddly entranced with this guy, and now it actually sounds quite tasty. "It might have a funny name, but Gewürztraminer is cheap and it tastes great. Make it in a big thermos and bring it to the beach." The beach? Wine at the beach?

"Now, if you don't have Gewürztraminer, Sauvignon Blanc will do—but you'll end up with what I call a Sauvignon Sour, which is a lot like a whiskey sour. So you might as well use sour mix instead of margarita mix. Pop in a maraschino cherry and you're set."

I respond, "You certainly are zealous about your job."

He reacts with a sidelong glance that seems to say, "Hey, this is not just a job." He picks up his towel and starts wiping away the stray drops of condensed water that fell from the cold martini shaker.

"Yes, well, the way I see it," he begins, "we've been devising unique ways to enjoy alcohol in one form or another for thousands of years. Keeping that tradition alive and well is the least I can do." With the bar now dry, he carefully folds the towel and sets it aside.

"You see," he continues, "creating a drink is an art form, like cooking or painting or composing music. It's a matter of starting with the right ingredients, knowing their individual characters intimately, being sensitive to subtlety, and balancing creativity with tradition."

Now I seem to be getting somewhere with this guy, even if the idea of equating martinis with Magritte seems a stretch. "That's okay." He shrugs. "You don't have to agree with me." By now I'm growing accustomed to his uncanny mind-reading abilities. "But, admit it, a good drink—just like good art—will make you stop, and think, and feel, and maybe even change the way you look at the world. Am I right?"

I open my mouth slightly to start verbalizing an automatic response of polite, if insincere, agreement until wisdom (or is it the wine?) restrains me. Stop and think, yes, I'll give him that, but change my world view? "Well, yes, you do have a point," I concede.

"Listen, how about that Margaret?" he asks. He picks up another glass from the bar behind him and resumes his eternal polishing. The glass sparkles occasionally between polished flicks of his angel-white bar towel.

"I don't know," I say, "it sounds good, don't get me wrong, but I think I'm in the mood for something a little more . . . solitary. A little more end-of-day. Maybe something red. What would you suggest?"

"Mmm, that's a little more difficult. Red wine usually doesn't mix well. The tannin, you know." No, I don't. "Tannin is the stuff that makes your mouth feel dry, like when you drink tea." Okay, yeah, now I follow. "Somehow the chemical structure of tannin doesn't take too well with most mixers." Hmm. "But I think I know what to try first."

He grabs a cocktail shaker and turns to an in-wall refrigerator. He opens the door, holds the shaker under a white box on the shelf labeled with a photograph of what looks like a vineyard, and pulls some sort of a spigot. Deep red liquid flows into the shaker. He closes the refrigerator door and turns back to the bar.

"You're kidding, right?" I say. I know enough about wine to pass right by the boxed stuff at the grocery store, and I can't believe this guy is actually going to serve it to me.

"Tell me what's wrong with boxed wine," the bartender says, his eyebrows arched.

Uh-oh. Wait a minute. Watch your step. "Well, I guess, for one, it's boxed."

He withdraws a plastic jug full of maroon-colored juice (fruit punch?) from the bed of ice under the counter and pours a few glugs into the shaker. He adds a few cubes of ice, slips the cover on, and starts shaking it. "Let me tell you this," he states. "Bag in a box is one of the safest, most effective ways to package wine. Especially for a bar. Every glass tastes fresh, like you just opened the bottle."

After a few precise moments of agitating the shaker, he stops and strains the deep rhubarb-colored concoction into a heavy pint glass. "I wish I could get all my wine that way." A twist of lime completes the drink and he sets it in front of me on a fresh paper coaster. "The house sangria. Three parts fruit juice, one part dry red wine, and a dash of Framboise, or really any fruit liqueur, if you want to experiment. Three bucks."

Oh yeah, money. For the heck of it, I put on my best poker face and let my mind dwell on the potential cost of my experimentation. Sure enough, the bartender continues, "But don't worry, I'll help you out. It's quiet, and I'm having fun, too." Jeez, maybe this guy really is some sort of angel. He replaces the shaker and wipes his hands with his towel.

"Thanks," I say, looking at my new drink. Boxed red wine—refrigerated, no less—mixed with juice, served in a beer glass, garnished with a lime. I'm willing to rock the boat, but this almost seems like sacrilege. Fancy name or not. "But I was hoping for something a little more . . . traditional."

"Listen. Spaniards have been drinking sangria for hundreds of years. What could be more traditional than that?" He replaces the now-empty shaker in its rightful position, where it will wait for its next drink. "We're just about the only society in the world that doesn't make mixed drinks with wine. Except for wine coolers, of course, but they're just prefab. That doesn't count in my book." The drinking practices of world cultures certainly wasn't my undergrad major, but somehow I get the feeling that this man's wisdom shouldn't be doubted.

So I nod and take a tentative sip of the sangria. And I'm pleasantly surprised. The drink is fruity, easygoing, and just a touch spicy, with a subtly intoxicating kick. The perfect party companion.

"Let me explain myself a little more. Look at the wine section. See how I've divided it into shelves, just like the booze?" Sure enough, the bottles took up three rows of shelves, a bottom shelf, a middle shelf, and a top shelf. "Just like booze, the bottom-shelf wine is the cheapest. It might not be the best wine in the world on its own, but it's great for mixing. The boxed wine is certainly a bottom-shelf wine—but it makes one heck of a sangria, no?"

"Yeah, it's not bad," I say with a slight nod. "But I think I'd need a pitcher to share with a bunch of friends to appreciate this one."

"Aha! Do you realize what you're saying?" I look up, startled by his sudden ardor. Back in hand, his white towel is quivering with excitement. "Nothing, no one, is an island unto itself. In order to value the individual, you must consider its environment. In other words, you can't judge a drink on its own. You have to consider the context." He returns his attention to the countertop and wipes furiously.

How the conversation drifted into a philosophy lesson, I have no idea, but I must admit that he makes a lot of sense. Sure, I might not order a pitcher of sangria for a business dinner, but on the other hand, beer isn't the only thing I can take to the beach, or a barbecue, or a tailgate party, for that matter. Suddenly a whole world of ideas is opening up to me.

The bartender stops wiping and nods enigmatically. "Mmm-hmm," he murmurs, and puts down his towel. "Here, let me take the rest of that sangria. That one's on the house. I have something that might be just perfect. Do you like chocolate? And Merlot?"

"Very much, on both counts." Probably the only other thing I know about wine is that I can always count on a Merlot for an easy-drinking red.

"Then it's no question." He reaches for a bottle of chocolate liqueur. "For this one I'll start with a second-shelf wine. See, the less you add to the wine, the better-quality wine you need to start. Now, with a really good top-shelf wine, I wouldn't recommend adding anything. Get it? It already has a mouthful of flavors, like chocolate, and raspberry, and lemon, and so on. They're subtle, and you might not notice them at first, but they're in there. That's what good wine is all about."

I taste my new drink. Cherries and chocolate immediately come to mind. "Hey, I thought you added only chocolate," I said.

"I did. Why, what's wrong?"

"Oh, nothing's wrong, it's just that I'm tasting something more than just chocolate. Like cherries or something."

The bartender leaned back and folded his arms. His gravelly eyes were sparkling almost as brilliantly as the rows of polished rocks glasses. He looked, dare I say, proud.

"Hold that thought," he said, grabbing a big bowl of a wineglass from the counter behind him. He takes a bottle from the top shelf of wines, uncorks it, and pours some into the glass. Wine the color of liquid ruby splashes out of the bottle and coats the sides of the glass with a luminescent red sheen. "My best wine. You don't want to know how much it costs. Also on the house."

I bring the glass to my mouth, but my nose gets there first. What a fragrance! No, it's a perfume. Like roses! And cranberries. Cherries and a little chocolate, too, but they're much more gentle than the last drink. And something else, something earthy but also kinda sexy . . . maybe leather? Wow. Suddenly all that flowery language on the back of wine labels is starting to make a lot more sense. I can just picture this one. "Heady rose-petal aroma, layered flavors of cranberry, cherry, and chocolate, with a hint of leather . . ."

It used to sound like so much bullshit, but I can actually taste all those flavors now. And they're delicious. Maybe I just never noticed them, or maybe I've been buying only so-so wines, or maybe the chocolate liqueur from the last drink just helped me to notice all these subtleties. Whatever the reason, I feel like a new world of flavor has opened. It's like I've been seeing in black and white all my life, and suddenly I realize the hues that once appeared to be a few shades of gray are really a Technicolor spectrum of colors. What a revelation!

"Nice, huh?" says the bartender.

"It's . . . " I throw up my hands, speechless. The bartender nods, his eyes glowing and the furrow of his brow melting away.

"Here's something to chew on," he says. "What if I told you that a wine made by the same winemaker, at the same winery, with almost the same grapes, only from a different section of the vineyard, will taste entirely different?"

"What you're saying is, the flavors of the grapes themselves are affected by where they're grown?" I ask. The bartender nods, still grinning with pride. "So you're not only tasting the grapes, but the land as well?"

He delivers another excited nod.

I'm straining to make sense of all this new information. Finally I understand everything. I can't believe what I'm about to say, but I can't help myself. "So in a way, savoring a good wine is like subconsciously communicating with the planet." The bartender is positively beaming. "Wow." I look into my glass and give it a spin. The ruby depths of the wine whirl mysteriously within the bowl of the glass, reflecting the neon glow of the bar sign and every so often my face. This is too much.

My trance is finally broken by the growing din of my surroundings. The bar, cozily light against the growing darkness outside, starts to fill with the more active, early-evening crowd. Still reeling from my dialogue with the philosopher behind the bar, I savor my wine as he busily attends to the new customers.

At length, noticing that my glass is now empty, he walks back. "How about something for dessert?" he asks. "You like Port? It's sweet, and it's strong. Mix two shot glasses with three scoops of vanilla ice cream, and maybe a dash of chocolate liqueur, and mix it all in a blender."

"You mean a wine milkshake?" Something fun and frosty sounds like a refreshing way to end the evening.

"Sure, if that's what you want to call it," he says.

"I usually don't have dessert before dinner, but what the heck, right? I'm an adult. Let's have it."

He grabs another bottle—back to the middle shelf this time—and pours some into a blender. He reaches into a freezer under the counter and pulls out a pint of vanilla ice cream. Sure enough, three scoops tumble on top of the Port. He tops the mixture off with some chocolate liqueur and starts the blender. In the meantime, he grabs another empty wineglass and a can of whipped cream from the refrigerator. When the blender has done its job, he pours the contents into the fresh glass. The concoction is a beautiful creamy shade of lavender. The bartender then tops it off with the whipped cream, sprinkles a bit of cinnamon on top, and serves the glass with a small dessert spoon.

"Voilà. A Port milkshake, as you call it," he says, and takes a step back.

Yum. It's frothy, mildly sweet, with a mellow kick and a mysterious depth of flavor unlike any milkshake I've ever had. "This will work just fine," I say gratefully, and pay my tab with a generous tip. "Thank you. I've learned a lot. You've really made me think. I'll never look the same way at wine again."

"It was my pleasure," he says with a nod.

A fresh group of patrons arrives at the far end of the bar, and he steps professionally away to collect their orders. One of them points to the section of dark glass bottles and asks, "Hey, what're those? I don't think I've seen them here before." The bartender turns to me as if to see if I heard, nods again, and turns back to the patron.

"That's wine, my friend," he replies, picking up his angel-white towel. "Always been here, you've just never noticed."

The Recipes

All recipes are open to experimentation. If you have concocted a brand-new combination of your very own, or if you simply found a better way to make any of the following recipes, please share your wisdom with your fellow shakers at WineRave.com—an on-line wine lounge open twenty-four hours a day, seven days a week. See you there!

Martini Grigio

4 oz. Pinot Grigio (Sauvignon Blanc an acceptable substitute)
Crushed ice
Vermouth to taste (better quality preferred—try Duckhorn King Eider)
Lemon peel, cocktail olives (for garnish)

Add ice, wine, and vermouth to cocktail shaker. Shake for approximately ten seconds. Rub lemon peel around rim of martini glass and add to glass with two cocktail olives. Strain shaker contents into glass.

Margaret

4 oz. Gewürztraminer (no substitutes)
2 oz. margarita mix
Crushed ice (to taste)
Dash of Triple Sec (or to taste)
Wedge of lime (for garnish)

Add ice, wine, margarita mix, and Triple Sec to cocktail shaker. Shake for approximately ten seconds. Salt the rim of a large rocks glass or a large red-wine glass. Pour entire contents of shaker into glass. Garnish with lime. Serves one—for party-sized quantities, increase proportions accordingly.

☖ Sauvignon Sour

4 oz. Sauvignon Blanc (Pinot Grigio an acceptable substitute)
2 oz. sour mix
Crushed ice (to taste)
2 dashes of Triple Sec (or to taste)
Maraschino cherry (for garnish)

Add ice, wine, sour mix, and Triple Sec to cocktail shaker. Shake for approximately ten seconds. Pour entire contents of shaker into large rocks glass or a large red-wine glass. Garnish with cherry.

☖ Wine Cooler/Wine Spritzer

2 oz. fruity wine (any "jug" or boxed white or red; also Sauvignon Blanc, Pinot Grigio, Gamay Beaujolais, Pinot Noir, Zinfandel, etc.)
5 oz. lemon-lime soda (plain soda water can be substituted for Spritzer)
Crushed ice
Wedge of lime (for garnish)

Fill a large rocks glass with ice. Pour wine over ice and slowly add soda. Garnish with lime.

♀ Red Kiss

4 oz. dry red wine (Cabernet Sauvignon, Merlot, or other red Bordeaux varietals preferred)
Dash of chocolate liqueur (better quality preferred—try Godiva)

Pour wine into large red-wine glass. Add chocolate liqueur. Swirl gently to mix.

♀ Sangria

4 oz. fruity red wine (see "Wine Cooler," above)
Dash of lime juice (optional—Rose's brand preferred)
Dash of Triple Sec
Wedge of lemon, wedge of lime
1 cup crushed ice (or to taste)

Combine all ingredients in cocktail shaker. Shake for approximately ten seconds. Empty entire contents of shaker into large rocks glass. Serves one—for party-sized quantities, increase proportions accordingly.

♀ Port Milkshake

2 oz. Ruby Port (preferably not tawny)
2 generous scoops vanilla ice cream
Dash of chocolate liqueur (better quality preferred—try Godiva)
1 cup crushed ice
Whipped cream and cinnamon (for garnish)

Add all ingredients to blender. Blend for fifteen seconds or until frothy. Pour into pint-sized beer glass or oversized red-wine goblet, if available. Garnish with whipped cream and a dash of cinnamon.

BRENDAN ELIASON

Yes, you've already met Brendan back in Part I prior to his piece on " . . . Deciphering and Using Wine Scores." As we'd mentioned, Brendan is studying enology at Cal Poly, which means he's a college student on a severe budget. There was no question that Brendan had to be the obvious choice on handling non-rules for junk food and takeout pairings for the book. We then tagged on some collective work by Joel Quigley, Darryl Roberts, Sarah Donnelly, and Stewart Dorman to round out "Fast Wines for Fast Lives . . ."

—j, j & m

Fast Wines for Fast Lives, or Quick and Easy Fast-Food Party Pairings

by Brendan Eliason and crew

Putting together food pairings for wine parties or even everyday life can often be like trying to become President to meet chicks—more expensive than it needs to be and a lot more trouble than it's worth. Anyone can pair wine with cheese. Red wine or Port with chocolate? Elementary. Champagne with strawberries? Been there, done that, bought the T-shirt. These are all classic pairings that have been closely nurtured by wine drinkers for hundreds of years to the point of restrictive boredom. Classic pairings work, but they just don't always mesh with the way people eat and drink today. After all, how much English Stilton do you have sitting in your fridge?

Snacks

The dirty little secret of wine-party snacks is that usually you don't have to go any farther than what you have in your cupboard now or the junk-food section of the supermarket to get party food that goes great with wine. If you want proof of this, look no further than Orville Redenbacher as a man who knew how to get funky. Microwavable popcorn is the perfect party food (unless you count whipped cream and licorice whips—in which case I want to be invited to your parties!). Popcorn is cheap (less than a dollar a bag), quick and easy to make (three to four minutes in the microwave), and, most important, it goes great with white wine (red wine works, too, sometimes, but I personally prefer white). My favorite pairing? Pop Secret Homestyle Popcorn with a dry Sauvignon Blanc (sparkling wine/champagne also kicks ass).

Don't let my preferences limit you, however; throw a popcorn party! Grab three or four different brands/flavors of microwavable popcorn and get a variety of white wines together and let people choose which wines they like with what popcorn. If they could have had microwaves in sixteenth-century France, I guarantee this would be common practice today. (Warning: The only disadvantage to serving microwavable popcorn is that it is very difficult to pull off the "I slaved for hours over a hot stove" look, but if you can pull it off, more power to you.)

I can understand why microwavable popcorn has taken some time to catch on among wine drinkers. After all, many great ideas take decades and sometimes even centuries to be recognized for their genius. I am quite confused, however, why every bag of chocolate-chip cookies does not come with a recommended red-wine pairing, or why every bottle of Zinfandel sold in this country does not come with a bag of Pepperidge Farm Sausalito Chocolate Chip Cookies preattached. Why doesn't everyone know that red wine and chocolate-chip cookies are possibly the greatest American pairing of all time? Even better than Jennifer Love Hewitt and silicone. Somebody, somewhere messed up.

Luckily, I don't think that it's too late to repair the damage if we are able to start a grass-roots campaign. The plan is simple. First, it must be considered every right-thinking person's duty to tell as many friends as possible. Be forewarned, this might require a party. Second, either make or buy chocolate-chip cookies and red wine (Zinfandel, Syrah, Cabernet Sauvignon, and Sangiovese are some of my personal favorites). Third, and last, simply eat them together.

Takeout and Such

All right, now that I've ranted and given up my most intimate snacktime secrets, let's build on the fast-food/takeout food concept. The following list of mealtime pairings, whether for one or twenty, offers hints on how to grab a quick dinner and a bottle of wine without having to sacrifice time, money, or the pleasure of your palate! You'll notice we didn't list vintage dates (the year the grapes were actually harvested), because these aren't as important as simply enjoying the wines. We've also made music/video/scene-setting selections to enhance your experience.

Love American-Style

DiGiorno's Rising Crust Cheese Pizza has given frozen food a good name. The crispy crust, tasty cheese, and spicy sauce are a perfect match with Kenwood Vineyards' Sonoma Valley Zinfandel, which is loaded with berry fruit flavors and black pepper overtones. Plant yourself in front of the tube with a lover and pop *Moonstruck* into the VCR.

Fightin' the Fat

After dashing through the produce section of your corner grocer and scooping up a pile of fresh greens and mixed veggies, snag a bottle of Australia's Seaview McLaren Vale Chardonnay. The wine's crisp, citrus acidity will stand up well to a good dose of vinaigrette dressing and Midnight Oil's hit album, *Diesel and Dust*. Now hit the floor for a few tummy crunches.

Jack and Jimmy Catch a Cab

The Ultimate Cheeseburger from Jack in the Box (don't drink and drive-thru!) is a good friend to Gallo of Sonoma's Cabernet Sauvignon. The red wine's luscious fruit and well-balanced tannins are only enhanced by this carnivore's delight: We suggest you super-size this one over and over by hitting the "Repeat" button on Jimmy Buffett's "Cheeseburger in Paradise."

The Deli Dash

You've already scored a bottle of Korbel's Chardonnay Champagne, a sparkling wine with all the fruit and no pretension. Now whip over to the deli counter for a turkey club sandwich and bag of potato chips. On the way home, shove a copy of the B-52s' *Cosmic Thing* into your CD player and celebrate the upcoming flavor-fest. Note: Ignore the gawking people in the car next to you as you rock to "Love Shack."

Kung Pao Chow on the Rhineland

Takeout Chinese has become an American staple. We suggest making Germany's P. J. Valckenberg Riesling its international partner in culinary diplomacy, especially when chowing kung pao chicken from the box. The high acidity of the Riesling will take the sting out of the heat, while the heat will balance the sweetness of the wine. Trio's *Da Da Da* should lend rhythm and dexterity to your chopsticks.

Washin' Back the Wrap

All right, how are you going to make that leftover veggie avocado wrap you picked up yesterday at the neighborhood trendy pit stop fresh again? First of all, play something crisp and new, like the Sundays' *Static and Silence*. Then pop open a bottle of Beringer Vineyards' Alluvium Blanc. This white blend's full and creamy flavors are made to bring food alive. However, if the veggie wrap is too far gone, simply sip Alluvium Blanc as a cocktail, while waiting for the pizza delivery.

Hey, You Ribbin' Me, Porky?

Sure, your domicile might not be much fancier than the first little pig's straw hut. And yeah, you might be the culinary equivalent to the Big Bad Wolf, but that doesn't mean you can't eat and drink with the best of 'em. Next time you're hunting the fertile land of heat-lamp meats at the grocery store, pick up some spicy ribs, a bag of sourdough, and a bottle of Sutter Home White Zinfandel. It's that sweet-meets-heat balancing thing again. When you get back to the shack, toss some frozen green beans into the microwave, then plant yourself in front of the tube for a delicious meal and an evening with the Cartoon Channel. Th-th-that's all, folks!

Jackie's Big Sub Marathon

You just cut out of work early and picked up a stack of videos for a Jackie Chan Friday Night Movie Marathon, then made a classic pit stop for a couple of Philly cheese steak subs. Now it's time to call your roommate at work and ask him to pick up a bottle of Nathanson Creek Merlot before meeting you back at the pad. No doubt, you've got to have something bold to wash down all that blood and cheese. Hey, who said wine wasn't for real men?

Tortellini Down Under

The new revolution in vacuum-packed fresh pasta makes Contadina's Cheese Tortellini and Marinara Sauce a friend to the working class. Australia's Rosemount Shiraz (same as Syrah in America) is an excellent match to the rich and spicy marinara with its huge, dark-berry flavors. While you're heating the water, we insist that you pull the cork for a predinner taste and crank up Chumbawumba's "Tubthumper." Ah-h-h-h, nourishment for the angst-ridden soul.

Steak 'n Potato Sinkfest

Go to the grocery store: Take a jumbo can of Campbell's Chunky Steak and Potato off the shelf. Hit the wine racks: Match big stew with Gundlach-Bundschu's Bearitage red blend. Back at the apartment: Eat beef stew over the sink while sipping Bearitage from a jelly jar. Nothing feels quite so liberating as a sinkfest, wiping your chin on your shirtsleeve, tapping your toe to the Red Hot Chili Peppers' *Blood Sugar Sex Magik*, and sippin' vino.

The Mexican Revolution

Before stopping by that Strip-Mall-Mexican-Food-Dive for your favorite spicy pork burrito, we recommend you pick up a bottle of fruity French wine. Robert Sarrau's Beaujolais-Villages, with its clean berry and grape flavors, will cool any animosity that this Mexican dish might have wrapped deep in its tortilla. Humphrey Bogart's classic *Treasure of the Sierra Madre* is the video to watch with this explosive pairing because "We don't need no stinking beer!"

DO THESE PEOPLE REALLY EXIST?

*Like Lora White (EDU.2.: Adventures in the Wine Aisle . . .), Rosina
Tinari Wilson is yet another journalistic enigma to the Wine Brats.
We've read and admired her progressive writings both in magazines
and her cookbook,* Seafood, Pasta & Noodles: The New Classics *(Ten
Speed Press). We've heard rumors and tales about the high quality
and style of her educational classes at California Culinary Academy
in San Francisco. As a senior editor at* Wine X *magazine, where they
refer to her as their* Token Boomer, *she's enlightened us with such
topics as pairing wines with fusion cuisine and quick holiday dinners
without the bird. We're sure she exists. Unfortunately, we've never
met her face-to-face in the kitchen or over a glass. What a shame.
Hey, maybe we should throw a potluck wine dinner as an excuse to
get all the Wine Brats Coalition contributors together and put an
end to all the mystery! But how the heck would we go about doing
that? How could we coordinate such a party? Ahhh! Seek professional help. Take it away, Rosina.*

—j, j & m

The Art of Culinary Delegation, or It's Potluck Party Time

by Rosina Tinari Wilson

W hen it comes to throwing a party, there are two extremes. You know them both, and though they're as different from each other as Chardonnay and Cabernet, the odds are that, at this point in your life, you don't really relate to either. The first, a specialty of college dorms and singles apartment complexes, takes zero planning—you just stick your head out the window and yell to drum up your guest list, then order up pizza and beer when people show up. Been there, done (way too much of) that! Luckily (except for the occasional lapse triggered by *Monday Night Football*), we've pretty much outgrown this mode, and never (well, hardly ever) party like this anymore.

At the other end of the spectrum, we have the seriously glitzy, obsessively planned bash, choreographed down to the last detail—with written invitations, color-coordinated theme decor, a hyperchic dress code, and lavish food that you spent all week preparing. Not long ago, throwing a party like this used to be a rite of passage into full-fledged adulthood, a way for newlyweds and bachelor/ettes to make their mark on the social scene. But that was then. This is now—the cusp of the twenty-first century—time for a whole new look at entertaining. It means parties that are well-planned but not fussy. With lots of flexibility. Room for creativity for you and your guests. Most of all, it means plenty of fun, plenty of good eats, and a focus on quality wine that will set your parties apart from everybody else's from here on out.

You can gear such details as dress code, decor, and music to the season, to the mood you want to set, and to any special events you might be celebrating. If the birthday girl is a jazz buff, for instance, put on some of her favorite CDs for a smooth, mellow background. If the anniversary couple is into sports cars, or mountain bikes, or (oh, nooo!) karaoke, find a way to work that into the mix. Use the ideas in this chapter as a springboard for your own imagination, and soon you'll be dreaming up great parties that express your own personal style. (Also, feel free to mix and match ideas from throughout the book to create hybrid parties.) What a great way to start the third millennium—as a certified partymeister!

To get you started, we'll be looking at two very different scenarios—one for red wine, one for bubbly—designed to make you a party legend in your own time. They'll work for as few as four or six or as many as your place will hold. They're flexible: day or evening; indoors or out; buffet or family style. And best of all, they're dead easy for you to carry off. So start assembling your eats, pull some corks, and add friends and stir. It's a simple recipe for entertaining and it makes for a great party. Enjoy!

INVITATIONS

Gone are the days of stuffy, formal invitations with their raised lettering and prestamped reply envelopes. You've got too much going on in your life to deal with all that paper; besides, who wants to do in all those trees? Not to mention that you can upgrade your wine choices with all the cash you save on postage.

Instead, after you've figured out your guest list, and the necessities of when, where, what to wear, and what to bring, either get on the phone (draft someone efficient to help make the calls if the guest list is large), or, better yet, let your E-mail and/or fax machine do the work. Just make sure to ask for RSVPs (although technically this translates to "respond if you please," it actually makes a yes-or-no answer mandatory) and remember to list your own phone, fax, and E-mail to make it just as easy for your guests to reply as it was for you to invite them.

No matter which party scenario you're choosing, keep your invitation simple—and be sure to let everyone know exactly what to bring. That way you don't have to do all the work, everyone feels tied to the success of the party, and best of all for you, you're in complete control.   *—Rosina Tinari*

Scenario 1: Grown-up Barbecue

In some parts of the country, barbecue season lasts all year long. And despite rainy winters and occasional frost, intrepid grillers will, whenever the urge strikes, gleefully fire up the covered kettle or propane firebox faster than you can say "latent pyromaniac." But barbecue's not just about burgers and dogs and a six-pack anymore. We're after something much, much classier now, even though it still has to be casual and fun.

A well-planned barbecue, fortunately, is practically a guaranteed success. Ever since our ancestors discovered fire, gathering around the communal flame has had the power to bring us together, and to turn even total strangers into fast friends.

This fun, easy barbecue menu will make your party both upscale and down-home. Anyone can pull it off—even if you don't know the difference between mesquite (FYI, it's a hardwood charcoal that makes even tofu taste terrific) and mosquitoes (burn citronella candles to keep 'em away!). Get your guests to bring some ultra-easy side dishes and desserts to wrap around your hot-off-the-coals main course. And now's the time and place to start your own new party tradition. Forget the brewski—instead, pour some good juice of the grape throughout.

The secret of the food is super-simple: two ingredients max for all recipes—dips, BBQ sauces, sides, even dessert! So invite your most laid-back friends (along with a few who need a little loosening up!) and delegate like crazy; then just focus on the fire and get set to enjoy the heck out of your own party.

No-Brainer Apps

Slice-it-yourself whole salami
Marinated mushrooms
Veggie platter (see suggestions below)
Blue corn, mesquite BBQ, and plain potato chips
Two-ingredient dips (see recipes below)

The first two appetizers come ready-to-serve at your nearby Italian deli or well-stocked supermarket. For your veggie platter, get anything that looks good, wash well, cut if necessary, and lay out a quick pattern (spokes-on-a-wheel works well) on a big round plate. Go for a variety of colors, textures, and shapes: tiny raw carrots, yellow and green zucchini sticks, rings of red and green bell pepper, broccoli and cauliflower florets, chunks of red, white, yellow, and/or purple potatoes (steamed twenty minutes). Use as few or as many as you like.

The chips are for crunch; just put them next to the veggies and use the dips for both. As for the dips, you can probably throw together all three in two minutes flat. Just mix each one in a bowl with a fork or spoon. (Yes, *do* attempt this at home—even if your usual MO involves just twisting open a jar of that infamous salsa from New York City!)

No-Brainer Barbecue—The Main Event

When I do a party like this, I like to grill up a little bit of everything I can get my hands on. You can, too, or you can just zero in on one main type of protein—a thick chuck roast, individual T-bones or filets, assorted sausages, juicy pork chops, meaty salmon steaks—whatever looks best and suits your crowd (or your wallet). (My own money-saving secret, by the way, is to raid the close-to-the-pull-date, half-price-or-less bin in the meat section of my local yuppie grocery. After two or three visits, and with a designated corner of the freezer to store my stash, I'm ready to roll whenever. I've even scored such exotica as ostrich meat, squab, lamb tenderloin, and prime-grade chateaubriand. Everything but your standard burger 'n dogs!)

Although four to six ounces of meat normally constitutes a standard serving, the aromas wafting from the grill have a way of jump-starting our primitive carnivore appetites. So double the expected amount, and you'll appease the (two-legged!) beasts. Once you've figured out your protein, stir up the crowd-pleasing two-ingredient barbecue sauces. Choose one or use all three. They serve triple duty: to marinate your meat before cooking, to brush or spoon on while grilling, and to use as hot dips at the table. **See PARTY.1: The Surreal Circus, topic "Be Accommodating," for alternative diets.**

If you've never touched match to charcoal, make sure to invite someone who has either experience at the grill or an ego that's so big that she doesn't dare mess up. And ask everyone to bring a side dish or dessert with only two ingredients. The last time I did one of these on the spur of the moment, my crowd showed up with some dynamite jalapeño corn muffins (packaged mix plus canned peppers), twice-baked potatoes stuffed with cheddar sauce from a jar, buttered white corn (grill or oven-roast in the husk ten to fifteen minutes), steamed green beans with canned cream of mushroom soup topping (warm in a 375-degree oven for fifteen to twenty minutes), wheatmeal crackers and after-dinner cheeses, toasted pecans and apple slices, and a watermelon. (Sounds like all the basic food groups to me!)

Your best bets in wine here are medium-weight reds such as pepper-spicy Zinfandel, Rhône-style blends from France, Australia, or California, and Italians such as Chianti (or its Cal-Ital equivalent, Sangiovese). Although bone-dry, these wines are fruity, easy to drink, and unlike, say, tannic Cabernets, they're easy to like. They also have the added advantage (rare these days) of a reasonable price tag. **See REF.5: Variety Is the Spice of Life.**

Open all the bottles at the beginning and let everybody taste what they want. Compare notes, if you like, by having a "comments" sheet next to each bottle. Tasters write down impressions of each wine; by the end of the evening, not only will you have a pretty good sense of what the wine's about, but you can also award prizes for things like "coolest wine buzzword" or "most off-the-wall food-pairing suggestion."

Your reds can carry through into dessert if chocolate is part of the picture. Add a bottle or two of decent Port or sweet sherry if you like—in a pinch, you can even pour them over your ice cream! Get some funky ice cream flavors, surround the cartons with bowls of interesting add-ons, and let everyone help themselves. Try chopped toasted nuts, chocolate chips, crumbled chocolate or shortbread cookies, dried cherries or cranberries, chocolate-covered raisins, warm-from-the-nukebox chocolate or butterscotch sauce. You can try doing the "comments" thing again—but don't expect the notes to be legible this late in the party!

Recipes

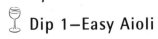 Dip 1—Easy Aioli

2 cloves fresh garlic, finely minced or squeezed through a garlic press
1 cup mayonnaise

🍷 Dip 2—Easy Creamy Salsa

1 cup salsa (your favorite brand and heat level)
1 cup regular or low-fat sour cream

🍷 Dip 3—Easy Guacamole

1 large avocado
1 package instant guacamole powder
*(If you're not chained to the two-ingredient rule, you can tang it up with a
    squeeze of lemon or lime.)*

Barbecue Sauces
🍷 Sauce 1—Smoky Java

2 cups bottled smoky BBQ sauce
½ cup coffee concentrate

🍷 Sauce 2—A1 Red

2 cups A1 steak sauce
1 cup dry red wine

🍷 Sauce 3—Soy with a Snap

2 cups soy sauce
1 cup Dijon-style mustard

Scenario 2: Sparklers, Apps, and Sweets

There's nothing like bubbly to get people into the party mood. More than
any other wine—more than any other beverage at all, for that matter—it

has that built-in aura of festivity and celebration. Even the rituals add to the fun: peeling back the foil and twisting off the wine muzzle; seeing whether the cork will blast out of the bottle with a sonic *POP* or slip out with a near-silent *phhht*; clinking the tall, slim "flute" glasses (buy, borrow, or rent them if you have to, to enhance the theme over standard wineglasses) full of mesmerizing little dancing bubbles.

For this party, you're starting a new tradition by serving bubbly, and nothing but bubbly, from start to finish. This is a great one for the December holiday season, for a special event, or for any time of the year when you want to make a really big, festive splash. Not only will your "bubbly only" theme make your party unique and imaginative, you'll pull it all off without even worrying about a main dish. Instead, you'll have enough bubbly-friendly apps to keep everyone busy for the first couple of hours, then enough desserts, with dessert sparklers to match, to wind things down.

A great icebreaker here is a toast-a-thon. You can ask your guests beforehand to come prepared with an original or borrowed toast for the occasion. Or surprise everyone and have them invent toasts during the party. Word-play is a plus—try starting with "Champagne to our real friends and real pain to our sham friends," and see where things go.

As for food: Although some say that bubbly goes with everything, there are certain types of flavors and textures that work especially well. Salty foods, for instance. It's the "pretzels and beer" or "chips and cola" effect. The salt, very simply, brings on the bubbles. (You can see this for yourself by shaking some salt into a glass of soda and watching it fizz up.) The bubbles then trap flavors from both the food and the drink, then blast them into your mouth when they burst. That's why champagne and caviar can be such a magical combo. And smoked fish. And salty cheeses. And . . . well, let's just put some recipes together and see.

Meanwhile, sparkling wine can also handle mild spice. It's usually made with a hint of sweetness, which can work wonders to temper heat in food. (Call this the "chutney with curry" effect.) And because sparklers can also show flavors of citrus, nuts, and even fresh-baked bread, using any of these flavors in your food will help make the bond with the wine that much stronger. Here's our party menu of appetizers geared to sparkling wine. Do as many as you like, then fill in with bowls of salted nuts and olives, plus breadsticks, bakery-style rolls, and fruit. It's substantial enough, and varied enough, that your guests won't even miss the main course! Lay in the bubbly, get the gang to bring desserts, and you're set.

Easy Apps for Sparkling Wine

🍷 Beefozolas

Get some thin-sliced rare roast beef at the deli; cut each slice into three pieces. Spread each piece along one edge with a tablespoon of Cambozola cheese (soft and spreadable like Brie but with a mild blue-cheese kick) and roll it up. Stick in a toothpick and top with chopped chives or green onions. (Can't find Cambozola? Blend cream cheese two to one with your favorite blue cheese.)

🍷 Avocado di Parma (or Genoa)

Wrap lengthwise slices of ripe avocado with thin-sliced prosciutto (classier) or salami (cheaper). Stab with a toothpick.

🍷 Smoked Salmon Toasts

Pick up a quarter-pound or so of good smoked salmon and cut it into half-inch slices. Smear some herb-flavored cream cheese on melba toast squares and top with the salmon. Optional: Decorate with lemon slices.

🍷 Green and Red Cream Cheese Spread

Get two packages of cream cheese. Place one on a serving plate and spread thickly with pesto (supermarket deli case or freezer). Top with the second block of cream cheese and a heap of chopped sun-dried tomatoes. (These come in jars, packed in oil. Drain before using.) Serve with thin slices of baguette. Perfect for a holiday party!

♟ Curry-Coconut Chicken

Cut leftover roast chicken, or supermarket smoked chicken, into bite-sized cubes. Get a packaged "mild curry" mix and follow the directions. At serving time, sprinkle on some grated toasted coconut and serve warm with wedges of pita bread.

♟ Ravioli with Pignoli

Pick up some ready-made small ravioli (there are several brands and quite a few flavors to choose among) from the supermarket dairy case. Cook the ravioli according to package directions, toss with butter and grated Parmesan cheese, then sprinkle with pignoli (pine nuts, an Italian favorite—substitute almonds or walnuts in a pinch).

♟ Super Frittata

Beat six to twelve eggs and stir in your choice of the following ingredients: chopped ham or bacon, sliced green onion, slivered red onion, bits of roasted red bell pepper (from a jar), chopped marinated artichokes, frozen peas, grated carrot. Add salt and pepper to taste and pour into a nonstick baking pan. Bake at 350 degrees until just cooked through (test with a knife or toothpick), about thirty to forty-five minutes. Serve warm or at room temperature in small squares or wedges.

♟ Caesar Nicoise

This brings together the best of two classic salads. On a serving platter, lay out a bed of raw spinach (prewashed, from a cello bag) and top with canned tuna, anchovies (if you like 'em), sliced hard-boiled egg, and assorted cherry tomatoes. Drizzle some good bottled Caesar dressing over all and sprinkle with capers.

Wine

The bubbly you serve doesn't have to be pricey. There are plenty of good domestic sparklers and Spanish Cavas out there, plus Italian sparkling Muscats (Asti Spumante is the easiest to find) for dessert, costing $12 max—far less than a Chardonnay or Cabernet of equal quality. Blush-colored Blanc de Noirs versions are extra festive. **See REF.5: Variety Is the Spice of Life.**

DESSERT WINES

Often people think that white zins or any other slightly sweet off-dry wine are dessert wines. Usually dessert wines will be anywhere from 7 to 35 percent sugar, whereas the others range from 3 to 5 percent. Their higher levels of residual sugar give them more viscosity, meaning the thickness, body, weight, and mouthfeel of the wine. Because of their higher sugar content, and even more so if they're fortified, they stay fresh longer once they're opened than dry wines. Enjoy them up to a month or so after they're opened. If not fortified, keep them refrigerated.

—Kim Caffrey

TERMS FOR DESSERT WINES

BOTRYTIS—The "noble" rot, this fungus (given the right conditions of cool, moist air and warm, but not too hot, afternoons) softens the grapes' acidity and concentrates its sugars, lending a honeyed aroma/flavor. Sauternes, Barsac, Auslese, Beerenauslese, and Trock-enbeerenauslese are the most well known.

FORTIFIED—When Brandy or a neutral spirit is added to fermenting wine, arresting the fermentation and leaving some residual sugar in the wine. Examples are Port, Sherry, Madeira-styled wines, and vermouths, flavored with herbs.

ICE WINE—When grapes are left on the vine until the first frost and then picked and pressed. Notable producers are Germany, Austria, Switzerland, and the Niagara area in the United States.

LATE HARVEST—When grapes are left on the vine to increase and concentrate sugars and picked after normal harvesttime is considered over. Often they are shriveled, raisinlike. They are frequently affected by botrytis.

RESIDUAL SUGAR—The percentage of (natural grape fructose) sugar left in the wine after fermentation. Most people begin to detect RS at levels of about 1 percent. Most "dry" wines fall under those levels. Off-dry wines can go up to 6 or 7 percent before you enter dessert wine territory, where the wines can go up to 35 percent, or roughly one-third sugar by weight. High residual sugar will help to preserve the wine when combined with alcohol and acidity.

—Kim Caffrey

CHAMPAGNES/SPARKLING WINES

We won't go into the purist versus New World issue of "Champagne can only come from Champagne" and everything else is sparkling wine. This goes back to naming wine by region versus varietal. What matters most in quality is the blend, and that the sparkling wine be made by the champagne method, "methode champenoise," wherein the secondary fermentation that traps the CO_2 takes place in individual bottles. One of the costliest but most important steps of the methode champenoise process is riddling. This process involves turning the bottle and tilting it slightly downward over a long period of time following the second fermentation, to get the **lees** (dead yeast) into the neck of the bottle, which is then frozen, blown out, and refilled with the "dosage," a splash of wine with possible sugar to determine its sweetness, then corked, wire-caged, and foiled. The longer the wine stays in contact with its lees in the bottle after that second fermentation, the smaller the bead (bubble). Sparkling wines made by methode champenoise outside of France's Champagne region include Cremants, Saumur Mousseaux, Cava (from Spain), and most good bubbly made in the United States.

LEES—The dead yeast and bits of skin and pulp that fall to the bottom of the tank/barrel after fermentation. Aging the wine "on the lees" (or French—*sur lie*) after fermentation is said to give a richness/ toastiness to the nose. Stirring the lees (*battonage*) is said to give the mouthfeel of the wine more creaminess.

The transfer method avoids the labor-intensive riddling and instead transfers the twice-fermented wine into pressured tanks, where the lees are filtered out, and then put once again into the bottle. Due to decreased lees contact, transfer-method sparkling wine will not have the same depth or richness as methode-champenoise wines.

The bulk or charmat method has the least character of all. Its second fermentation takes place in pressurized tanks with little lees time. Its bubbles tend to be rather large, often referred to as toad's eyes or cola bubbles. This is the stuff you use to make Mimosas. Don't make them from fresh-squeezed orange juice and Dom Perignon. Make them from inexpensive bubbly and OJ outta the carton.
                                                                  —Kim Caffrey

A COLLECTIVE KNOWLEDGE WITHIN THE COALITION

Now that you've gotten a mishmash collection of ideas for parties, pairings, recipes, and just plain fun, all of which can happen within the confines of one's personal digs, we've decided to share some of the insight we've gathered over the past few years concerning organizing tasting groups and Bigger Bashes. This following little ditty is not the work of one, but of a collective within the coalition, and mainly those working directly with Wine Brats National and a few friends both past and present. As with all ideas offered within this here book, we highly suggest you mix and match ideas to suit the needs of each given event . . . be creative!

—j, j & m

Hosting the Big Bash, or What You'll Need to Know to Survive Large Events

by a collective within the coalition

So maybe you're already a Wine Brats' regional chapter leader—or thinking about it—or someone who would just like to host an event centered around wine. Of course, we're talking about something bigger than a Surreal Dinner Party or a Potluck Tasting Party designed by Rosina Tinari Wilson. There are so many different kinds of events you might host that it is impossible to provide you with specific "instructions" on how to host one. However, what we've tried to do in the following pages is give you some basic guidelines and advice. If you've ever hosted a party at your house, that experience, combined with the information in this section, should allow you to host a successful wine event.

If you feel you need further advice, we suggest you seek out the help of the special-event professionals in your community. You'll often find them at party rental stores, hotels, ad agencies/PR firms, restaurants, and independent event planners. There is also an organization called ISES (International Special Events Society) with chapters worldwide. You can reach them at (800) 688-4737 or snail-mail them at 9202 N. Meridian Street #200, Indianapolis, IN 46260.

Types of Events

Chances are you will want to start with a fairly simple event, like a mixer. A mixer is almost exclusively a social event. It is a lot like having a party at your house: You'll want good wine, some good food, a little music, and people to have fun! You may want to give a short "thanks for coming" speech and explain the goals and mission of the mixer. If it's a Wine Brats event, explaining the mission is a must. But keep any speech brief; boring diatribes are a sure way to kill the mood.

Mixers are pretty easy. One person can probably do all the setup and cleanup, although two or three people to help will make it much easier. Another kind of event you might host is a formal tasting. Tastings are fun and educational. You can do varietal tastings, where several different bottles of the same kind of wine are tasted, such as Pinot Noir or Sauvignon Blanc. At vintage tastings, different types of wines from the same year are tasted. **See PARTY.2: Flying Blind.**

Formal tastings require a few people to "work" them. Depending on how many guests you have and how many wines you pour, you could need five or more people to pour the wine. Consider having one person to open and pour the wines for every twenty or twenty-five guests. You might also host a wine dinner, probably in association with a restaurant. Different wines would be matched with all the parts of the meal. With any luck, you'll be able to talk the restaurant's staff into pouring the wine (if you buy the wine from them, the law might in fact require their staff to open and pour the wines). We recommend that you have a couple of people on hand to lead these tastings. Always check local laws concerning alcohol.

A few other event ideas are: concerts, comedy shows, etc.; wine festivals; scavenger hunts; barbecues, cook-offs, and other food events; murder mystery dinners; and on and on . . . **See Part II: It's Party Time!**

Really, any event where wine can be showcased is a perfect event. Here are some things to remember.

In most states, if it appears you are selling alcohol (as it would if you charged admission to a tasting, for instance), you are required to have an alcohol permit or license. It is essential that you find out what, if any, permits or licenses you need well in advance of your event. Your state Alcoholic Beverage Control office or, sometimes, the local police can help you obtain the permit. Many times you can ride on the license from a restaurant or bar's existing license. If you choose a venue such as an art gallery and the event is open to the public, you will need a permit or license! Sometimes being a nonprofit organization exempts you from some of these regulations. But don't assume anything! Check all laws!

Insurance can also be an issue. Whenever large groups of people are brought together by the actions of an organization, that organization can be held liable for anything that might happen. Your organization's general liability policy may cover special events or it may be possible to modify it for events on a case-by-case basis. A good independent insurance agent can also sell you event-specific insurance, but it can be incredibly expensive.

Getting Wine

For most events you host you'll need help with obtaining wine. At events like mixers or informal tastings, you can ask guests to bring a bottle and probably have more than enough wine. However, for larger events you'll need other sources.

If there are wineries in your area, they are, of course, the best places to start. If they sponsor Wine Brats or believe in your cause, they may be willing to donate wine. If you run into tightfisted bureaucrats who just won't donate, offer to buy the wine at a discount (ask for 50 percent off and you'll probably get it).

If there aren't wineries near by, try writing to some of your favorite producers. Your letter should be concise (use the journalist's five Ws), specific (we need five cases by May 1), honest (we need your help), sent well in advance (two months or more if possible), and addressed to the right person (call the winery, if possible, and ask who handles donations).

Local wine distributors may also be a source for wine. Call or write them using the same guidelines as when asking wineries for product. The best results with distributors will probably come from personal contact. Ask your associates if anyone knows/works for a distributor.

Retailers might also give you wine. The only way to find out is to ask. The offer to buy at a discount is probably a good tactic here as well.

Checklists

The type of event you are hosting will dictate what specific supplies you'll need, but the following list includes things you need for most events. Some of the things listed might sound pretty obvious, but . . .

- **Corkscrews.** The waiter's corkscrew is often most useful because it has a little foldout knife and can also be used to remove bottle caps from mineral water and the like.

- **Dump Buckets.** Any container can be a dump bucket, but re- member, if they're small, you'll be running around emptying them all the time.
- **Glasses.** You can rent large quantities of glasses from party rental stores for about fifty cents each. You might also consider pur- chasing an inventory of glasses. Watch for sales at discount stores like Target or contact a restaurant supply company.
- **Tables and Tablecloths.** You can also rent these from party rental stores. However, costs can add up quickly when both are going for anywhere from $6 to $12 a pop. If you're working with a restaurant or venue that has tables and tablecloths, ask for their support.
- **Nonalcoholic Beverages.** Nonalcoholic beverages are essential. Mineral water, sparkling and still, is usually all you need. You could add juices or iced tea if you like. Coffee at the end of the event is also a good idea—don't forget the cream and sugar and paper cups!
- **Coolers and Ice.** White wines must be kept cold, or at least cool. Ice chests are the best bet, but if you don't have enough, there are other solutions. The cardboard case box that the wine comes in can be turned into an ice chest of sorts by removing the dividers and lining it with a plastic bag. Restaurant bus tubs can also work.
- **Miscellaneous Stuff.** Bring some felt-tip pens, masking or duct tape, a staple gun or office stapler, some string, note paper, garbage bags, scissors, and thumbtacks or pushpins.

Location

Finding a location for your event shouldn't be difficult. If you're lucky, there's a receptive wine bar, restaurant, or wine store in your area that would be glad to host your event. If not, you can always rent event space at a hotel, conference facility, or community center. Art galleries and other al- ternative spaces can be even better; however, be prepared to carry *every- thing* in and obtain special alcoholic beverage licensing.

If finding a location proves difficult, get creative! Consider your own home. A local college campus may be a possibility. Is there an abandoned warehouse you drive by every day on the way to work? Does your office building have a lobby or atrium you could commandeer? Does one of your members live on a farm with a funky barn? Is there a parking structure at the local mall that's never full? Is there a big patch of lawn at your apartment building?

As you can see, holding a large-scale wine tasting can be more logistically challenging than simply pouring hard drinks into plastic cups or tapping a keg. However, the rewards are also far greater as the addition of wine to any event elevates the overall experience. Instead of the event being focused on "quantity," the heart and soul of the night becomes "quality." Hopefully this section has given you enough information to be comfortable hosting your wine event. If you need more advice or information on ideas or events, please contact the Wine Brats anytime.

Responsible Hospitality

It is the policy of the Wine Brats to promote responsible hospitality at all events. The information below is adapted from several publications produced by the Responsible Hospitality Institute. They are a great organization and are always willing to help organizers promote responsible consumption at events. Contact them at (800) 443-7277 or snail-mail them at 4113 Scotts Valley Drive, Scotts Valley, CA 95066, for more information. We highly recommend that you always share such information with everyone involved in producing your event and that they read and understand it.

Two Important Laws

1. It is illegal to serve alcohol to anyone under the state's legal drinking age.

2. It is just as illegal to serve alcohol to anyone showing signs of intoxication as it is to serve a minor. Above and beyond these laws, as hosts of special events/tastings that serve alcoholic beverages, being responsible about alcohol consumption is vital to the success of the Wine Brats

mission. Individual federal and state laws must be reviewed by anyone hosting a wine event to ensure compliance.

Promoting responsible hospitality is fairly easy. To ensure the safety and well-being of those attending the events, here are some tips from the Responsible Hospitality Institute's publication *Hospitality Insighter*. Classic signs of intoxication (there are others, but chances are you will know an intoxicated person when you see one):

- Changes in speech (louder, quieter, slurred, or foul language)
- Personality changes (bravado, uninhibited behavior, anger/belligerence, flirting)
- Physical impairment (problems standing/walking, unfocused/red eyes, slowed movement, and clumsiness)

Logistical Nightmares

Creative locations can be fun, but they can also be logistical nightmares. Some things you should keep in mind:

- You'll need water, and it's heavy if you have to haul it in.
- You'll probably need electricity for lights and a sound system. However, it can be expensive if you have to bring in a generator.
- Convenient restrooms are a necessity. Portable toilets are the solution to sites without any other facilities, but you're probably better off choosing a site with restrooms.
- And certainly, if the site doesn't have toilets, it won't have a kitchen for food preparation.

Doing the Math

Earlier in the book when we talked about blind tastings and theme parties, Tina Caputo suggested, "One bottle of wine for every two guests should be sufficient." A 750 ml bottle contains about four/five glasses of wine—

this equates to approximately one case of wine for every twenty-five guests. However, when we plan for larger events, where guest numbers can fluctuate greatly and lots of wine can end up in the dump buckets, we go by the two-cases-per-twenty-five-guests equation. This should protect you from running out of wine, and if the producers who supplied the product are present, they simply take the leftovers with them. So . . .

example: 4 cases for 50 guests, or 8 cases for 100 guests

We highly suggest you divvy up the commitment for product support among multiple producers so that the cost is shared. Also, it's a good idea to ask each producer to pour two to four different wines! If you bring in four producers and each pours three wines, your guests will be able to sample twelve different wines.

example: 50 guests = 4 cases ÷ 4 producers = 1 case each, then 4 producers x 3 wines each = 12 wines

example: 200 guests = 16 cases ÷ 8 producers = 2 cases each, then 8 producers x 4 wines each = 32 wines

Try to work the equation so that you never ask any one producer to bring more than two cases each. Depending on the theme of your event, you may also set parameters on the types of wine they pour. If you are planning a Wine Brats event, we can help you with lists of what producers have what types of wines. Many times, producers are excited to be involved with theme events that fit their products. Let's say you're planning a Rhône varietal tasting. The obvious choice is to pour wine from France's Rhône region; however, you could also include California and Australian producers of Syrah, Shiraz, Grenache, Viognier, and the like. Not only can Part II help with ideas, but our reference sections focusing on regions and varietals can also spark thematic ideas.

Here are some other equations that can help with planning a wine tasting:

- One eight-foot table for every two wineries
- One dump bucket and wine opener for each eight-foot table
- One cooler or chilling tub for each eight-foot table
- Five pounds of ice for every case of wine that needs to be chilled
- Glasses for Mixers: one wineglass for each guest, plus 20 percent
- Glasses for Sit-Downs: comparative tastings require one glass for each wine tasted times the number of guests, plus 20 percent

Part III:

Gettin' Dirty with the Wine-makers

WINEMAKING: FROM THE TOP DOWN TO YOU

As we've traveled the country over the past several years, we've come to realize that many people have the perception that winemakers are reclusive, dusty old men in caves who quietly tend to their wine barrels. Nothing could be further from the truth. Take Darryl Groom from Geyser Peak Winery. He splits seasons between winemaking in California and Australia. Remember, we're talking Northern and Southern Hemispheres with opposing seasons. Or Gina Gallo, granddaughter of Julio Gallo, now in her early thirties and a winemaker for Gallo of Sonoma Winery. From cellar rats to marketing, the industry seems to be taking on a new face, a wide-eyed, youthful, and visionary enthusiasm that bodes well for the future of fine wine.

To open Part III, we asked Gina Gallo to share her early wine experiences and the inspirations that led her to become a winemaker. We weren't so concerned with her opinions about the details of winemaking, such as "How much time should a Chardonnay spend in oak, if any, and what percentage of malolactic fermentation . . . ?" No. That's another book. We wanted to know if her ascendancy within wine giant E&J Gallo was automatic? Was she always comfortable with wine. Does she love her job as a winemaker?

But winemaking is more than just families handing down a tradition from generation to generation. What about newcomers with a dream? What about you personally? That's why, within this section, we move to Stewart Dorman's diary, which chronicle's the day-to-

day life of Adrian Fog, a small upstart winery, and its challenges and triumphs. And finally, yet another contribution from Joe Naujokas, detailing the framework for one of the most successful home wine-making clubs we've run across to date, so that you might find the in-spiration to start one of your own. But first things first. Let's hear what Gina Gallo has to say about wine.

—j, j & m

BREW.1 # Stepping into Grandpa's Big Rubber Boots

by Gina Gallo

The tricky thing about wine for me, having grown up in a winemaking family, was figuring out for myself just what makes wine so special. Ironically, the most important message I try to get out to people who are just starting to enjoy wine is exactly the opposite: Wine is not so special. It's simply part of life.

Easy for me to say, certainly. I've been around wine since I was yay high to a grape. And while I never drank wine as a child, or watered down, as children often do in Europe, I do remember my father offering it to me as a teenager. My dad would say, "Would you like a glass of wine?" It was a very open, natural thing, like asking if I wanted some more sauce. The wine was almost always red, and usually straightforward and good, just like the food. They were both parts of the same meal; there was food and there was wine, and neither ever seemed as important as the family around the table.

It was different in college. I remember getting carded, like everyone else, and I drank beer at parties. But at dinners I would drink wine, which was very uncommon for a lot of people, especially in college. Some friends saw the wine there, and we'd share some and enjoy it. But the catch, I discovered, for most of the people my age was just getting over that hump of thinking about picking a wine, any wine, to begin with.

Fear of wine seemed unthinkable to me, until I learned the hard way. I went out to dinner with a boyfriend's family. Everyone said they wanted wine, and then they all turned to me. Suddenly I felt the pressure. *Don't pick anything stupid!* was all I could think. The wine list didn't have any of my family's wine, so I did what I figure most everyone does in that situation: I played a safe bet, a Napa Cabernet Sauvignon. The pressure took away from the whole experience. And then, to top it off, I can remember thinking the wine was corked. It tasted a little off. But there was no way to go back and change it, because so much was expected of it, and me.

Looking back at the experience, I simply allowed myself to be cornered because I was naive and put on the spot. Why is ordering wine in a restaurant like taking a test? Hey, they don't do that with food! You just try something you think you'll like, whether that means something exotic or an old favorite. It's sad when pressure changes everything. Wine should leave room for whims, for moods, and it should never be so momentous that people expect a genie to pop out of the bottle when you uncork it.

Maybe that was the beginning of my education about wine in the real world. I still hadn't decided that I'd make wine my profession, but I suddenly had a taste of how wine can be something other than the simple part of a meal I had grown up with. It's not surprising really that so many people's eyes glaze over at the mere mention of wine. There are just so many choices. It can be overwhelming. But **complexity** never entered into the picture for me because I never lost sight of the reason I was choosing wine in the first place: because it adds pleasure to life.

COMPLEX(ITY)—When a wine has depth, many aromas, flavors, and nuances.

Wine is actually a lot like people in this respect. On the most basic level, wine brings pleasure and people bring pleasure. We seek out people who make us feel good, and the more time we spend with them, the more we appreciate them. Ditto for wine. It's no wonder, really, that wine lovers talk about particular bottles that have soul, character, or personality. The simple fact that wine brings pleasure becomes a starting point for going farther, trying new ones, learning more, and discovering even more things to like about wine.

Of course, drinking wine for pleasure is one thing. Making it is another thing entirely. As far as I knew growing up, wine came from the vine and wound up on the table. I had no idea what happened in between. There was no mystery because I had never considered the transition. After college, I started in the business, selling wine in San Francisco. A "box jockey" is the industry nickname. It was only then that I grew curious about how wine is made, to understand what I was selling. I started sitting in on some basic viticulture classes at the University of California at Davis. Then I knew that I wanted to get involved on the grape side of the business.

In becoming a winemaker, however, I was again in a position of having the simple pleasures of wine overwhelmed by the details. Fortunately, wine has a built-in focus. It all starts in the vineyard. Whether it's Pinot Noir in Burgundy, Sangiovese in Tuscany, or Chardonnay in Sonoma, our job is to help the grapes along their way. It's a very humbling profession, because we always rely on Mother Nature to get things started.

I've made more than five hundred wines now, and even though the weather in California tends to be more temperate than in other wine regions of the world, each vintage is different. **Crush** is by far the most exciting time of the year. That's when everything happens. It's a month and a half of hands-on work, seven days a week, sometimes around the clock. What intrigues me about winemaking is that you never master it. Even when you feel like you're getting ahead, there's always something new, something to learn, like tasting when the grapes are ready to be brought in, or knowing when to take the wine out of the barrel before the tannins upstage the fruit.

CRUSH—Term for either harvest time or the actual crushing of the grapes.

Needless to say, I now look at wine in a completely different way than I did when it was just something Grandpa or Dad brought home and put on the table. And in a completely different way than I did in college when I was surrounded by people who thought of wine as a special-occasion thing that has to be planned out and prepared in detail.

But, thankfully, I've never let go of the feeling that wine, like people, is first and foremost about pleasure. And wine has never stopped surprising me. Once someone asked me what was the greatest wine I'd ever had. And two came to mind. One was a famous red Burgundy, La Tâche (hey, gotta splurge sometime), which I shared on Valentine's Day with my husband, my brother Matt, and his wife at a restaurant in Carmel. The other was a nameless red table wine I had at a trattoria just outside Florence with a great pizza, watching people walk about on the streets. A couple of bucks for a pitcher versus an extremely expensive bottle. Both were equally awesome. And both are reminders of how wine and food can really bring out the best in each other, and in people.

HEY, WHO'S THAT YOUNG WHIPPERSNAPPER WITH THE BARREL THIEF?

Stew-baby. Wine Brats' Poster Child. The Man with the Mousse (it's a hair thing). We've got a thousand monikers for one of our favorite people on the planet, all of them meant to be as endearing as our Director of Education, Stewart Dorman. Executive Director Joel Quigley first hooked up with Stewart at a coffee bar sometime back in early '95. Stewart had requested the meeting to discuss the development of our Wine Brats' educational programs. Basically, he wanted the opportunity to work with a group that would support some of his fresh ideas for not only making wine education approachable, but outright fun. After a lengthy discussion on philosophies and several fifty-cent refills, they shook sweaty hands.

Since that first meeting, Stewart's delivered on his promise, and together we've traveled the country, creating such educational wingdingers as Fast Wines for Fast Lives *(WineRave Chicago),* Yo Mama's Grape Juice Never Tasted Like This *(U.C. Berkeley Haas School of Business),* Variety Is the Spice of Life, So Why Not Drink It! *(Cronkite-Ward's* Wine 101 *series),* A Potluck of Chefs with a Mish-Mash of Wines *(C/Net Central),* 2 Bachelors in the Kitchen *(Taste of Cincinnati), and* Wines for the Holidaze: Pairing Wine with Gifts *(CNN).*

And now, as a next step in the educational process, and in tandem with Stewart's preparation for the first release from Adrian Fog Win-

ery (he's co-owner and winemaker), we asked him to give us a blow-by-blow report on bringing a bottle of wine from the vineyard to America's table. So if you're interested in the art, science, nightmares, and joys of winemaking, feel free to take a peek inside Stewart's journal entries and notes. Following his diary, our old buddy Joe Naujokas will give you some great ideas on how to put together your own home winemaking club, based on one of the most successful groups ever to attempt such a feat, the Woof Woof Wine Company. He'll also point you in the direction of some great references for home winemaking, since such a subject is a book in and of itself.

—j, j & m

In the Vineyard of Good and Evil, or Days in the Life of a Winemaker

by Stewart Dorman

Diary Entries from Adrian Fog's First Year

January 3, 1998

In my lifetime I've done everything from selling insurance to piloting hot-air balloons. But I've never stopped thinking that there's a better life out there for me. I've been working in the wine business for the past eleven years and love it. I started out as a stock clerk in a winery and worked my way up.

Last night I had this crazy idea to start a winery of my own. I'm getting married this spring, and this could be a new life for both of us. My future wife, Janey, loves the thought of living in wine country, with all its rolling hills covered with vineyards and sunshine. Owning a winery is more than a business—it's a way of life. We'd want to make a wine of quality and to stay small so we could really know our customers as family, not just people who buy something we sell. Life's full of people who are just going through the motions. I want more out of my life. I want to live.

Wine is the very essence of passion. That and a well-placed French kiss. And my passion is Pinot Noir. Now all I need to do is find the right Pinot vineyard, one with a cool climate, well-drained soils, and lots of character. I'll also need a place to make my wine. That shouldn't be too hard. All my life I've been looking for something, something that challenges me, something that makes life what it should be—exhilarating! Sex is good, but I usually lose my place and forget what to do next. This I can do, this is very cool.

Janey loves the idea. She can get away from all that stress at the office and really get into what life is all about.

January 6, 1998

I'm having a hard time finding the right vineyard. They all seem so similar to each other. I want a vineyard with attitude and personality. Like me, but with less hair.

I don't know a lot of people in the wine business and not being born here doesn't help. I spent much of this afternoon calling every name in the phone book. I can't believe how hard this is. It's either "We don't have any Pinot for sale" or "Don't call us, we'll call you." My dream is driving a truck through the vineyards with mud caked into the wheel wells and dust on the dash so heavy you could write a novel in it with your finger. And I'd have to have some type of personalized license plates for this truck, like WINEU or DRINKME or 12WINE. The Wine Brats are throwing a bash at U.C. Berkeley tonight; maybe that'll help relax me and get my mind off of things for a while.

January 12, 1998

I met a guy at the Wine Brats event last night, George Hambrecht. His family owns a few vineyards in Sonoma County's Russian River Valley and Anderson Valley, the latter being in Mendocino County. He asked me if I would be interested in checking them out! This is very cool. I spend all day on the phone looking for fruit and then meet a guy last night with a vineyard full of Pinot Noir!

George seems like a pretty cool guy. He has this dog that's the size of a grizzly bear, but you can tell he really loves that dog. That's a good sign. A man that cares for something that much can't be bad. Janey and I are planning to go up the coast this weekend. We can meet George and check out the vineyard on the way back. During the winter, Mendocino is cold, rainy, and rough. I love sitting by the fire every night with some awesome Pinot Noir while listening to the ocean.

In the winter, wine country is so quiet. The vines look like skele-
tons. The rain is endless. Clouds seem to get caught in the coastal
redwoods as if they were cotton, while the sun hides behind the
mist for weeks at a time. You can almost hear the vines sleeping.
My therapist says as long as I don't hear the vines talking to me I'm
okay. I look forward to seeing George again and checking out the
vineyards on Sunday. Looks like El Niño is going to dump a lot of
rain on us this year. That means a lot of erosion in the vineyards,
but the cover crops should help keep the land in place.

P.S. Cover crops are the plants and grasses planted between the
rows of a vineyard to hold in the top soil and create a home for
beneficial insects that eat bad bugs (pests).

January 20, 1998

The coast was incredible. The B&B we stayed at let us trade wine
for the room. I guess they drink a lot of red wine in the winter to
stay warm. I bought a pair of binoculars on the trip. Janey can't figure out why, though. I guess it's a guy thing.

We looked at the vineyard on the way back from the coast. It's
located by a little general store much like the one on The Waltons.
The store's called David at the Flood Gate. I don't know what that
means, but we found out that the vineyard is called Flood Gate, so
go figure. The vineyard sits atop a small mountain where the fog
rolls in below the vineyards, forming what looks like an island of
vines surrounded by fluffy snow.

The truck we just bought got pretty muddy, and we got stuck going up the vineyard road. It was great! I couldn't believe how beautiful it was up there. All the worries I had about starting up a
winery just slipped away. It started to rain while we were walking
through the vine rows and it didn't bother me or Janey a bit. For the
first time in my life I felt like I found home.

Our next job is to figure out which vineyard sections we'd like to
get fruit from. Pinot Noir is the only wine I want to make, and this
location just screams of world-class-quality fruit. The climate is
cool to allow the fruit to ripen slowly, achieving maximum richness

for a big cherry characteristic in the finished wine. The vineyards are terraced, so they're well drained, putting stress on the vines, concentrating flavors into the fruit. The terracing also allows each vine to get equal sunlight. This vineyard has personality, all right. Now, if I could just come up with a name for this world-class Pinot Noir.

March 5, 1998

The weather has been warm for the last few days, and the buds on the vines are starting to push out new shoots. The vineyard is waking up. The '98 vintage has started. I worry about the frost this year. We've had so much rain that we're sure to have mildew problems.

At home here in Sonoma County, every morning we wake to the sounds of tractors mowing the grasses in the vineyards, or the blowing of sulfur on the vines to prevent mildew. Living in the middle of a vineyard outside Healdsburg has its prices. Getting up at five-thirty A.M. is one of them.

We go up to our Pinot vineyard every other weekend. The four-hour round-trip drive is long, but the scenery is a nice distraction. We came up with the name for our winery the other evening. Adrian Fog. After a few glasses of wine we started to get creative. First it was Dorman Cellars. But who'd buy a wine with a name like that? We did a little research and found that Adrian is Greek for dark and rich, just like the style of wine we're making, and Fog is what surrounds the vineyards. Thus, Adrian Fog Winery. Very cool.

P.S. The Fog, my favorite movie, had Adrienne Barbeau playing one of the lead characters. That's the real story of how we came up with the name for our winery; the other version is for PR.

April 12, 1998 (Janey's Birthday)

Barrels, barrels, barrels. I never realized how many producers, styles, types, and regions there are to buy barrels from till now. Every little change in the barrel ultimately changes the way the wine will taste. American oak has a heavier vanilla flavor. French is more on the toasty side. And Hungarian oak, I'm not so sure about. Then you have the choice of two- or three-year seasoned staves. The longer you air-dry the staves, the less aggressive the oak becomes in the wine.

Each producer has their own style of barrel, which means the wine will taste different from barrel to barrel. And the cost for just one barrel is somewhere between $255 and $755. Ouch! This wine-making thing is expensive. I love the idea of the barrels being handmade. The craft of coopering a barrel takes years to perfect, and when the barrel is finished it's watertight—no glues, caulks, or pastes used. I can't get over how old the art of making wine is. It goes back over six thousand years and is still pretty much the same game. I sometimes wonder if it'll still be the same "game" in another six thousand years. History is the best part of getting older.

April 15, 1998

I decided to use French oak for the wine. So I called a few producers to place an order. Guess what? They're all out. None in stock. Can't help you. Try us again next year. Not too promising.

We still need a place to make the wine. Just a small concern of ours. And because of El Niño, this year's crop is looking kinda iffy. Too much rain! Selling all of our stocks and cashing in our savings doesn't sound so appealing all of a sudden. Too late now, it's all or nothing. I can always go back to selling insurance. I hate selling insurance.

April 30, 1998

Finally found a few French oak barrels. It took some talking—and a few bottles of wine—but we got what we needed. The weather's still rainy. We're going over to Angwin (in Napa County) to pick up the barrels tomorrow. I hope I can borrow a truck. We can only get two barrels at a time into our Explorer.

We met with a label designer today. Ten thousand ($10,000) to have a label designed. Maybe we can sell Amway to pay for it.

FERMENTING IN OAK

The use of oak in winemaking dates back over two thousand years. Originally, oak was used as a flavor addition, along with herbs, to improve the taste of crudely made wines of the time.

The barrel's purpose, aside from being a vessel, is to age wine and add a subtle oak flavor. Most barrels used in California are French, although American oak is gaining popularity. There are many aspects of the manufacturing process that influence wine flavor, all of which the winemaker must consider when ordering the precise barrel needed.

A winemaker has many considerations when choosing barrels. Each wine style requires a different oak influence. Barrels fashioned from the same tree, fired to the same toast level, made by two different coopers may have totally different flavors. So winemakers have the opportunity to choose the cooper, wood type, forest, size of barrel, and toast level that best suits their wine. Some barrel makers have a "house toast," which is their own particular style. (You get it their way.)

Forests: *A winemaker can choose from a number of oak forests. Many of the popular forests or wood types, from loose (open) grain to tight (closed) grain, are Limousin, Nevers, Bourgogne, Trancais, Allier, "Center of France," and Vosges. Wines aged in looser-grain barrels age and acquire oak flavors faster. Oak types also offer subtle differences in flavor. Some impart more vanillin characteristics, while others offer stronger spice flavors.*

Firing: *Aside from wood choice, firing is the most important process to the winemaker. Once can choose from light, medium, or heavy toast levels, each of which has a significant flavor profile ranging from slightly toasty to caramelly to smoky. A heavily toasted barrel can even be brought to the slightly burnt point.*

American versus French Oak: *French oak, in general, tends to be tighter in grain structure; thus, the oak flavor it imparts tends to be subtle and less "woody." American oak tends to be looser in grain; thus, the woody elements tend to be more prevalent. Also, because* of the environment (soil, weather, etc.), American oak tends to give more vanilla flavor to the wine.

Oak versus Stainless Steel: *The reason some winemakers age their wines in oak, even if the barrel is neutral or gives no "oak" flavor to the wine, is for the purpose of "breathing." Because the wood staves of the barrel are porous, there's a transfer of oxygen. The oxygen bonds with the wine and (without getting too technical) results in a smoother, more integrated product. Stainless steel does not allow the wine to breathe; thus, no transfer of oxygen occurs. But remember: It all depends on the wine and the winemaker's styles to whether oak is used or not. No one method is better.*

Size: *The standard barrel size used is 225 liters, or 59 gallons. If every drop of wine from a barrel is bottled, it would amount to twenty-five cases (three hundred bottles) of wine*

—Kim Caffrey

I hope the rain stops soon. Yesterday we drove up to the vineyard to mark off the vineyard sections we want for our Pinot. We picked out one section that faces north to south running down a slope. The other two sections face east to west and are terraced on a hillside. All three sections are different clones of Pinot Noir and are about the same age. This means three different styles of Pinot, which I'm really excited about! I think the section facing north to south will be the most interesting. Janey thinks it's one of the east to west sections. We named that first section after her dad, John J. The other sections are named 1A and Bullwinkle. "Bullwinkle" came up when I asked Janey what she thinks of when I say rocky (as in rocky soil). She said Bullwinkle, so Bullwinkle it is.

P.S. A clone is a slight variation of a type of grape (see glossary).

May 9, 1998

We still don't have a place to make wine yet. There was an article in this morning's local newspaper on how all the new vineyards that've been planted over the last five years are mature enough to *start producing fruit. That means that finding a place to make wine this year just got harder. Production's over capacity.*

It would take about half a million dollars to build a small winery. And then you'd have to get all the permits to go along with it. That's out of the question for us. No wonder the wine business is full of people who made their fortunes somewhere else and got into the wine business as a hobby. We just want a small winery that makes world-class wine. We've even thought of making our wine in the basement of our house. But we'd still need the permits and equipment. Even if we bought used equipment, we'd still have to come up with about $100,000 or so.

I remember growing up in southern Indiana, where all of my friends lived on farms. I especially remember how hard it was for their families. The farm was everything to them, and if the weather was bad that year, the crop was bad too. I could never understand why someone would put themselves through that every year. The hardships and the struggles just to keep the farm going. What's the point to have to work so hard just to be at the mercy of Mother Nature. I never knew until these past few months. I get so excited every time we go to the vineyard. It's like going into a garden that provides everything you could ever want. The work is hard, the sun is hot, and I never felt better about myself. I've never slept so well as after a day of work in the vineyard. I guess I'm a farmer after all.

June 20, 1998

I ran into George today and he said that his family was building a small winery to produce only red wine. High-quality stuff and very small production. He said it'd take a few years to get the case production they wanted. That got me to thinking: So if they were only producing a small amount of wine the first year, then maybe there'd be a little extra room for Adrian Fog! I tried not to get too excited as I asked him if they had a little room for us. He said he wasn't sure but would check into it. I told Janey. We're both excited and nervous about this new possibility. If it doesn't work out, then we're out of options.

July 5, 1998

The Fourth of July was great. We had a house full of friends, a fridge full of food, and a closet full of wine. There's no better way to enjoy Independence Day than with friends, food, and wine. God bless America. The fireworks display was quite nice. Unfortunately, we sat in the fallout zone. Our wineglasses were full of ashes and small pieces of paper, but you could still drink the wine. The paper and ash gave the wine character.

George called today. I tried to call back but missed him.

July 7, 1998

Happy, happy, joy, joy! We have a place to make wine. Yee-ha! I finally got ahold of George, and he said no problem. Life is good!

July 12, 1998

Janey saw the first signs of verasion today—the change of color in the grapes. The ripening has started. Pinot is very fussy. If the weather gets too hot for too long or too soon, you can get a very herbal or green flavor in your wine. The fruit is looking very nice, though. As each day passes, it gets a little riper. Usually the weather in California is dependable—not too hot and no rain this time of year. That's one big advantage to making wine here—the sunny weather. I'm convinced Anderson Valley is the place to grow great Pinot Noir. It stays cool in the summer and gets a lot of sun, which is perfect for tasty Pinot. From now on Janey and I'll have to go up to the vineyard two to three times a week to check on the fruit.

August 3, 1998

We measured the weight of a few clusters to get an idea of how much fruit we can roughly expect this year. A vine has one instinct—to grow. I've seen some vines grow as much as thirty-six feet in one year. A vine that grows that much usually doesn't make very good wine. I want a vine that grows slowly, having a little stress on its roots to help concentrate flavor and quality. The slower the vine grows and ripens, the higher the concentration of color and flavor in the finished wine. Right now our guess is about two and a half to three tons per acre. That's just about right for the quality of wine we're looking to make for Adrian Fog; any more tonnage would dilute the flavors of our wine.

September 8, 1998

Today we did our first field sample of our Pinot Noir. It takes a while to pick three hundred separate berries, put them in a Ziploc bag, squeeze all the juice out of them, and then measure the sugar content of the juice with a refractometer. We did this for each of the three sections. 1A was 19 Brix, John J. was 20.2 Brix, and Bullwinkle was 19.4 Brix. At this point in the growing season they say you can get anywhere from 1 to 1.5 Brix a week. At this rate we'll be picking in October, just in time for the start of the winter rains. If we get heavy rains, it'll not only dilute the flavors in the wine, but we could lose the ripeness in the grapes. It takes about twenty-four to thirty-six hours after a rain for the vines to start soaking up the water. The water has only one place to go and that's straight into the berries. Disaster. I told Janey that we'd pick our grapes at around 23.5 Brix. We're going to wait until we get 23.5 Brix.

P.S. Brix are a measurement of sugar in the grape juice; roughly, it is a percentage of sugar. A refractometer is a simple handheld tool designed to measure the Brix level in the grape juice. See **REF.6: Wine Mumbo Jumbo.**

October 2, 1998

The weatherman is predicting rain this weekend, and lots of it. The best section of our Pinot is at 22.5 Brix. I'm a little nervous. I heard there's a few wineries picking already. It's a gamble. If it doesn't rain and we get some sun, we'll get what we're shooting for.

On the other hand, if it rains, we just might make some of the worst wine on record.

We decided to do a little proactive vineyard management by cutting off some of the grape clusters that're still a little green. This'll speed up the ripening process a bit and focus more flavor into the remaining clusters. While Janey and I were in the vineyard, some heavy clouds moved in, and you've never seen two people move so fast. We worked as fast as we could, but we couldn't beat the rain. As it fell my heart sank into my back pocket. I thought it best that we just stop, load up the truck, and come back tomorrow. But Janey just kept saying, "We'll work until we're done." We did just that. Soaked to the bone, dead on our feet, we finished thinning out our vineyard. I'm so proud of what we can achieve. Sometimes life is tough, but that just makes you stronger or stranger as the case may be. We treated ourselves to a great dinner in Boonville and had a well-earned night's sleep.

Today, our vineyard became the vineyard of good and evil.

October 5, 1998

The big rain they predicted for today only amounted to a heavy mist. We checked the Brix and found we hadn't lost any of our ripeness. The weather is supposed to be sunny and clear for the rest of the week. We're set to pick on Saturday, and have the 23.5 Brix we were waiting for. I feel like I just made the biggest gamble of my life and won!

I need to pick up some picking bins for our grapes. There's this special food-grade plastic bin that actually looks like a giant Tupperware container. Great for Pinot. It keeps the fruit cool after it's picked, locking in the fresh fruit flavors. They cost a lot more, but there are no shortcuts in making great wine. I feel like an expectant father—nervous and excited both at the same time.

Saturday, when we harvest our Pinot Noir, will be the proudest day of our lives. Once we pick, we'll have to load the bins into a climate-controlled truck and deliver it to the winery so they don't overheat. And that's where the fun begins. Destemming the fruit is the first step. From there it goes straight into a small half-ton to one-ton bin for a nice long soak to bring out all of the flavor that we've worked so hard for all year. (You see, nearly all the flavor in the grape sits in the skin.) The rest is easy. Tomorrow will be one hell of a fun day.

October 6, 1998

One hell of a long day. The weather was great and picking was a breeze. I can say that because we're smart enough to know that picking is one of the hardest jobs in winemaking. Thus, we knew we needed help. We hired a picking crew that rocked through the vineyard like Matchbox 20. In less than two hours, we had three acres picked while the fog was still hugging the hillside, keeping the fruit nice and cool.

The ride down to the winery was nice, but that's where the party ended.

It was supposed to be a simple task—gently dump each half-ton bin of fruit into the destemmer. That's all there was to it. I told Janey and our friend Craig that it'd only take fifteen minutes, tops. And after that I'd treat them to a nice breakfast.

We woke up at four-thirty A.M. The plan was to be done by eleven A.M. We finished at nine-thirty P.M. Nine-thirty P.M.! Seventeen hours later. My God, what a day. The problem was none of the new equipment had been tested, and we didn't realize that everything needed to be scrubbed and cleaned before we could start. We were bringing in the first load of grapes to a brand-new winery.

Once we cleaned the destemmer, bins, cellar floor, crushpad floor, and all the equipment within sight, we started the destemming process. The destemmer didn't work. And, of course, we found that out after we filled it with our grapes. Two hours later we fixed the problem. Now we should be out of here in fifteen minutes, tops. Next problem: The one-ton bins that we bought wouldn't fit under the destemmer, so we had to hand-bucket 3.9 tons of fruit, five gallons at a time, into the bins. Craig, a good friend of ours who was up for the weekend from L.A., did all the bucket work, all 3.9 tons of it. If not for Craig's help, we would've been in bad shape. Craig, thank you from the bottom of our hearts. Thank you.

I was the only one that knew how to drive the forklift or, should I say, the only one that was willing to drive the forklift. Janey was like a mongoose—she was everywhere and doing everything. She's the best thing that ever happened to me. By sundown we had destemmed all the fruit into the bins. I forgot that we still had to return the rental truck, adding another two and a half hours to the day from hell. On my gravestone I think I'll have written, "We'll be done in fifteen minutes, tops." At the end of the day we had some great fruit in a very clean winery, not a bad day's work. Adrian Fog was born today. And thank God, after seventeen hours of hard labor, she (Adrian, of course, is a girl) was born healthy.

October 9, 1998

The past three days have been pretty easy. We go up to the winery four times a day and punch down the fruit by hand. Punching down gently breaks the skins of the grapes and allows the juice to escape. By making wine this way, we're able to highlight the natural fruit quality of the juice (retain its true personality) without bruising the fruit. The seeds of a grape are very bitter and can produce a harsh bite in the wine if the fruit is not handled with utmost care. In the next day or so we'll induce natural fermentation by letting the sun warm the bins. Yeasts multiply quite quickly as they're warmed by the sun. Natural fermentation produces complexity in Pinot Noir but can be risky because of the unknown populations of yeast.

P.S. There are two ways of starting fermentation: with a cultured yeast purchased from a lab, or by letting wild yeast ferment the wine naturally.

October 10, 1998

Moving the bins into the sun worked, and fermentation has started in two of our four bins. We expect the other two to start in the next day or so. Now that we have fermentation, around-the-clock punch-downs begin. Every three hours we'll punch down our four bins. It shouldn't be too bad. Piece of cake.

October 15, 1998

Sleep deprivation is killing us. It's like having a baby—every three hours we have to do a feeding, I mean a punch-down. Getting up four times in the middle of the night is making us whacked. I think I saw a unicorn in the vineyard today. I'll just keep that one to myself. As soon as fermentation is over, we'll cut back to two punch-downs a day. Thank God that looks to be in the next day or so.

October 20, 1998

The wine finished fermentation two days ago, and we did a brief extended maceration, meaning letting the wine stay in contact with the skins. If we let the wine stay in contact with the skins for a little while after fermentation, it can gain a bit more complexity in flavor.

The wine smells great, and that alone is the biggest part of making wine. If it smells bad, there's a problem. And if it stinks, there's a big problem. We went through fermentation without any off odors— that's a good sign.

Today we pressed off the wine in a very expensive Italian bladder press. A bladder press is a cool tool that uses air pressure inside a rubber bladder to gently press the wine away from the skins. And after all the juice has been pressed out, the grape skins come out bone-dry. No juice is wasted. And if you have a slow press cycle, the wine doesn't get a bitter flavor from the seeds.

From the press the wine is collected in a stainless-steel tray and pumped by air pressure into our new French oak barrels. We moved the now-filled wine barrels into a nice, clean, cool cellar where they'll rest for the next twelve months. The aging process is the slowest part in winemaking and the most rewarding.

Every few days we'll go to the winery and check how each barrel is tasting. We'll also make sure each barrel is filled to the top with wine. Topping off the barrels ensures that no spoilage (from **oxida-tion**) will ruin the wine. Air (oxygen) is the biggest enemy of wine. We're now the caretakers for our baby, Adrian Fog.

P.S. Oxidized is when the wine has been exposed to oxygen and has taken on a smell similar to sherry. It usually kills any fruit smells.

November 17, 1998

We checked our wine today and she's tasting like a warm kiss from a cool stranger—sweet and mysterious.

In a few more weeks we'll start going back up to the vineyard because the new vintage will begin. I can't believe a whole year has gone by already. Life in the vineyards is like a summer vacation that never ends. I get to play in one of the most beautiful places in the world, and what I make I get to share with my friends and family. There's no better satisfaction than to drink good wine with the people you love. In a world of confusion I found my home in the vineyard of good and evil.

STAINLESS-STEEL FERMENTATION

To some it doesn't look as romantic as it did in "the old days." Huge wooden tanks and glass-lined cement tanks used in the past for fermenting wines have been replaced by stainless-steel tanks. Why? They are nonporous, to eliminate the transfer of bacteria which can cause spoilage within a winery's wine supply. You can drain Cabernet Sauvignon out of a stainless-steel tank, rinse it, and minutes later have Chardonnay in there, with no color or flavor transference!

The tanks have a double layer of stainless steel (with a kind of coolant between), which can regulate temperatures. They can keep the longer, cooler fermentations of the whites, rosés, and light reds going (about 55°F) while allowing the heavier reds to ferment

quicker at warmer temps (about 80°F) without getting too hot.
Voondabah!

With a few exceptions (Chardonnays especially), most wines are
fermented in stainless steel. Reds ferment with their skins, and it's
much easier to maintain the maceration (broken skins' contact with
the juice) in a stainless-steel tank. As a result of the yeast convert-
ing the sugar in the grape juice to alcohol (hey, that's fermentation!), the heat and CO_2 released cause the skins to float to the top,
forming a "cap." Fresh wine must be either "pumped over" the cap to
break it up and distribute the skins in the juice, or the cap may be
"punched down" manually to get the skins back down amongst the
juice.

Wine in stainless tanks can be pumped through a network of
hoses/pipes to another area. They're clean, they're strong, they're
stainless steel!
                                                              —Kim Caffrey

ROSÉS/PINK/BLUSH

To Pink or not to Pink? That is the question ... whether 'tis no-
bler to produce a dry French (Rhône or Loire) style rosé or a fruity
"blush" style rosé (very pale color) with some residual sugar?

Rosés are essentially white wines made from red grapes, meaning the skins are pressed away from the juice prior to fermentation
(as with whites) and don't ferment with the juice throughout fermentation (as with reds). In the production of some rosés, the
grapes are pressed immediately (skins and juice separated) and red
wine is added after fermentation, prior to bottling, to achieve desired color. In others, the skins are allowed to sit with the juice prior
to fermentation to extract flavor and pigment. Then there's the
"saignee" method, letting the skins sit with the juice, perhaps
through the beginning of fermentation, then "bleeding" the colorful
free-run juice/wine from its skins, then finishing fermentation. To

try to retain as many fruit aromas as possible, the wines are generally cold-fermented in stainless-steel tanks to optimize freshness. Any contact they see with wood is negligible. It's essential that rosés maintain their fruitiness.

Hint: Rosés are light and refreshing and fit the bill when even light reds might be too heavy. Color is not always an indication of sweetness. Try going by the alcohol. The lower it is, the sweeter the wine. Blushes go great with hot and spicy, teriyaki, barbecue, and sweet and sour! Yeooooowwwwwwwwwww!   —Kim Caffrey

HOW TO MAKE FRIENDS IN FOUR HUNDRED
EASY STEPS

Joe, meet our, readers. Readers, meet, Joe. Oh, you've already met? At a bar? Ah, that's right, Joe gave us some great recipes back in PARTY.5 for wine cocktails. Not to mention a bit o' insight into what makes him tick upstairs—as in the noggin. If you're not too troubled by Joe's liberal use of fantasy and fiction within a nonfiction book to move forward, and if your interest in wine goes beyond merely imbibing the juice, we suggest you pull out your notepad. Joe's following recipe, based on the Woof Woof Wine Company, for organizing a home winemaking club—which goes way beyond brewing a batch in the closet of your apartment—may be the perfect elixir for the socially impaired. Now go! Get out! Share the fruits of your labor!

—j, j & m

Home Winemaking Comes Out of the Closet, or How to Organize a Winemaking Club

by Joe Naujokas

"Micro" is not exactly the first word that comes to mind when thinking about winemaking in Modesto, California, corporate home to E&J Gallo, the world's largest wine producer. However, a small group of young, creative, and energetic Modestans have established one of California's most active and innovative home winemaking cooperatives that never bottles more than two hundred cases a year. They named their co-op "Woof Woof Winery" after the dog of a wine that, over a decade ago, was their first attempt at winemaking. Since that inaugural vintage, the quality of their wines and their methods have improved dramatically, reflecting the wisdom gained over years of squeezing and fermenting grapes.

It's Not About a Cheap Buzz

They don't do it just for the pride of making their own wine, either. See, Modesto is not exactly the most cosmopolitan city in the world, and many locals (including several Gallo employees) feel socially and creatively stunted. The cooperative gives them a chance to party, meet people, exercise their creativity, and make their own juice.

Here's How It Works

Every year, about one hundred members "buy into" the co-op by paying $150 to the group's treasurer. Only about $100 of the money is used to buy grapes and equipment. The rest pays for several work "parties" throughout the whole year. "One of the most important lessons we've learned about making our own wine," said Pat Dodd, one of the group's founders and ironically Gallo's Director of Fine Wines, "is that there's nothing mysterious about it. You can make wine, you can drink wine, and you can have fun doing both."

How Many Parties Does It Take to Make Your Own Wine?

Four, according to this bunch. Their year begins, of course, with the harvest, which always and everywhere is a good excuse for a party. Some brave Woof Woof souls even help pick the grapes, while others wait at the "crush-pad" (actually a garage) to do the stompin' and squeezin'. All that work calls for a mighty celebration at the end of the day. After all, it takes good wine to make good wine.

Every So Often

A few months later, in the doldrums of winter, after the raw wine has mellowed out for a few months in barrels, Woof Woof holds its annual barrel tasting. This is really the first glimpse of what the vintage has to offer—you can't judge a book by its cover, and you can't judge a wine by its juice at harvest. To cheer their January spirits, the group puts on black ties and evening gowns and goes formal. "It's one of the only black-tie events in Modesto—and it's a great excuse to get dressed up," admits one member. But throughout the year, of course, someone must take a nip from the barrels "to ensure quality control."

Oh, But the Labels

As time marches on and the wine develops, the group gathers to brainstorm label concepts to match the character of the emerging wines. They pass these raw ideas to their two label designers (on loan from guess which winery . . .), who take the ideas back to their studios for creative fleshing out. Judging from their past labels, the brainstorm party must be one of the most bizarre of them all.

For the last party, the designers return with label prototypes. During this gathering the members take a final vote for their favorite designs. Not long after that party, one case of the newly bottled and freshly labeled wines is delivered to each member as their yearly "ration." A hundred and fifty bucks isn't bad for a case of pretty dang good wine, four parties, and a way to meet like-minded new friends.

"We Like Conan Wines!"

Fine winemaking can be a delicate task, requiring complex equipment and round-the-clock attention. Woof Woof Winery can afford neither (their crushpad is a garage, the barrel room basically a converted garden shed), so they make Barbarian wines that are durable yet also benevolent and gentle enough (like the superhero, Conan) to be drinkable while still young. "Our group is looking for immediate gratification," Dodd said, admitting, "We don't want to age."

Their favorite varietals are all red: Zinfandel, Petite Sirah, and the red Bordeaux varietals (Cabernet, Merlot, Cabernet Franc, etc.), but they're also currently experimenting with a rather hearty Pinot Noir from the Russian River Valley in Sonoma County.

Planet Grape

Every year, every harvest, every varietal, and every vineyard teaches them something new, introduces them to someone different. And after all those years, the members have developed bonds with each other that stretch beyond mere bottles of wine, beyond a few parties. It's not just a good buzz, it's not just a few casual friends, it's not just individual gratification. Celebrating humanity is what it's all about. This is why we're all here . . . this is the ancient magic that is wine and winemaking at its best, in Modesto or anywhere on Earth.

Are you ready to get started? Here are our book and magazine picks for making the juice:

Winemaking: Recipes, Equipment, and Techniques for Making Wine at Home
by Stanley F. and Dorothy Anderson
Harcourt Brace Jovanovich, 1989

Even a beginner could make a case of wine with this guide. Instructions are broken down with easy-to-follow tables and quick reference charts. Recipes include: various fruit wines; fruit-juice-concentrates wines; champagnes and liqueurs. Sections are devoted to issues of safety and sanitation and in-depth equipment discussions for more advanced winemakers. There are no guarantees that your attempts will be drinkable. But with this book, you'll have fun trying.
$21.00

WineMaker Magazine
For creating your own great wines. Published annually, *WineMaker* offers articles on bottling, finding the best fruit, and choosing the best kit. The advertisements can be great leads for getting the goods you need.
$4.95
Phone: (530) 758-4596
E-mail: byo@byo.com

Part IV

The Eternal
Search for
Knowledge

LIVING THE DREAM

We figured, since we've already introduced you to the likes of Darryl Roberts and Rosina Tinari Wilson, we'd take up this white space thanking Sophia Schweitzer for collaborating on our wine regions section. Sophia is yet another prolific young writer who hails from a place many consider a romantic paradise, North Kohala, Hawaii. In her home at the end of a jungle road, she writes, focusing on food, wine, and travel, in addition to novels. Novel writer: yet another romantic fantasy for many. Her forthcoming books are 51 Words of the Soul *and* Liquid Obsession.

—j, j & m

Around the World in Eighty Bottles, or Wine Regions of the New and Old Worlds

by Darryl Roberts, Sophia Schweitzer, and Rosina Tinari Wilson

New World Wines

North America

United States

There's an old expression, "You can take the people out of wine country, but you can't take the wine country out of people." Okay, it's not an old saying, we just made that up. But it's true. When Europeans settled the United States in the late sixteenth century, they brought with them the rich tradition of enjoying wine. Once the settlers discovered the abundance of native American vines, it was the aim of Virginia and Carolina colonies to establish winemaking in their communities. Thomas Jefferson and William Penn tried their hands at growing grapes and making wine. And, even though their quest was never quite realized on the Eastern Seaboard, that's how the wine industry took hold in the United States.

CALIFORNIA: The leader, by far, in both production and status, is California, which produces 90 percent of all American wine. Its near-perfect conditions for grape growing—lots of warm sun during the day followed by cool nights—has helped California prove itself to be a world-class region. With instantly recognizable appellations, such as Napa Valley, Sonoma County, Mendocino, Monterey, and Santa Barbara County, and the ability to grow everything from Sauvignon Blanc to Viognier to Pinot Noir to Sangiovese, California has almost become synonymous with American wine.

Franciscan missionaries planted the first **vinifera** vines in California in

1779. The first wines were made from the Mission grape, which dominated production for the next century. When the U.S. annexed California in 1847, winegrowing spread rapidly through the state, with vineyards being established as far north as Amador County. But it wasn't until the 1970s that the big boom hit in California. In a span of about thirty years, Chardonnay and Cabernet Sauvignon grape acreage rose from 700 to more than 90,000 acres, which was as about as much as the French national total. Combining all other grape varieties, California, in 1991, was producing wine from about 290,000 acres of vines.

> VINIFERA—The European species of vitis; the vine most used for making wine, i.e., Chardonnay, Cabernet Sauvignon.

Despite what some people believe (or want to believe), winemaking doesn't stop at the California border. Currently, forty-four of the fifty United States grow grapes and almost every state has a winery. Let's take a look around the country at some of the other areas that grow and produce wine.

NEW ENGLAND: (Maine, New Hampshire, Vermont, Massachusetts, Connecticut, Rhode Island) At a latitude that makes it just slightly more southerly than France, the New England area has two officially recognized appellations: Western Connecticut Highlands and Southeastern New England. There only a handful of commercial wineries here. Those close to the coast are buffered by the Atlantic Ocean, while wineries inland suffer from the severe winter weather. Chardonnay is grown and made here, as well as some **hybrid** wines, such as Seyval and Vidal Blanc. There is also an abundance of fruit wines made in this area, ranging from raspberry to cherry to pear.

> HYBRID—A cross between two different species. They can occur naturally, through cross-pollination, but are mostly produced by man to incorporate certain qualities from each parent for specific reasons, i.e., Seyval Blanc, which ripens early and withstands cold climates.

LONG ISLAND: The majority of wineries on Long Island are located on the North Fork, a 159-square-mile band of well-drained soil that experiences the longest, coolest growing season of any viticultural region in the northeast. Because the surrounding water cools slowly in the winter, it reflects heat back onto the land, so harsh winter freezes are mostly unknown here. The first commercial vineyard was planted in 1972, and since then there has been a boom in plantings, mostly of vinifera vines such as Chardonnay, Gewürztraminer, Pinot Noir, and Cabernet Sauvignon. Some critics argue that Long Island wines are as good as any made in the world.

LAKE ERIE: (Pennsylvania, Ohio, and western New York) Lake Erie is the largest grape-producing region in the nation outside California and is an official appellation, the first tristate **AVA** in the United States (1983). However, less than 10 percent of the grapes grown here are used for wine. The vast majority are native American varieties, such as Concord and American **Labrusca,** which are supplied to the grape juice industry.

> **AVA or AMERICAN VITICULTURAL AREA**—Like appellation, a geographic area for growing grapes, this title requiring approval by the BATF. Many AVAs have sub-AVAs (or appellations), such as Napa with its Howell Mountain, Carneros, Stags Leap District, etc., and Sonoma with its Russian River, Knights Valley, Alexander Valley, etc.

> **LABRUSCA**—A species of the vitis genus that's native to North America.

At the turn of the century, Ohio was the largest wine-producing region in the country. But Prohibition all but destroyed Lake Erie's wine industry. Recently, however, there's been a resurgence in the area. Wines produced here range from Riesling to Gewürztraminer to Cabernet Franc to Pinot Noir. There is also fruit wine made in the area.

LAKE MICHIGAN: (Michigan, Illinois, Indiana, Wisconsin) The majority of wineries in this area are located on the eastern shore of Lake Michigan. All four states grow grapes, supplying this small winemaking community with hybrids and a few vinifera varietals. The lake moderates the extreme climate, cooling nights in the summer and moisturizing the air during winter to provide a blanket of snow, which protects the vines from the severe low temperatures.

MID-ATLANTIC STATES: (New Jersey, southeastern Pennsylvania, Maryland, West Virginia, Virginia) There are more than fifty wineries in Pennsylvania, the majority of which are located in the southeastern region of the state. Most of New Jersey's wine industry is around Egg Harbor, which is better known for boat building than winemaking. Maryland's Boodry Vineyard is well-known for supplying rootstocks and French hybrids to East Coast vintners, and West Virginia is mostly known for producing hybrid wines, such as Vidal and Seyval Blanc. Perhaps the greatest growth in eastern viticulture has been in Virginia. Grapes have been planted here since Jamestown was settled in 1607, and Thomas Jefferson was responsible for importing French varietals to plant on his Monticello estate. Chardonnay and Bordeaux varietals, such as Cabernet Sauvignon and Merlot, do well here, and the wineries now number more than fifty.

MIDWESTERN STATES: (Missouri, Arkansas, Iowa) The first AVA (American Viticultural Area) in the U.S. was Augusta, Missouri, approved in 1980. The winemaking in this area is deeply influenced by the German and Swiss immigrants who migrated west across country in the 1800s. French missionaries also influenced early viticulture before the territories achieved statehood. Most of Arkansas's wineries are located in the western part of the state near Altus, near the Arkansas River. Iowa's wineries are predominantly in the Amana area, about seventy-five miles west of the Mississippi. Few wineries in the Midwest grow vinifera grapes, the vast majority of vineyards being planted to hybrids and Labruscana.

SOUTHWESTERN STATES: (Texas, New Mexico, Arizona, Colorado) New Mexico is the oldest winegrowing region of the U.S. Franciscan priests first produced sacramental wines here (the Mesilla Valley) in the sixteenth century. There are currently more than eighteen wineries in New Mexico, producing everything from sparkling wine to Cabernet Sauvignon. Arizona, with its extremely dry climate, has a similar growing season to New Mexico's, but focuses more on vinifera grapes, the most promising being Pinot Noir and Cabernet Sauvignon. Colorado's vineyards lie primarily west of the Continental Divide and east of Denver. As with Arizona, vinifera grape varieties are the focus. Texas wine country has seen the biggest boom of all these states over the past decade, as viticulturists tackle the challenge of the hot, dry terrain. Chenin Blanc is the state's most productive grape, followed by Sauvignon Blanc, Chardonnay, and Cabernet Sauvignon. There are currently more than twenty-five commercial wineries in Texas.

SOUTHEASTERN STATES: (Georgia, North and South Carolina, Florida, Tennessee, Louisiana, Mississippi) **Vitis** rotundifolia vines, also known as Muscadines, dominate the Atlantic seaboard from Virginia to Florida. There are more vinifera grapes going into the ground, especially in Georgia and North Carolina, but with the hot, humid climate during the summer and frosts in winter, growing high-quality vinifera grapes is difficult. Besides the Muscadines, Labruscanas and some hybrids are grown.

VITIS — The genus of the plant kingdom which includes the vine.

NORTHWEST STATES: (Oregon, Washington, Idaho) Of all the aforementioned regions (except California), the great Northwest offers the most diversity and promise for high-quality wine production. Oregon's modern winemaking history dates back to 1961, when Richard Sommer established Hillcrest Vineyards near Roseberg. Others followed, like David Lett of Eyrie Vineyards and Dick Erath of Knudsen-Erath Winery, who had decided that California wasn't the place for their style of wine. It was Lett's 1975 Pinot Noir that put Oregon on the map, but today Pinot Gris, Riesling, and Chardonnay are quickly emerging as major forces behind the state's wine initiatives. The principal wine region in Oregon is the Willamette Valley, a ninety-mile stretch of land just south of Portland. The region produces two-thirds of Oregon's wine, and most of the reputable producers reside there. The moderate maritime climate is especially suited to Pinot Noir, Pinot Gris, and other varietals.

In 1969, when the wine boom was sweeping California, there were only two wineries in Washington State. Since then, however, the state has crept into second position (way behind California) as an American vinifera wine producer, but its reputation isn't far behind. The vast majority of wine here is varietal, with Chardonnay, Riesling, and Semillon the forerunners of the whites and Cabernet Sauvignon and Merlot leading the pack for the reds. One grape that Washington seems to have a monopoly on is Lemberger, which a few wineries produce very well. The majority of vineyards are located east of the Cascades, where desert-dry soil and hot summers marry to produce near-perfect growing conditions. The major regions here include Yakima, Columbia Valley, and Walla Walla. West of the Cascades, in the damp proximity of the Pacific Ocean, is Puget Sound. The focus here is cooler-climate varietals, such as Chardonnay and Pinot Noir.

Idaho's viticultural region has more in common with Washington than its other neighbor, Oregon. Summers are hot, with cooling nights providing the relief the grapevines need. Dominated by Ste Chapelle, which sits along the Snake River to the west of Boise, the region is well-suited for growing Riesling. Chardonnay and Cabernet Sauvignon also grow here, but need a longer growing season to shine.

Canada

Canada grows wine in four of its provinces, Ontario, British Columbia, Quebec, and Nova Scotia, but the majority of production is centered in two—Ontario and British Columbia. The major concentration of vineyards in these two regions is planted on the same latitude as Languedoc and Chianti, but the harsh winters and unpredictable springs make them very cool growing areas. Thus, most of the vines planted are winter-hearty hybrids, such as Vidal and Seyval Blanc for whites and Marechal Foch and Baco Noir for reds. However, more vinifera vines have been planted recently, especially in regions such as the Niagara Peninsula (Ontario) and Okanagan (BC).

Due to the freezing winters, icewine is regularly made each year. There are generally two kinds of icewines made: one made from Vidal and one from Riesling. Both can produce exceptional wines. More recently, producers here have been experimenting with grapes like Chenin Blanc, Sauvignon Blanc, Pinot Blanc, Chardonnay, and even Cabernet Sauvignon as alternatives.

ONTARIO: This region's weather is buffered by two bodies of water—Lake Erie and Lake Ontario. The majority of vineyards are planted in the Niagara Peninsula area, which is further protected by the escarpment, the shore on an Ice Age lake. (The bluff encourages off-shore winds to dissipate fog and minimize frost damage.) A wide variety of grapes are grown here, everything from hybrids to Chardonnay to Riesling to Cabernet Sauvignon. And, of course, icewine, which is garnering a world-class reputation, with Niagara leading the way.

BRITISH COLUMBIA: The vineyards of British Columbia are mostly concentrated in the Okanagan Valley, which lies just north of Washington State. On the east side of the Cascades, the valley shares the same stretch of rich soil and arid climate as the Columbia Valley in Washington but benefits from Lake Okanagan, which warms the vineyards in the winter. The emphasis here is on white varietals, such as Chardonnay, Riesling, Gewürztraminer, Chenin Blanc, and Pinot Blanc. However, more recently, work is being done with red varieties, such as Merlot and Cabernet Sauvignon. Icewine is produced, with some wineries experimenting with Chenin Blanc and Pinot Blanc.

QUEBEC: Most wines produced in Quebec are hybrids, with the majority of wineries centered around the town of Durham. A bit of Chardonnay is made, but most of the whites are Seyval Blanc, and the reds are generally made from Marechal Foch and Chancellor. Some icewine is produced here, also, with the vast majority of production being sold at the wineries.

NOVA SCOTIA: Only three commercial wineries exist in this province, all located around Malagesh on the Northumberland Strait. Some funky old Russian grape varieties still thrive there as well as Marechal Foch.

Australia

Although the Land Down Under has been producing wine for more than 175 years, it's only been within the last twenty that Australia has been recognized as a producer of world-class wines. Table-wine production just recently surpassed that of fortified wines, as Australians shift from a cheap, wholesale product to a more refined, quality-oriented market. This shift is a result of a keener focus on vineyards planted in cool-climate districts, such as Coonawarra and the Adelaide Hills. Aussie winemakers have realized the need to concentrate on wines with more elegance, clarity of fruit flavor, and complexity in order to satisfy discriminating palates worldwide. Areas once abandoned because of their inability to produce ripe fruit are now back in production, as winemakers use the strengths of this continent's diverse growing regions.

Wine production in Australia is concentrated in four states: South Australia, New South Wales, Victoria, and Western Australia. Some of the more famous regions producing the majority of its world-class wines are: Hunter, known for Semillon and Shiraz (the Australian name for Syrah), and more recently Chardonnay; Barossa, producing high-quality old-vine

Shiraz and Grenache, along with Cabernet Sauvignon and Riesling; Coonawarra, with its Bordeaux-like climate producing Cabernet Sauvignon, Shiraz, and Riesling; Padthaway, known for its intense Chardonnay, Cabernet Sauvignon, and Riesling; Adelaide, with its Chardonnay and Pinot Noir for sparkling wines along with Riesling; McLaren Vale, producing fine Shiraz, Cabernet Sauvignon, Chardonnay, Sauvignon Blanc, and Grenache; Clare Valley, which recently has been praised for outstanding Riesling and Shiraz; and Margaret River, which excels in Cabernet Sauvignon, Sauvignon Blanc, and Merlot.

As for the most famous and consistently best Australian red wine, it is Penfolds Grange from South Australia. It's also the most expensive. Extremely expensive. Produced from the Shiraz grape and capable of aging for decades, it's one of the most sought-after red wines in the world.

New Zealand

Vines were first planted in New Zealand in 1819, yet it took more than 150 years for producers to realize that their maritime climate was ideal for growing world-class wine grapes. The country's wine production is still small by world standards (about one-tenth that of Australia), but vineyards now flourish in nine growing regions—Gisborne, Hawkes Bay, Marlborough, Northland, Auckland, Wairarapa, Nelson, Canterbury, and Central Otago—spanning the country from the North Island to the South Island.

The largest wine region in terms of vineyard acreage is Marlborough, situated at the northeastern tip of the South Island. Here, the three most recognized grapes planted are Chardonnay, Riesling, and Sauvignon Blanc, with the latter being responsible for putting Marlborough on the international map. Sauvignon Blanc is probably the best-known grape from this region and is the most-planted variety. New Zealand Sauvignon Blancs tend to be rather pungent, aromatic, and a bit herbaceous—a style for which the country has become known. Chardonnay is the second most widely planted grape, with the style of wines made from this variety more dependent on the winemaker than on the vineyard. Rieslings range from dry to very sweet, botrytis-affected dessert wines, which can be produced almost every year. **See REF. 6: Wine Mumbo Jumbo.**

Centered around the town of Napier is one of New Zealand's oldest and best winegrowing regions, Hawkes Bay, where Chardonnay is king. With intense flavors and bold elegance, Hawkes Bay Chardonnays are seldom matched by those of other regions. In the red-grape category, Cabernet Sauvignon is the predominant variety, often showcasing intense flavors with a hint of herbaceousness. And depending on the winemaker, these wines can exhibit a strong oak influence from aging up to two years in new French barrels.

Africa

South Africa

South Africa has been a major wine producer for more than 350 years, and its wine-producing regions centered around the Cape of Good Hope are what many believe to be some of the most picturesque in the world. With mountains jutting straight up more than 1,600 feet from valley floors, South Africa's ten proclaimed areas of origin (wine-producing regions) are home to more than 4,500 wineries. The country currently ranks eighth in the world in total wine production, but it wasn't until the recent abolition of apartheid that the country's wine market was opened to the United States. Even so, only 80,000 to 100,000 cases of South African wine are imported into the United States each year.

In general, South African wines are more European in style than other New World wines, because many South African winemakers study viticulture and winemaking in France. In addition, South African wines have been favored throughout the world for their style, as they incorporate finesse and charm rather than brawn and forwardness, like their Australian counterparts. Their fingerprint is a cross between Bordeaux and Tuscany, with red wines generally exhibiting slightly lower alcohol levels, higher acids, and firm, ripe tannins. They are also less opaque in color and tend to age very gracefully.

Of South Africa's ten areas of origin, Stellenbosch is considered the center of gravity. Situated east of Cape Town and bordered on the south by False Bay, wines from this area reflect the fertile soils and coastal influence needed to produce a world-class product. With the highest concentration of wineries and widely diverse **microclimates,** Stellenbosch consistently produces this country's best wines.

MACRO/MESO/MICRO CLIMATE—Macroclimate is a larger area—say, Napa Valley. Mesoclimate is a more specific area, as an

AVA—say, Carneros. Microclimate is the climate immediately surrounding the vines, within a vineyard, for example.

Wines originating from the regions of Paarl, Constantia, Walker Bay, and Elgin should also be considered for purchase. Paarl and Constantia, like Stellenbosch, focus heavily on fine-wine production, while Walker Bay, a newer, cool-climate area, produces some very good Chardonnay, Pinot Noir, and Riesling. Elgin, an area that until recently was known primarily for its apple production, is also turning out some fine cool-climate grape varieties.

South America

Chile

New World wines from this South American country are steeped in European history. The first vineyards in Chile took root in the mid-1500s, when missionaries planted the black Pais grape to produce sacramental wines. After the revolt of 1810, which ended 275 years of Spanish rule, vintners looked to reshape the future of their industry. They began importing vinifera vine stocks from Bordeaux and other prominent wine regions of Europe to increase both wine quality and production.

This importation of European vine stock proved ironic when, in 1870, the **phylloxera** louse began its devastating march across Europe and North America. Chile's vineyards, protected by natural barriers, remained untouched. Thus, when Europe began its monumental task of vineyard restoration, it turned to Chile for young, healthy plants for grafting onto phylloxera-resistant rootstocks. Today, Chile remains a rare example of a country where pure, ungrafted European vines still flourish.

PHYLLOXERA—The tiny louse that attacks and eventually kills a vine through its root system. It first devastated Europe in the late 1800s, nearly wiping out France's entire wine industry. The pest appeared in California in the 1980s in a mutated form, causing around 95 percent of California's vineyards to have to be replanted at a cost of around $500 million over fifteen years.

Recent interest from foreign investors in Chile's wine industry has boosted the country's recognition. France's Domaines Barons de Rothschild (Lafite) purchased a 50 percent equity share of Vina Los Vascos in 1988. Mumm, the Seagram's-owned sparkling-wine house, was the first to build a winery there more than two years ago, and Napa Valley's Franciscan Estates has purchased five hundred acres for its new Chilean property, Alto de Casablanca. In addition, Robert Mondavi has established a $12 million joint venture with Chile's Vina Errazuriz, Sebastiani is buying Chilean bulk wine to bottle for airline use under its Vendange label, and American vintners Kendall-Jackson, Firestone, and Hess Collection are currently scouting and courting potential partners. With high quality and low prices, more and more vintners worldwide are importing Chilean wine juice for use in blending in their own portfolios.

Argentina

Argentina is perhaps one of the world's few remaining major wine-producing regions yet to be fully exploited. This is due to the fact that, up until 1980, Argentina's annual per-capita consumption rate of wine was more than twenty-two gallons. By 1992, however, that figure dropped by almost half (and is still dropping), and wine producers began giving serious consideration to exporting their product.

Unlike Chile, Argentina failed to draw a substantial amount of outside investment in the 1980s and '90s. However, Michel Rolland from Pomerol, Italian vermouth producers Martini & Rossi, and the French Champagne houses of Chandon, Mumm, Deutz, and Piper-Heidsieck all have held interests in Argentina vineyards for the past several decades.

BUYING TIP

Because New World wine regions in Australia, New Zealand, South Africa, Argentina, and Chile are south of the equator, their harvests are the calendar opposites of those of North America's. Vines in these countries come out of dormancy in our late fall, and harvest occurs in spring. Therefore, south-of-the-equator wines are technically six months older than North American wines of the same vintage. —Darryl Roberts

Argentinean wine regions are widely dispersed but mostly confined to the western strip bordering the foothills of the Andes Mountains. The first recorded vineyards were planted at Santiago del Estero in 1557. The city of Mendoza was founded in 1561, and vineyards in the area known as San Juan to the north were established on a commercial scale between 1569 and 1589. In the 1820s, and again in the early 1900s, there was a massive influx of European immigrants which brought new vines and winemaking skills, thus laying the foundation for Argentina's mammoth domestic wine industry.

One of the most distinctive white-grape varieties grown in Argentina is Torrontes. With three different strains—Torrontes Mendocino, Torrontes Sanjuanino, and Torrontes Riojano—the third, Torrontes Riojano, is by far the most prominent. Torrontes wines are generally light in body and tend to exhibit strong Muscatlike aromas. With the idea of exporting (to the United States and Britain), Chardonnay is now the white wine that everyone wants to produce. Argentina has its own clone of Chardonnay—the so-called Mendoza clone—that was developed at the University of California at Davis. These wines tend to vary in style from winemaker to winemaker.

Argentina's signature red grape variety is Malbec (also spelled Malbeck), which has found its true home in upper Mendoza. Wines tend to be deep in color, exhibiting robust fruit characteristics worthy of oak aging. Cabernet Sauvignon, Merlot, Nebbiolo, Dolcetto, and Tempranillo are also prominent red-grape varieties grown here.

Old World Wines

Europe

France

With vines planted well over two thousand years ago, French winegrowers know their land and their fruit. The key to their wines are appellations: pieces of land as small as a vineyard or as big as a region defining the type of a wine. Remember, when you buy French wine, you base your decision on origin—not on varietal. **See EDU.4: Unraveling the Mystery of Wining and Dining.**

SOUTH AFRICA'S ZINFANDEL: PINOTAGE

South Africa is home to a varietal grown in few other places: Pino-
tage—a cross between Pinot Noir (the red grape of Burgundy,
France) and Cinsault (a red grape grown in France's Rhône region).
It's often compared to California's Zinfandel grape, and although
developed at the University of Stellenbosch in 1922, it wasn't
planted until some thirty years later. Its unique flavor characteris-
tics—a deep berry with spice, smoke, earth, and a bit of game—per-
fectly complement heartier red meat dishes such as lamb and
venison. You might even want to drink it with a cigar. In its youth,
Pinotage shows smoky raspberry and red fruit flavors, reminiscent
of its Rhône grape heritage. As it ages, though, it leans more toward
its Burgundian roots, retaining its red fruit flavors but exhibiting
more earth, truffle, and tobacco characteristics.   —*Darryl Roberts*

The appellations, which started in the 1930s in an effort to assure authenticity, have developed into a maze of areas and classifications. Unfortunately,
the structure of this maze varies from district to district. Generally speaking,
winegrowing zones nestle as circles within circles of sub-appellations, and
wines are named after the appellation—Appellation d'Origine Controllée
(AOC). The smaller the zone the higher the price.

A new category is the new, dynamic class of Vins de Pays. Far more affordable, these uncharted wines, created to give winemakers outside of the
AOC zones an incentive to make better wines with identity, are almost always worth trying and offer great value for money.

Let's look first at the six traditional regions where appellations reign.

BORDEAUX: Overall, the unpredictable weather along this western maritime coast, bordering the river Gironde, makes the vintage of a Bordeaux
wine extremely important. Of all Bordeaux wines, 80 percent are red.
The region counts fifty-seven AOC zones which are subclassified in about
nine thousand properties called Chateaux—vineyards with winemaking
facilities.

When these Chateaux were given their power in 1855, sixty-one of the
Chateaux earned the title Grand Cru Classé. The Grand Crus were subdi-

vided into five growths, with the top five permitted the label First Growth: Lafite-Rothschild, Latour, Margaux, Haut-Brion, and Mouton-Rothschild.

Now, here's the catch: Today we still buy into this classification. But the Chateaux, with the exception of one, grow Cabernet Sauvignon in the Medoc, just a narrow strip of land. Merlot-producing regions like Saint-Emilion and Pomerol, or Graves and Pessac-Leognan, were deemed so inferior in 1855 that they never entered the system. That means that outside of the Medoc, and in the lesser-known Chateaux, you can find more affordable and equally excellent wines. In Bordeaux, by the way, also lies Sauternes, with its sexy, sweet Semillon.

BURGUNDY: There are rumors that Burgundian farmers, after heavy rain, hike down the hills, shovels in hand, to recapture their precious, fugitive soil. Buying a Burgundy is like buying a designer label: You pay for the land and its name. The 185-mile stretch of golden hills counts nearly 120 appellations, some as small as 2.1 acres. The fickle Burgundian weather makes vintage equally important.

Burgundy's best-known grape varietals are easy to remember: Pinot Noir, Gamay, and Chardonnay. Pinot Noir accounts for all the red wines in five of Burgundy's six main regions, while in the Beaujolais (south)—famous for its marketing gimmick Beaujolais Nouveau—Gamay is the designated varietal. Within these six regions—Chablis, Côte de Nuits and Côte de Beaune (Côte d'Or), Côte Chalonnaise, Maconnais, and Beaujolais—hides a labyrinth of villages and, within them, vineyards, thriving as appellations in their own right. The vineyards are titled either Grand Cru (best), producing the essence of Burgundian wines, or Premier Cru (second best), judged better than the village wines but not as good as the Grand Crus. **See REF.5: Variety Is the Spice of Life.**

RHÔNE: Wines from the fertile valley south of Burgundy have always been friendly, big, and warm. These days they are also fashionable and expensive. In the northern region, the appellations Côte Rotie, Hermitage, and Crozes Hermitage create remarkable Syrah wines, sometimes lightened with Viognier. Southern Rhône, with its overall appellation name Côtes du Rhône, relies on Grenache as its varietal, and blends it with Syrah, Cinsault, Mourvedre, Roussanne, and Marsanne. An inner circle of sixty-four communities may label their wines Côtes du Rhône Villages, and sixteen villages are entitled to their own name. In the valley also lie Tavel, famous for its dry rosés, and Châteauneuf-du-Pape with its powerful, passionate reds of thirteen different varietals.

LOIRE: The romantic Loire Valley, dotted with medieval castles, starting a mere thirty miles north from the Rhône and then flowing in a horizontal line to the Atlantic, knows over sixty appellations but only a few dominant styles. In red wines, Cabernet Franc is important, but whites are what give the Loire fame. Toward the Atlantic, Muscadet names the region, its predominant grape, and its low-acidity sensuous wine. In the middle of the valley, Chenin Blanc results in refreshing whites from Touraine and spirited wines from Vouvray. Here also lies Anjou with its money-making rosés. At the source of the Loire, Sauvignon Blanc translates in sensuous Sancerre and the delicate, full-bodied Pouilly-Fumé.

ALSACE: This appellation differentiates itself from its German neighbors in that Alsace wines are fully fermented without residual sweetness and have a higher alcohol content. Alsace is the only region in France where the wine is named after the varietal. It must contain 100 percent of the fruit mentioned. You'll find Riesling, Gewürztraminer, Pinot Blanc, Muscat, and Pinot Gris. Pinot Noir is emerging as a leading varietal. Wines are clean-cut, aromatic, and light. About fifty sites in the Alsace, offering superior wines, may add the words Grand Cru to their label.

CHAMPAGNE: To the purist, true Champagne must come from France's northernmost vineyards planted with Pinot Noir, Pinot Meunier, and Chardonnay. Again, to the purist, the bubbles of the methode Champenoise—natural fermentation in the bottle—are secondary to the cuvee, designed by the monk Dom Perignon, a precise and secret blend of thirty or forty different varietals and vintages, that determines greatness.

Champagne is classified by its degree of sweetness, from extra brut (the driest) to brut, to extra dry, to sec or dry, to demi sec (semi-sweet).

As for the lesser-known appellations of France: affordable wines, free from stuffy traditions and ratings, tasting unbelievably good. They have AOC status or belong to the more than 140 different Vins de Pays. Some, like those from the Jura and the Savoie, never make it to the United States. Others, especially those from the Midi, are flooding our markets. They are based on Mediterranean varietals such as Carignan, Cinsault, Grenache, Syrah, and Mourvedre or names after well-known grapes like Merlot or Cabernet. The same is true for Rhône-style wines of the sensual Provence. The southwest of France produces unique wines with fiery Basque influences and regional grapes. Even sun-drenched Corsica is coming out with promising Vins de Pays.

Italy

Italy, the largest wine producer in the world, has remained an enigma when it comes to the quality of its wines. The Mediterranean temperament blazes in the most sensuous table wines and brave winemaker revolutions. It blows up in an unpredictable legislation, intent to develop an appellation system that takes the fun out of the ancient vine. And it sure makes you question the purpose of setting rules when it comes to tasting the noble grape!

It helps to know that in Italy wine is like daily bread and has been produced there for well over three thousand years. For centuries there were no wine laws, no clear labeling regulations, and yet there were thousands of winegrowers totally dedicated to their art. With rural and simple technology, wine was not a business but a lifestyle. Wines never traveled. They were drunk in the village where they were made. In short: Italians love their wine.

But then, in 1963, following the rest of Western Europe, the Denominazione di Origine Controllata (DOC), a government-sponsored agency patterned after the AOC in France, set out to control minimum standards and regulate wine production. Also that year the government initiated an even higher quality category called Denominazione di Origine Controllata e Garantita (DOCG), which added "guaranteed" to "controlled," a label that was intended to be reserved for the country's elite wines. **See EDU.2: Adventures in the Wine Aisle.**

Regardless of laws and quality standards, Italy is most known for its robust red wines. From its world-famous, spicy, medium-bodied Chianti (made in the Tuscany region mostly from the Sangiovese grape) to the fuller-bodied Barbaresco (made in the Piedmont region from the Nebbiolo grape) to the powerful Barolo (also produced in the Piedmont region from the Nebbiolo grape), these are serious wines for serious foods.

Germany

German wines offer some of the best values in the market today. The problem is understanding all those vowelless words on their labels. Well, for a quick lesson in understanding German wines, the grapes they use, and the regions they come from, keep reading. Let's explore these life-threatening issues, and maybe, just maybe, understand a little more about this wine-producing region.

REGIONS: Most vowelless words on German wine labels are the regions from which the wines come. And, as with French wines, understanding the complexities of these regions is basically useless to all non–wine geeks. However, what is important is remembering what grape varieties are grown in these regions, i.e., Burgundy (France) = Pinot Noir and Chardonnay. So, here are Germany's major growing regions and the wines produced there:

Ahr: red wines from Pinot Noir and Portugieser; a few whites from Riesling and Müller-Thurgau

Mittelrhein: white wines from Riesling, Müller-Thurgau, and Kerner

Mosel-Saar Ruwer: white wines from Riesling, Müller-Thurgau, and Elbling

Rheingau: white wines from Riesling; red wines from Pinot Noir (Spatburgunder)

Nahe: white wines from Müller-Thurgau, Riesling, and Silvaner

Rheinhessen: white wines from Müller-Thurgau, Silvaner, and Riesling; red wines from Pinot Noir (Spatburgunder)

Pfalz: white wines from Riesling, Müller-Thurgau, Kerner, Silvaner, and Morio-Muskat; red wines from Portugieser

Franken: white wines from Müller-Thurgau and Silvaner, usually bottled in a squat, green flagon called a Bocksbeutel

Hessische Bergstrasse: white wines from Riesling, Müller-Thurgau, and Silvaner

Württemberg: largest red-wine region in Germany; red wines from Trollinger, Mullerrebe (Pinot Meunier), Spatburgunder (Pinot Noir), Portugieser, and Lemberger; whites from Riesling, Müller-Thurgau, Kerner, and Silvaner

Baden: white wines from Müller-Thurgau, Rulander (Pinot Gris), Gutedel, Gewürztraminer, and Riesling; reds from Spatburgunder (Pinot Noir). (A popular rosé wine is Spatburgunder Weissherbst.)

Saale-Unstrut: white wines from Müller-Thurgau, Silvaner, and Weissburgunder (Pinot Blanc)

Sachsen: white wines from Müller-Thurgau (Rivaner), Weissburgunder (Pinot Blanc), and Traminer

GRAPES OF GERMANY: With names like Gewürztraminer and Spatburgunder, grapes used to make German wines sound more like a sobriety test than a complement to fine food. However, even if your pronunciation isn't quite exact, it's understanding the aromas and flavors of varietals that'll benefit you the most. So here goes.

WHITE

Müller-Thurgau: flowery bouquet; milder acidity than Riesling; slight Muscat flavor; best consumed young

Riesling: fragrant; citrus-and-peach fruit bouquet; pronounced acidity; potential for aging but enjoyable young

Silvaner: neutral bouquet; mild acidity; full-bodied; best enjoyed young

Kerner: light Muscat bouquet; racy, lively acidity; similar to Riesling

Scheurebe: lively acidity; bouquet and taste reminiscent of black currants

Rulander/Grauburgunder: robust, full-bodied, smooth, soft, and full on the palate

RED

Spatburgunder: full-bodied, with hints of almonds

Portugieser: light, mild, easygoing, best consumed young

Trollinger: fragrant, fresh, fruity, good acidity, hearty

QUALITY

There are three levels of German wine quality:

1. Tafelwein, which designates an ordinary table wine, made from normally ripe grapes and usually served in one-liter jugs. In other words, a good cheap drink.

2. Qualitätswein bestimmter Anbaugebiete (QbA), German for "Quality Wines from Specific Regions," an official designation for a good quality wine from a specific region, Bereich, or village. Wines with pretensions to quality but that don't quite cut it (sugar had to be added to the grape juice in order for the finished wine to reach minimum alcoholic strength).

3. Qualitätswein mit Pradikat (QmP), German for "Quality Wine with Distinction," an official designation for quality wine from a specific Bereich, village, or vineyard. This is the highest classification of German wine and can be further defined as to the village or vineyard and as to the following categories:

Kabinett: lightest of Pradikat wines
Spätlese: means late harvest, though not necessarily sweet
Auslese: usually, though not necessarily, sweet
Beerenauslese: made from overripe grapes (e.g., sweet dessert wines)
Eiswein: icewine, very sweet
Trokenbeerenauslese: made from raisined grapes, super sweet, honeylike
  wines

GERMAN TO ENGLISH DICTIONARY: Of course, no German lesson is complete without translation. Without getting too involved, this list will get you through a basic German wine list . . . hopefully.

Bereich: a district or subregion
Diabetiker-Wiensiegel: a diabetic wine
Einzellage: single vineyard
Grosslage: not a piece of land but the name a grower may use to designate
  a blend of two or more Einzellage wines

Konsumwein: ordinary daily wine

Liebfraumilch: means, quite simply, Rhine wine

Moselblummchen: an approximate equivalent to Liebfraumilch

Oeschle: percentage or degree of sugar in the grape

Suss-reserve: sweet grape must be added to wine before bottling to add
   freshness and elevate the percentage of residual sugar

Well, there you have it. Everything you ever wanted to know about Germany and its wines. Well, close. But if you remember anything, remember this: The degree of grape ripeness at harvest determines the quality of German wines.

Spain

Although Spain is no larger than, say, Texas, its climate and terrain vary literally all over the map. Wedged between France and Portugal, with the Atlantic on its north and west edges, and the Mediterranean along the east and south, Spain has everything from mountains to near-deserts to sunny coastal plains, making for a multitude of microclimates in which to grow grapes for everything from delicate sparklers to seriously gutsy reds to that quintessential Spanish specialty, sherry.

In the northeast, just inland from Barcelona in the foothills of the Pyrenees, the Penedes region of Catalonia (Catalunya to the locals) produces Spain's best-known sparkling wine. Known as Cava and made in the classic *methode champenoise*, it features native grapes such as Parellada, Macabeo, and Zarel-lo. Recently, some Cava producers have begun adding or substituting classic Champagne varietals such as Chardonnay and Pinot Noir, especially in their high-end blends. Even so, it's hard to pay more for Cava than about $12—and most of them run well under $10.

Reds make up the major output of the Rioja region, in north-central Spain, and account for Rioja's world-class reputation. Mostly based on the grape Tempranillo (thought by some to be a clone of Pinot Noir) and Garnacha (Spanish name for Grenache), and aged in quality oak, they're Spain's best-known reds. Softer and fruitier than the Cabernets and Merlots of Bordeaux (which lies just over the Pyrenees to the north), red Rioja is often lightened up, as they do in Italy's Chianti region, with whites such as Viura—in fact, the vineyards often have a mix of reds and whites planted side by side. There's also a small but growing amount of white wine in Rioja, too: some crisp, light, and traditional; some rich and creamy from barrel fermentation.

Just northeast of Rioja, the ancient kingdom of Navarra, known as "Spain's California," grows a great deal of the country's fruits and vegetables in addition to a wide range of wine grapes. Though it's best known (partly thanks to Ernest Hemingway) for its fruity, easy-drinking rosés, Navarra also turns out some high-quality white wines (mostly Viura and Chardonnay, which are sometimes blended) and age-worthy reds (Tempranillo, Garnacha, Cabernet, and Merlot, as pure varietals and in various combinations).

Along the lower west coast in the province of Andalucia, just above Spain's southernmost tip, lies the town of Jerez de la Frontera. Here, and in the surrounding region, the chalky soil, sizzling heat, and unique winemaking methods turn the Palomino grape into the sun-baked, golden elixir called sherry. Sherry can range from pale, delicate, and bone-dry to thick, sweet, and toffee-colored—and it's great with everything from a simple appetizer of olives and bread to a slab of fruit-and-nut tart. Sherry tastes unlike any other wine for two main reasons. First, a crust of flor yeast can form on its surface, flavoring it as it matures. Second, it ages in a multilevel solera system of giant racks, in which the wine moves from barrel to barrel, top to bottom, blending younger lots into older ones and delivering the finished product from the lowest tier.

Portugal

Portugal has long been known for producing some of the finest fortified wines in the world—Port. It hasn't been until recently that the country's table wines have gained attention. From the crisp, acidic whites of Vinhos Verde to the deep, rich reds of the Douro, Dao, and Bairrada, Portugal is producing world-class table wines to rival those of any Old World producers.

If you have the opportunity to travel the country, you'll see that it seems as if every house in northern Portugal has its own little vineyard. Grapevines are usually trellised high on arbors, draped like canopies covering walkways, around the perimeter of the small yards. This old traditional trellising on pergolas of granite post and chestnut lintel serves several purposes: It slows the ripening process, producing a desired sugar/acid balance; it keeps fungus diseases to a minimum; and the traditional practice allows the planting of crops underneath.

The prominent producing regions of Portugal include: Vinhos Verde, which is Portugal's largest wine region, accounting for about 20 percent of the country's harvest. Its name means "green wine," derived from the region's proximity to Costa Verde, or Green Coast. Wines are usually light, dry, and a bit fizzy, but more recently commercial brands are lightly sweetened to appeal to overseas markets.

Another is Douro, arguably one of the most beautiful winegrowing regions in the world. Dominated by the Douro River, its terraced vineyards sprawl in a virtual amphitheater, creating a heaven for growing well-balanced, flavorful grapes. The Douro is known for its Port wines. However, it's recently made great strides to upgrade the quality of its unfortified table wines.

A third is Dao, centered around the old cathedral city of Viseu in north-central Portugal. It has the reputation for producing some of the country's best red wines. Its name comes from a river in the high country not far south of the Douro and well inland from the sea. Touriga Nacional, one of the principal Port wine grapes, is regarded as the best in the region.

Last we have Bairrada, whose wines are perhaps the only real rival to those made in Dao. The region sits between Dao and the Atlantic, north of Coimbra and south of Oporto.

Check out www.winebrats.org for downloadable wine region maps!

INSIDER TRADING

Steven Van Yoder is a great example of how the Wine Brats' network has evolved. At first he became a familiar face around events. Then a friendly introduction came about through mutual acquaintances. Next, we discovered he was a freelance writer wanting to break into food and wine writing. Then he went on to doing interviews with us and covering Wine Brats events for BUNG!online. Now Steven is a member of the coalition, helping expand "insider" information through our network of members concerning our country's "hot spots" to sip wine.

—j, j & m

Driving Between the Vines, or America's Hot Spots to Sip and Drink Wine

by Steven Van Yoder

Traveling Like a Wine Brat Means Following Rumors, Ignoring Conventional Wisdom, and Staying on the Road!

One rainy day in 1991 I made my first trip to Napa Valley. As a fresh arrival to California, I had dreamt about visiting wine country for some time, and I was ready for an excursion of epic proportions. My friend Dan—having been to the Valley several times, and claiming he knew of the friendliest places—volunteered to drive his truck from winery to winery.

We had a good day overall, managed to learn something about wine, and didn't encounter too much in the way of intimidation—except for the last stop of the day, where the tasting room staff were less than enthusiastic about dealing with newbies. We left the winery, ready to head back to San Francisco. Then suddenly, to my shock and surprise, before even leaving the winery property, I found myself in the middle of a vineyard, a few yards from the driveway, Dan's truck axle-deep in mud.

"I don't believe you did that!" I shouted. "I really can't believe you did that!"

"But you told me to," he responded emphatically. "You said to take out that row of vines, and that's what I tried to do." He proceeded to laugh maniacally.

Yeah, I told Dan to take out a row of vines. I've also told people to go to hell—I just don't expect them to do it. In the end we managed to get out of the situation without much embarrassment. In fact, we were victorious. A couple of workers from the vineyard pulled us from the ditch, invited us to their apartment, and invited us to drink from their "special collection" well into the night. Yes, way.

What interests me about this totally ridiculous memory is how my previous life back East, and my new life in the West, somehow came into play at that moment while stuck in the mud of a vineyard. I had just graduated college with a Bachelor of Philosophy, after four grueling years nose-down in the writings of Kierkegaard, Nietzsche, and Kafka. College was great for a while, but academia (and those who lived it) became oppressive. I was sick of arrogant professors more concerned with "one-upping" each other than capturing the interest of their students.

About the same time I discovered my love of wine while innocently taking an introductory wine course. Until then, my favorite wines came in a box. I spent most of my undergraduate years drinking cheap beer, assuming the pomp and seriousness over wine was a sham. But after a few classes I realized that wine, a new source of endless pleasure, would be part of my life.

When I arrived in California, armed with a little wine knowledge, I hit the vineyards (literally) of the Napa and Sonoma Valleys, and the restaurants and wine scene of San Francisco, eager to experience wine firsthand. Most of the "wine" people I encountered were approachable, while a few were just like the sarcastic professors from college. I soon discovered that wine snobs, like some college professors, were cut from the same cloth: intellectual bullies who were proud of their privileged and exclusive "secret handshake."

That's when I started "collecting" my own private list of places that were conducive to drinking and learning about wine in a relaxed and friendly atmosphere. The world of wine, like academia, can be an intimidating place for a newcomer. But if you are serious about enjoying wine, you don't want to limit your pursuits to the safety of your living room. Getting out and about—to restaurants, wine bars, wineries, wine tastings, and events—is one of the best and most exciting ways to learn about and enjoy wine.

As any traveler knows, the best "finds" usually occur by accident . . . or through the recommendations of others. So, my advice? When Wine Brats hit the road, they have to think like sleuths. Nothing can replace tips from friends and fellow travelers, browsing Internet chat rooms, and seeking alternative sources to ferret out the stuff of personal, authentic, unintimidating experiences for the wine traveler.

So read the following barrage of wine-friendly establishments gathered from Wine Brats around the country before you plan your next outing. Sift through the tidbits, chart your wine travels, and start your own list of cool places to drink and explore wine. Also understand that by no means is this list comprehensive, yet it sets a standard where places are recommended for their progressive friendliness and knowledge, rather than lofty attitudes and untouchable wine lists. We also encourage you to post your finds at wineRave.com, or E-mail us at info@brats.org so that we might share them with our friends! And finally, if anybody gives you attitude while out and about in pursuit of wine: Smile, rise above the situation, never patronize them again . . . and whatever you do, stay on the road!

Recommendations: à la Wine Brats/Wine Rave Web Sites

Okno
1332 North Milwaukee
Wicker Park, IL 60622
(773) 395-1313

Walking into Okno gives one the feeling of being transported via space tube to another dimension. The decor looks like George and Astro took the long way to the Andy Warhol exhibit in the Bradys' kitchen. Freak show! While waiting for a table upstairs in what looks like the bridge of the Starship Enterprise, listen to techno-house and try some tasty wines by the glass: Iron Horse Brut, Storybook Mt. Zin 1991, Coppola Rosso. The wine list comes in a compact disc case. Very cool.

—Andy Pates, Chicago

Webster's Wine Bar
1480 W. Webster, Clybourn Corridor
Chicago, IL 60614
(773) 868-0608

"Welcome to the fine art of leisure" is the Wine Bar's motto. Opened on a shoestring budget, the Wine Bar has since become a major player in the Chicago wine scene. It is usually packed. Webster's wine list is comprised of ample wines by the glass that change regularly. There are also monthly features and flights such as Rhône Rangers, Southwest of France, Alsace, etc. There is a light menu of salads, cheeses, pâtés, pizzas, and other knash to get you through the evening. A new party room has been added upstairs to accommodate overflow from the bar as well as private parties and special tastings. Also check out "Mo Music Mondays."

—Andy Pates, Chicago

Rudi's Wine Bar and Café
2424 North Ashland, Clybourn Corridor
Chicago, IL 60614
(773) 404-RUDI (7834)

I have always been partial to Rudi's—a place to go and escape the wine asses of the world. It should be treated with respect. Grasshopper, you may now enter. There is no last name. Don't ask. Like Cher, Madonna, and the Artist (formerly known as Prince), Rudi is just Rudi, and dammit if he doesn't bare a striking resemblance to Robert Goulet. This is a cozy, dark, and romantic hangout. The food is Country French bistro fare. The menu rarely changes but is very tasty and ridiculously affordable. Try the escargot and mussels for starters. The lamb and rabbit are some of my favorite entrees. The approximate ten wines by the glass range from $3.50 for J. M. Arcaute Bordeaux Merlot 1995 to $7.25 for Chateau Graville LaCoste Graves Blanc 1997.

—Andy Pates, Chicago

Aquitane
569 Tremont St.
Boston, MA 02118
(617) 424-8577

Although opened at five-thirty P.M., it was worth the wait on our Sunday tour. Yum. They serve fifteen wines by the glass, good bottle list both French and American. Excellent appetizers and entrees. Sophisticated interior dinning with eight-seat bar. French bistro–type food. Jazz is the music playing in the background.

—Joanne Fantini, Boston

Franklin Cafe
278 Shawmut St.
Boston, MA 02118
(617) 350-0010

Hidden amoung the rowhouses and brownstones, you will find the Franklin. This place is great to bring friends when you can share a bottle of wine. This list is mainly American with an occasional French. With a regular bar and about ten booths, morning finds breakfast or brunch until three P.M., closing until five P.M. for dinner. Funky atmosphere at night with techno-funk music. Wearing black is a good thing. Not many wines by the glass. Best price for bottle wine selection. Can get a great red zin for $23 (U.S.)!

—Joanne Fantini, Boston

Enoteca I Trulli
122 E. 27th St.
New York, NY 10016
(212) 481-7372

Trulli restaurant is on 27th Street, just off Park Avenue South. Forty-five wines reside on the all-Italian Enoteca list, all by the glass, and there are ten "flights" of three wines each, grouped for your tasting pleasure, ranging from $7.50 to $27 per flight, or pick a full glass for $4.25 to $30 (for the legendary Italian wine Gaja Barbaresco 1994). The staff is well-informed and can help you with a wine or food selection. There is a substantial Enoteca menu, with appetizers, pastas, and entrees. Quick, go and taste before everyone finds out!

—Wayne Young, New York

Bar Six
502 Sixth Ave.
New York, NY 10011
(212) 645-2439

Aside from the excellent Moroccan-influenced French bistro eats, the wine list there is unique. Mirrors line the walls of the dining room in back, upon which is painted the list of available wines: seven whites and seven reds, with easy, broad categories like "Southern French Red" and "Alsace." The staff is happy to describe them to you in simple detail. All come $5.50 per glass or $23 per bottle. There is always a selection from Morocco. (Believe it! It's good!) Don't overlook the well-selected beers, bubblies, and stogies, too, if you're so inclined. A deejay spins great music Wednesday through Sunday from eleven P.M. until two A.M. right on the bar, and the kitchen will feed you until three or so. I love this place!

—Wayne Young, New York

Divine Bar
244 E. 51st St.
New York, NY 10022
(212) 319-9463

A mecca of tasty things. Seventy wines are available by two-ounce taste, by the glass, or by the bottle. Divine Bar features flights of matched wines from all over the planet. There are also forty-five different beers, a bunch of sparkling wines and champagnes, and an available cigar list. Descend into the first floor lined with a big stainless-steel bar, backed by zebra-striped wine-dispensers. Ascend up to the très-cool lounge, complete with tables, comfy chairs, and couches overlooking the bar. Look out for the purple velvet couch . . . rumor has it that it magnifies the libidos of couples once the Barry White starts spinning.

The menu is neatly divided into categories like "land," "sea," and "garden," with two items called "Wild Tapas," which are Pepper-Crusted Ostrich Filet and Alligator Fritters (a couple next to me loved the alligator so much that they were losing their minds!). This is a very hip environment with lots and lots of fun stuff to put in your mouth.
    —Susan Balasny, New York

Firecracker
1007 Valencia St.
San Francisco, CA 94110
(415) 642-3470

Firecracker is a Chinese restaurant in the Mission District of San Francisco. Decor is something like Gothic meets Chinese, whatever. The wine list is short yet comprehensive, well chosen with excellent prices. It's great to see the fusion of wine with nontraditional ethnic food.
    —Tammy Dubose, San Francisco

Corks
1026 S. Charles St.
Baltimore, MD 21230
(410) 752-3810

Corks is actually a hub for the Baltimore Wine Brats. The place has tasty food and an extensive wine list offered just over retail. In fact, the wine list is an educational experience itself (an easy-to-read vino bible). You can contact them at corksemail@aol.com.

—Joel Shalowitz, Baltimore

E-mail Submissions from Wine Brats Members

Arizona

Christopher's is a friendly establishment in Phoenix, Arizona. Christopher and his wife, Paola, have one hundred wines by the glass, served with bistro food. It is also friendly to cigar smokers and has a microbrewery.

Biltmore Shopping Plaza
2398 E. Camelback Rd.
Phoenix, AZ 85016
(602) 381-8920

Submitted by Bruce H. Shelton

The Dish is the wine bar portion of the Rumrunner wine and gourmet foods shop. The Dish is small, dark, with a selection of over thirty premium wines by the glass. The staff is very friendly and unpretentious. Excellent food.

3200 East Speedway Blvd.
Tucson, AZ 85716
(520) 326-0121

Submitted by Len Napolitano, Pacific Palisades, California

California

There is a great bed-and-breakfast that is part of the Fitzpatrick Winery in Somerset, California. It is on the top of a hill with a killer view. There are many other wineries in this Eldorado County area (Windwalker, Latcham,

Granite Springs, Lava Cap, Oakstone, Single Leaf). A fun and romantic weekend getaway.

Fitzpatrick Lodge and Winery
7740 Fairplay Rd.
Somerset, CA 95684
(800) 245-9166 / fax (530) 620-6838
http://www.fitzpatrickwinery.com/

Submitted by Steve Pacheco, San Francisco

Bouchon. Need a Franco-infusion but can't foot the bill for a trip to Lyon? Head to Bouchon in Yountville, California, to see the roots of the just-drink-it wine philosophy. There aren't little dogs in people's laps, or clouds of cigarette smoke, but you can still imagine being in France!

6534 Washington Street
Yountville, CA 94599
(707) 944-8037

Submitted by Jack Bittner, Silverado Vineyard's Director of Public Relations and Wine Brat since birth

EOS Wine Bar is a wine-friendly joint with hundreds of wines in a wide range of prices. Because they want to encourage experimentation, the markup on each wine is only $5 or $10 above retail.

101 Cole St.
San Francisco, CA 94117
(415) 566-3063

Submitted by Tina Caputo, San Francisco

Fabio's is a little Italian restaurant in Tracy, California. They have the tastiest, freshest food you'll find in the Valley. The wine list is quite good and growing, but the atmosphere makes any wine fabulous. Or is it the other way around?

88 W. 10th St. @ B
Tracy, CA 95376
(209) 836-2012

Submitted by Johnny Leonardo, Tracy

The Hayes and Vine Wine Bar in San Francisco is a great place to taste a variety of wines from around the world. There is a good selection of wines by the glass that changes weekly. There is a back room with a purple velvet sofa that makes the experience relaxing and fun. Contemporary tunes, a knowledgeable staff, and tasty appetizers complement the wines nicely.

377 Hayes St.
San Francisco, CA 94102
(415) 626-5301

Submitted by Karimah I. Tennyson, Santa Clara

Colorado

Mattie's is a historic brothel house located in the Lower Downtown (LoDo) district of Denver. Mattie ran the brothel in the 1800s, and legend has it she still walks the halls today. Mattie's recently held the Inaugural "Nouveau en LoDo," where we highlighted the release of Beaujolais Nouveau from France as well as Gamays from Napa Valley. There is a restaurant and the wine list contains selections mostly from California.

Mattie's House of Mirrors
1946 A. Market St.
Denver, CO 80202

Submitted by Jason Ornstein, Denver

Idaho

Boise, Idaho's, premiere summer music and wine festival takes place each June–September at Ste. Chapelle Winery and features some of the hottest jazz, Zydeco, blues, and rock musicians from around the country. Jazz at the Winery draws huge crowds and talented musicians. Lots of winemaking tours, vineyard tours, and tastings during the festival.

19348 Lowell Road
Caldwell, ID 83605 (twenty-five minutes west of Boise)
(208) 459-7222
http://www.winesnw.com/idhome.html

Submitted by Steven Roberto, Boise

Illinois

Rudi Fazuli's is a new restaurant I discovered on a recent trip to Chicago. The menu is contemporary Italian featuring a variety of entrees and appetizers. The wine list and staff are incredible! Each week they feature a "wine of the week" that is priced at a steal. A must for anyone in Chicago!

2442 North Clark
Chicago, IL 60614
(773) 388-0100

Submitted by Dave McKlveen, Providence, Rhode Island

Indiana

The ambiance is perfect, the food is terrific, the prices are reasonable at the Scholars Inn Gourmet Cafe and Wine Bar in Bloomington, Indiana. It has warm lighting, Latin poems on the walls, and a 1920s feel, with a small piano in the center room next to the fireplace. They have an *excellent* selection: ninety wines by the bottle, thirty by the glass, and "flights" in which you can taste four to six different dessert wines, Chardonnays, etc. The atmosphere is relaxed and unpretentious—you can show up in your best duds or your bar-wear and feel comfortable.

801 North College Ave.
Bloomington, IN

(812) 332-1892

www.monroecounty.net/scholars

Submitted by Cameron Blake Holtz, Boston

Massachusetts

I recommend the Silverstone Bar and Grill on Bromfield Street in Boston. Silverstone is casual and inexpensive. Their wine list isn't huge but it's interesting. They mark up full bottles by $10 and half bottles by $5, a real bargain for Boston. Josh and Katy, the owners, pick the selections carefully, and Josh is particularly good at recommending wine (ask about his secret selections).

69 Bromfield St.

Boston, MA 02108

(617) 338-7887

Submitted by Sharon Bostick, Boston

Michigan

Some of my best and most pleasurable experiences have been with the small family-owned wineries in Michigan. The ten or twelve wineries in the Leelanau Peninsula of northern Michigan make a great weekend getaway, with many bed-and-breakfasts and hotels to accommodate visitors to the area. These vintners make wine out of pure love and treat every visitor with friendly smiles and respect. Most were so friendly I had to go back two or three more times to make sure it wasn't a fluke!

Michigan Grape and Wine Industry Council

PO Box 30017

Lansing, MI 48909

(517) 373-1104

Submitted by P. Todd Reed

Missouri

The Mt. Pleasant Winery and the Stone Hill Winery and Restaurant are great after a day of touring Missouri Wine Country. Wine Brats will enjoy the history of Missouri wines and learning about the grapes grown in this region. The restaurant at Stone Hill is a great place to enjoy a meal with a bottle of Missouri wine.

Mt. Pleasant Winery
5634 High St.
Augusta, MO 63332 (about forty-five miles west of St. Louis)
(800) 467-WINE
www.mt-pleasantwines.com

Stone Hill Winery and Restaurant
1110 Stone Hill
Hermann, MO 65041 (about sixty miles west of St. Louis)
(800) 909-WINE
www.wine-mo.com/stonehill.html

Submitted by Tom Colgan, St. Peters

Gomer's Midtown is a liquor store under current ownership by Brad McLeroy, who is thirty-one years old, a graduate of culinary school, and a wine lover who spends two to three weeks a year in France traveling and playing tour guide through wine country for customers. Since he has taken over, he has created a reputation for carrying the finest and most unique wines in Kansas City (in all price ranges). Above the store is a large room and kitchen that are used for wine tastings, CellarMasters events, a twelve-week wine class, and Wine Brats meetings. Brad is hip and fun and always willing to offer his location for any wine event. No snobbery at this joint!

3838 Broadway
Kansas City, MO 64111
(816) 931-4170

Submitted by Chris Yonke, Wine Brats VP, Kansas City Chapter

In the Kansas City area there is a restaurant called The Classic Cup. It has a fantastic wine list, a knowledgeable waitstaff, and the chef turns out progressive, well-prepared dishes. The place is fairly small with an intimate atmosphere, and the restaurant has an amazingly well-stocked bar, including everything you need to make the perfect martini, pour the best Calvados, or choke down the finest Grappa. Prices are very reasonable and everyone is made to feel welcome.

301 W. 47th Street
Kansas City, MO 64112
(816) 753-1840

Submitted by Gavin Fritton, Overland Park, Kansas

New York

After growing weary of white Zinfindel and realizing that the wine with the nicest label was not necessarily the best tasting, a friend recommended Best Cellars. Best Cellars caters to novice wine drinkers by categorizing their wines as Fizzy, Fresh, Juicy, Smooth, Soft, Big, Luscious, and Sweet and displaying each type in full-wall wine racks. The staff is extremely helpful and patient and encourages questions. The best part is that all bottles—whether Californian, French, or German Rhine wines—are all $10 or under, so you don't have to spend a fortune learning.

1291 Lexington Avenue (at 87th St.)
New York, NY 10028
(212) 426-4200
www.best-cellars.com

Submitted by Janine Walits, Pine Brook, New Jersey

In the Finger Lakes, in the heart of New York State's wine country, Inn on the Lake is definitely worth a visit. Located on the north shore of Canandaigua Lake, you can enjoy the casual, relaxed atmosphere of the lounge or outdoor patio, or arrive by boat at the outdoor Sandbar and enjoy one of over fifty wines featuring local Finger Lakes vintages. The surrounding

Finger Lakes region has fifty-eight wineries, all just a short trip from the inn, and traveling from winery to winery is breathtaking during the fall foliage season.

770 South Main St.
Canandaigua, NY 14424
(716) 394-7800

Submitted by Dan Barnett, Canandaigua

Ohio

Mt. Adams Book Store is unique, with a friendly atmosphere. A real neighborhood establishment. Combines the best of a book store, newsstand, gift shop, coffee shop, and most importantly, a wine bar. Occasionally, they have live acoustic music sets. Don and Carol host a wine tasting every Saturday afternoon. It's always an entertaining and informative event.

The Mushroom Wine Shop has been a Cincinnati tradition (and the pride of the Mt. Adams neighborhood) for over twenty-five years. An amazing selection of wines of all sorts. A very informed and helpful staff treats each customer as a special guest. Wine tastings every weekend. A wine lover's paradise.

Mt. Adams Book Store
St. Gregory St.
Cincinnati, OH 45223
(513) 241-9009

The Mushroom Wine Shop
Hatch St. at Mt. Adams
Cincinnati, OH 45223
(513) 721-0016

Submitted by Joe Hull, Cincinnati

Rhode Island

About one and a half hours south of Boston there is an area straddling the Massachusetts/Rhode Island border that provides great bicycling between vineyards. Two notable vineyards are in the area, within biking distance of each other. Sakonnet Vineyards in Little Compton, Rhode Island, is New England's largest and oldest winery, specializing in varietals that perform well in New England. A few miles away, down country roads lined with stone walls, country stores, and ice cream shops, is Westport Vineyard and Winery in Westport, Massachusetts. Westport's sparkling wines can stand up to California's best. Killer Chardonnays, also. Both vineyards offer free tastings and tours.

Sakonnet Vineyards
62 West Main Rd.
Little Compton, RI 02837
(401) 635-8486
rockwellinn@ids.net

Westport Rivers Vineyard and Winery
417 Hixbridge Rd.
Westport, MA 02790
(508) 636-3423

Submitted by Jayme Lacour, cofounder of the Boston Wine Brats

South Carolina

Charlestonians are renowned for their hospitality, and the Peninsula Grill adds some glamour to that tradition. Visiting Brats should settle in at the bar, order oysters, and ask for the champagne menu. There are typically about a half dozen choices of champagnes by the glass, and some of the selections are quite unusual. (We were lucky enough to sample the Bollinger Grand Anee 1989.) The staff is knowledgeable and chatty, and the bar is elegant without being overbearing.

112 North Market Street
Charleston, SC 29401
(843) 723-0700

Submitted by Cameron Blake Holtz, Boston, Massachusetts

Texas

Without a doubt the coolest wine bar in Houston has to be Benjy's Restaurant and Lounge. They usually serve twenty-five properly stored wines by the glass, all of admirable quality and vintage. Cigar smoking is allowed in the wine room. Benjy's is located in "The Village" (Rice University Village for out-of-towners).

2424 Dunstan #125
Houston, TX 77005
(713) 522-7602
www.benjys.com

Submitted by Rob Eddlemon, Houston

Virginia

Virginia now boasts over fifty vineyards, and the number is growing. There are two Virginia Wine Festivals held every year at which to sample our great wines and to party like its 1999. The festivals are held at Great Meadows in the "Hunt Country" region. The Virginia Wine Festival is the largest of its kind on the East Coast. It does not get any better than this!

Submitted by Charley Barth, Alexandria, Virginia

Washington

Kaspar's Restaurant in Seattle has many options for the wine-philic. I like to make reservations for the wine tastings they have the first Wednesday of each month—they are typically $40 per person and include five (five!) wines and a fabulous food option to go with each course. Occasionally they host dinners with winemakers who discuss their wines accompanied by really, really great food.

19 West Harrison
Seattle, WA 98119
(206) 298-0123
www.kaspars.com

Submitted by Barbara Pittenger, Seattle

City Cellars Fine Wines is owned by three young people who have all had very interesting experiences in Europe and the States and who have, despite their age, a deep understanding of wine and its importance in our various Western cultures. And most important, they are down-to-earth and not snobby. They are friendly and have everything else you want in a great wine shop—including an amazing selection from around the world, chosen by taste and authenticity and not some stupid score in a dumb wine magazine.

1710 N. 45th St.
Seattle, WA 98103
(206) 632-7238
citycellars@eudoramail.com.

Submitted by Rafer Nelsen, Seattle

Washington, D.C.

Tasting Society International is based in Washington, D.C, and creates tasting events that are fun and educational. Speakers include wine experts who have traveled around the world tasting wine and food. We cater to the beginner wine drinker who wants to learn about wine. We hold "Wine Basics 101" nine times a year and it's open to the public.

Various venues throughout D.C.
www.tastedc.com
E-mail: wine@tastedc.com
(202) 333-8992

Submitted by Charlie Adler, President, Tasting Society International, Washington, D.C.

Cafe Atlantico in Washington, D.C., is a fun and exciting place to go. The cuisine is influenced by Latin America and the wine list is almost exclusively from there. Bright, loud, electric cuisine . . . a great excuse for a party!

405 8th St., NW
Washington, DC 20004
(202) 393-0812

There is a traditional George Duboeuf Beaujolais Nouveau party in town that is getting out of hand. On the eve of the release, they open one hundred cases at midnight and pour for free. This year the mayor showed up and the Washington Capitals hockey team came after they whipped Toronto. Many chefs and restaurateurs show up. I participated this year (in total excess!). What a party!

Les Halles de Paris
1201 Pennsylvania Ave. NW
Washington, DC
(202) 347-6848

Submitted by Andrew D. M. Schneider

SEEK AND YE SHALL FIND

One day, the national office received an E-mail from a guy named Jeff Moriarty. It seemed Jeff wanted to talk wine and the Internet. Turns out he's a Web geek and instigator from the New York Times Co. *This same publishing group happens to own our NorCal newspaper, the* Press Democrat, *known for its straightforward wine reviews and reporting on the biz. So our Executive Director, Joel Quigley, meets him for lunch at Cafe Lolo in Santa Rosa (Joel's fave spot for eats and wine). Jeff, because of* NYT*'s zero-tolerance policy, has to watch Joel sip a tasty zin, while he explains over lunch that he hoped we could work together. Four months later, with the help of* Wine X, *the three of us launch WineRave.com. Now Jeff has his hands even deeper into cyberspace's goblet of juice with WineToday.com. No other choice than Jeff to talk the subject you are about to explore.*

—j, j & m

Finding Wine on the Web, or Confessions of a Techno Wine Geek

by Jeff Moriarty

So, I'm standing there in this castlelike former monastery in Napa Valley, where, in another time, in fact just a few years before, wine had been made since the nineteenth century. It's a typical wine country affair, and while people taste top wines and gourmet foods, trapeze artists flip around the ceiling as chamber music fills the air and ballet dancers twinkle about the stone floors. All right, the trapeze routine and ballet dancers aren't quite so "typical."

My girlfriend, she's two steps away, talking to the chef of one of Napa's finest restaurants about how he made the Foie Gras spread that she's sampling on a wafer. The chef is waving a hand to indicate how the wine at the table next door complements the flavors.

Taking in the sites, the sounds, and savoring the flavors of an incredible Cabernet Sauvignon, I covertly meander back to the table with the lamb hors d'oeuvres that go with it so well. A knowing smile from the person working the table blows my cover. As is my standard nervous reaction to uncomfortable situations, I reach into the pocket of the suit jacket I had revived from the back of the closet for this event. To my surprise, I find a long-lost CD of one of my favorite punk-rock bands of days past—days when my social calendar may have included a stop off at the local pub for Nickel Beer Night or a Jack Daniels and Coke.

So here I am in the middle of this quintessentially wine country scene, savoring fine wines, and actually appreciating the differences between them. You know, how they go with the food, the music, and the scene itself. I can't even believe it myself: a punk-rock CD in my pocket, a Cabernet in one hand, and lamb in the other. This is where and when I realize that *this is the place to be.* Nickel beers be damned.

And guess who, actually what, I have to thank for this revelation? The Internet.

My appreciation of wine began when I started to research wine publications on the Internet. I had just moved from Florida to Sonoma County, California, to work for the local newspaper, a *New York Times*–owned publication that wanted to establish a wine magazine on the World Wide Web. As part of the research that would eventually help us build our wine publication, *WineToday.com*, I started to understand and appreciate that there's much more to wine than I had previously known.

As I became friends with people in the wine industry and people involved in the Wine Brats, I began to see that wine is an art and a science that pairs very well with the Web, another combination of art and science for which I have great passion.

If you had asked me a year before my research what a Zinfandel was, I would have suggested that it was the pink stuff my mother drank when she was out of Blue Nun. Not that there's anything wrong with either.

Two years later, I've got my first batch of homemade Zinfandel (the red stuff) fermenting in the basement. I made the wine with my own hands (not counting the squishing of the grapes by my girlfriend's feet), made from grapes and advice provided by a winemaker friend and instructions I found on the Internet. I'm tentatively labeling the vintage "Chateau Fancypants" in honor of our highbrow friends in the wine biz.

I have to admit, there's something very cool and exciting about going into a restaurant, reading a wine list, and making an educated decision on a wine with qualities that will enhance my meal. Or picking a wine to go with the movie that I'll be watching that night. Or finding a cold bottle that will refresh me on a hot summer day. Information is power, and there's no better place to find information on wine than the Web.

Wine Publications Are Your Friends

There are literally thousands of sites on the World Wide Web where you can learn about wine, research a specific topic, or buy a bottle to go with dinner—everything from *Wine X* wired, which pairs wines with music, to the old-school *Wine Spectator*, with wine reviews of the most coveted (and expensive) wines in the world to sip with your fancy food.

The Web is a perfect place to find wine information because you have this kind of variety at your fingertips. Take these two very different tasting notes, for the same wine, from two very different sources:

> "An openly fruity style, floral and spicy, with ripe apple, melon, fig and citrus flavors that are well focused."
> —*Wine Spectator*

> "Like the Spice Girls, this wine is bold, intense, in-your-face, and spicy. But unlike the Spice Girls, it's talented."
> —*Wine X*

Because of the nature of the Internet, I can compare two impressions of this wine before I plunk down the cash to buy it. Thanks to the power of hypertext, I can in minutes make a more informed decision.

Here's another example of the power of the Net: You've got a hot date tonight. Your usual "drink what I like theory" seems a bit too reckless, too chancy. Sure, magazines are shiny, readable, and portable, but how many magazines do you know that will let you search for a good Pinot Noir for under $20 with flavors of cherry to go with the duck breast with fig sauce that you're preparing? Paper and ink just can't do wine selecting justice. There are too many factors, too many variables in making a good wine selection to rely on the linear nature of printed publications.

The answer? Sites like the *Spectator* and *WineToday.com* let you search their vast wine databases with ease and with endless options. Looking for a top-ranked zin from Dry Creek Valley for under $15? No problem. Fill out a search form and wait for the matching wines to roll out.

I can't remember what I had for dinner last night, not to mention what wine I read about that was supposed to be good according to some magazine. When I'm standing in the store staring at hundreds of labels, I get stage fright and hope that something, anything, will stand out.

But if I have a printout of wines I've found on the Net or my Palm Pilot (yes, I'm a techno-geek), I can find a wine in no time and quickly, painlessly, and with a better chance of it being good. Finding a wine site with variety is a first step to finding the information that meets your tastes. These sites provide a good starting point to researching wine on the Internet. From there, you can find just about anything. Just be sure to write it down or print it out for use when you need it.

Wine, Beers, and Spirits of the Net

www.ryerson.ca/~dtudor/wine.htm
Since 1994, this has been one of the most simple, comprehensive, and noncommercial lists of links on the Internet.

Wine Spectator

www.winespectator.com
The venerable old-school publication is also on the Net, with a powerful database of more than 65,000 searchable reviews.

WineToday.com

www.winetoday.com
Wine news and reviews updated constantly with the latest happenings in the U.S. wine scene.

Wine Enthusiast

www.winemag.com
Another wine magazine ported to the Internet. One of the best wine accessories catalogs around.

Wines on the Internet

www.wines.com
A number of wine magazines update their content on this far-reaching site.

Winefiles.com

www.winefiles.com
A searchable list of sites, with site reviews and a "wine crawler" that traverses the Web for wine information.

Wine X Wired

www.winexwired.com

The Internet edition of *Wine X* magazine features past issues along with a searchable data base on wine reviews to educational articles to music and wine pairings.

Epicurious

www.epicurious.com

This Condé Nast site has food and wine databases with great searchability and great articles from top wine and food magazines.

And, of course:

Wine Brats

www.winebrats.org

Stay connected to the latest happenings in the Wine Brat world, with events, chapter information, and links at the Wine Brats' home page.

Skip the Store and Just Order On-line

If you live in an area without a good wine shop, or have a crummy wine selection in grocery stores, try buying on-line. If you combine on-line research of wines with the power of just clicking to buy them, you have entered a new world of wine purchasing. By logging on to a site like Virtual Vineyards (http://www.virtualvin.com), you can educate yourself about the wines they have available, and then with the click of a mouse, pick one to be delivered to your door.

Because laws in some states don't allow wines to be shipped into them, it can be complicated to order wine on the Web. Believe it or not, in some states it is a felony to ship wine directly. Companies like Virtual Vineyards have found ways to legally ship wine into most states, but there can be some supply problems that make it less convenient. However, there are many initiatives under way to lift these restrictions, which will make wine ordering on the Web more efficient. Until then, try these sites.

Virtual Vineyards

www.virtualvin.com
   The most well-known and Web-savvy merchant on the Internet. A unique selection of wines is available backed up by a reliable fulfillment service in most states.

K&L Wines

www.klwines.com
   This San Francisco merchant hosts one of the most comprehensive selections of wines available on the Internet.

Windsor Vineyards

www.windsorvineyards.com
   This site sells their own fantastic wines and allows for customized labels!

Winebid

www.winebid.com
   On-line auction format with rare and collectible wines up for bid.

Free the Grapes

www.freethegrapes.org
   Information on initiatives to change laws in states with restrictions on wine shipping.

Ask and Ye Shall Receive

It can be intimidating to ask the sommelier at a restaurant about a wine. This is where Web-based chat boards can come in handy. If you want to know what wine to buy to impress that woman you invited for dinner tomorrow night, throw the scenario up on a chat board and see what you get.

Sometimes there are other wine aficionados who know the answer. Like the following exchange on the WineRave (www.winerave.com):

Wednesday, October 8, 1997, 7:44 P.M.

I'm an ex–beer drinker who just discovered the whole wine thing pretty recently. I was making a big Italian dinner for this woman I was trying to impress, so I picked up a bottle of red wine and I liked it! A few months later I'm posting on this here conference.

After recommending a few wines based on this experience, someone replied in a message to ask how the plan had worked. The response:

Monday, October 20, 1997, 12:08 P.M.

The ploy with the woman worked beautifully. We're living together now.

If you're afraid of this happening to you, it might be best to blindly pick a wine. If you're not, then try any of these great discussion areas:

WineRave

www.winerave.com
Okay, so I helped build this one, but you will find thousands of postings ranging from pairing wines with rock stars to finding a wine to go with dinner.

Wine Spectator

www.winespectator.com
Solid discussions on a wide variety of topics

WineToday.com

www.winetoday.com
Discussions and content-initiated discussions. Read a review you don't agree with? Post your own.

Wine and Technology Come Together

In the future, it will become easier and easier to find the perfect wine. We're currently relying on a number of valuable resources on the Web, but because of limitations of the Web medium and antiquated shipping laws, we have a long way to go before the full power of the Internet can directly and easily enhance your wine-buying habits.

With that day in mind, consider these very real possibilities:

- You're wheeling your full cart down the wine aisle at the grocery store. A sensor determines what items you have in your cart, and a display screen on the cart handle lists some wine recommendations. "To complement your chicken, the Safeway Sommelier recommends a Kenwood Chardonnay, twenty feet ahead on the bottom shelf."
- Digital paper technology is expected to be developed in the next ten years, which would make it possible for digital wine labels to recommend recipes or display seasonal recommendations. "This wine is perfect for Thanksgiving!"
- Still clueless about what to buy? Log in to the Cyber Sommelier on the Net and ask a real human being for suggestions, twenty-four hours a day, whenever you need the advice. All this for just a few galactic chits.

Becoming a Techno Wine Geek

You can learn more about wine and enhance the whole experience by using the vast resources of the Web. You may find inspiration in a big site like the *Wine Spectator*, or maybe it's some guy in Alabama who has a homepage where he tells you about the wines he likes.

There's a source out there for everyone, and the trick is to find one that you like and that seems consistent with your tastes and lifestyle. You may use the Web for the most simple research into wine, or you may use it to become one of those wine geeks who tries to know everything.

I'm far from a wine expert, but what I have learned by surfing the Web has taught me a tremendous amount about wine. And at the least it's an excuse for this techno-geek to buy one more gadget.

My wine techno-geek status culminated recently while at a business dinner in a small town in Florida. I was surrounded by execs from mostly Southern newspapers, and they turned to me when the time came to pick the wine. As I glanced at the very slim wine list, I was perplexed with what to choose because I wasn't familiar with the quality of the labels they had on the list.

At the risk of looking like a total geek (and self-promoter), I reached into my pocket and pulled out my Palm Pilot hand-held organizer, on which I had installed Wine Master 2.0, a program that allows you to keep a database of your wine cellar or your tasting notes. It also lets you download reviews from WineToday.com.

I simply typed in the name of one of the wines on the list into the "find" function, and the program searched through six hundred wine reviews, finding four reviews of vintages from this winery. We ordered one that had gotten a four-out-of-five-star rating and was designated a "good value" wine. It turned out to be perfect with the meal.

Yes, my colleagues were intrigued, but I'm sure they secretly consider me "that California guy with the wine gadget." You may never become a techno wine geek, but if I see you in a restaurant discreetly pulling out your Palm Pilot and hiding it in the wine list, I'll be sure to say hello.

YOU'VE GOT MAIL

Since we're still on the techno-communications theme here, and Amy Reiley's piece happens to be next, we thought we'd talk about the power of E-mail. If you don't know, our membership growth and communication systems have been driven, for the most part, by E-mail and the Web. Amy is yet another great example. She originally contacted us sometime back in '95 about becoming a member and getting involved. We believe she even attended a few early events. Then she vanished for about a year. Next thing you know she responds to an E-mail blast, saying she's living in Australia, but "keep the E-mails coming!" We did. Jump ahead yet another year and we get an E-mail announcing she's back in the States and she'd like to write for BUNG!online. We responded, "Hey, have we got a project for you." We asked her to update our original list of books and periodicals by our longtime friend and chapter leader Katrina Walker.

—j, j & m

Page by Page, or the Wine Brats' Publication Guide

by Amy Reiley

I never touched a book on wine (except maybe to dust off one of those glossy picture books that sit around on coffee tables) until I began working in the tasting room of a Sonoma County winery. I was twenty-two years old, from the back woods of Pennsylvania. To put it quite simply, I was in over my head.

The first bit of wine salesmanship I learned in my new position was a humbling one. I had to master the phrase "I don't know" and deliver it with a dash of charm and a generous helping of honesty when customers' inquiries exceeded my meager knowledge, a frequent occurrence! The charm factor was especially important when dealing with a winery-frequenting "cork dork," or "wine bozo" (those sixty-something fuzz-headed customers in designer cardigans who only asked questions as a vehicle for showing off their impressive, yet often meaningless, wine vocabulary).

Soon after I mastered the magic little phrase, it became clear that "I don't know" was not a sufficient answer. And so began my eternal quest for wine erudition. Luckily, the tasting room had an admirable wine reference section with which I became intimately acquainted. My wine knowledge may have been slim, but my wine reference knowledge became quite impressive. (All right, I probably wasn't extremely popular with the customers who thought they were asking innocent questions and wound up cornered against a bookcase with the "Wine Nazi" waving leather-bound volumes in their faces. They may not have known what hit 'em, but they always left with the answers to their questions!)

Although I no longer work for a winery, I continue to rely on wine resources for the answers to my own questions. I've accepted that it is okay to say, "I don't know," but it's absurd to remain ignorant. Who knows, maybe someday I will use my knowledge to single-handedly stamp out irresponsible beverage consumption the world over. Or, at least, if by any chance I ever appear on *Jeopardy* and the final round is "Wine Varietals of the Coonawarra . . ." Sometimes you have to dream.

The Wine Brats' Guide to Books

1998 Wine Spectator Magazine's Guide to Great Wine Values $10 and Under
Wine Spectator Press, 1997.

This handy-dandy pocket-sized guide contains reviews of more than 1,200 wines for under $10. Skip the *Spectator's* self-promoting introduction and plunge right into the reviews. Featuring tastings from around the world, this annually updated edition is superb for planning Brat-style dinner parties. Drink, save, and be merry!

$9.95

Winemaking: Recipes, Equipment, and Techniques for Making Wine at Home
by Stanley F. and Dorothy Anderson
Harcourt Brace Jovanovich, 1989.

Even a beginner could make a case of wine with this guide. Instructions are broken down with easy-to-follow tables and quick-reference charts. Recipes include various fruit wines, fruit-juice-concentrate wines, champagnes, and liqueurs. Sections are devoted to issues of safety and sanitation and in-depth equipment discussions for more advanced winemakers. There are no guarantees that your attempts will be drinkable. But with this book, you'll have fun trying.

$21.00

The Surreal Gourmet: Real Food for Pretend Chefs
by The Surreal Gourmet a.k.a. Bob Blumer
Chronicle Books, 1992

Here is even more wisdom from our friendly neighborhood vegetable-headed chef. Complete with full-color surreal art, this book is great for those evenings you get a wacky inclination to throw on the chef's hat. All recipes can be assembled in less than thirty minutes and come with recommendations for wine as well as music to cook by—a multimedia affair! What's not to love about this book, which even includes a list of ten ways to avoid making dessert (use your imagination).

$14.95

(Also by Blumer are *The Surreal Gourmet Entertains* and, coming in the fall of 1999, *Off the Eaten Path: Inspired Recipes and Culinary Adventures.* For more info, call 1-800 FAUX-PAS.)

Wine Lover's Companion
by Sharon Tyler and Ron Herbst
Barron's, 1995

Here is the wine drinker's answer to Webster's Dictionary. From abboccato to zucchero, more than 3,500 definitions await your perusal. Memorize a few humdingers for your next cocktail party. (The pronunciation guide will keep you from tripping over those Italian vowels.) Or just keep the companion around to help decode French labels.

$12.95

The World Atlas of Wine
by Hugh Johnson
Simon & Schuster, 1994

This volume is one for the coffee table. Johnson's beautiful hardcover maps all the significant wine regions of the world, illustrating the relationship between geography and wine qualities. It is a classic reference with breakdowns of soil content, vineyard elevations, and photos that will make you want to jump on the next plane to France . . . or Australia . . . or Chile . . . or . . . !

Pricey at $50, but you have to splurge once in a while.

Wine Basics: A Quick and Easy Guide
by Dewey Markham, Jr.
John Wiley and Sons, Inc., 1993

This wine guide for "adults" is one of the few that actually manages to avoid pretensions. Although it is yet another guide to the basics, *Wine Basics* is a fairly fast read and a good reference to keep on hand. It addresses some tricky topics like restaurant winespeak and navigating those intimidating, zillion-page wine lists.

$14.95

Wine for Dummies (Second Edition)
by Ed McCarthy and Mary Ewing-Mulligan
IDG Books Worldwide, 1998

Here is the book that is not afraid to address all the "dumb questions" you've been too embarrassed to ask. This witty text will walk through the sometimes intimidating road to enjoying wine. From the wine shop to the table, this manual is packed with information geared toward every level of wine drinker. Cute icons add entertainment value. IDG also prints more in-depth *Dummies* guides for white varietals, reds, and buying wine.

$19.99

In Praise of Wine: An Offering of Hearty Toasts, Quotations, Witticisms, Proverbs and Poetry Throughout History
by Joni G. McNutt, Foreword by Robert Mondavi
Capra, 1993

The title says it all. (Try repeating it five times, fast.) For those of you who aren't running to the bookstore already, they threw in a few drinking songs for added enticement. You could build an entire evening—heck, try a week—of entertainment around this book! Besides, you should never leave home without a choice witticism.

$12.95

Harvests of Joy: My Passion for Excellence; How the Good Life Became Great Business
by Robert Mondavi
Harcourt Brace Jovanovich, 1998

This autobiography describes in lurid detail how Mondavi built one of the world's greatest wine empires. It is a fairly candid reflection on the "godfather of wine." Pick it up for a good read, and you may even learn a thing or two about good business policy.

$27.00 (look for the cheaper paperback edition due out by September of 1999)

Parker's Wine Buyer's Guide (Fourth Edition)
by Robert M. Parker, Jr.
Simon & Schuster/Fireside, 1995

Known by some in the industry as "God," the author of *The Wine Advo-*

cate also produces a frequently updated manual evaluating recent vintages. Although wine is all a matter of taste, Parker's taste buds are considered some of the best in the business. He puts together one of the most extensive guides available, including tasting notes on more than 4,500 wines. You may need a forklift to pick it up, but you're guaranteed to pick a good wine with the aid of this book.

$25.00

Tasting Pleasure: Confessions of a Wine Lover
by Jancis Robinson
Viking Penguin, 1997

The diva of wine writing, Jancis Robinson, exposes her personal side in this series of reflections on her twenty years of industry experience. Wine guru becomes human being as she shares pleasures and mishaps in an extremely intimate style. This is a woman who is not afraid to proclaim, "I don't want to manage my wine cellar. I want to drink it."

$24.95

The Frugal Gourmet Cooks with Wine
by Jeff Smith
Avon, 1988

Yes, TV's favorite chef even has a wine book. If you can get past the cheesy cover shot of Smith grinning over an empty pot, you'll find this book is packed full of cooking hints and wine-pairing ideas. His practical instructions range from such basics as how to chop vegetables (as opposed to fingers) to choosing the right wineglasses for your next dinner party. The recipes are simple and include wine varietal recommendations. Smith's book will soon have you de-boning duck, de-glazing pans, and de-lighting guests. Bon appetit.

$6.99

Windows on the World Complete Wine Course
by Kevin Zraly
Sterling Publishing Co., Inc., 1998

The founder of the Windows on the World Wine School, Zraly is one of those rare experts who can actually make study entertaining. A sensibly arranged self-study course, this book will take you through major wine regions, addressing such topics as wine-buying strategies, food and wine pairing, restaurant wine lists, and regional styles from around the world. It is down-to-earth and packed with information for enthusiasts and professionals.

$23.95

The Wine Brats' Guide to Periodicals

Because wine is an ever-changing business, periodicals are the only means for keeping entirely current. We've assembled some of our favorite information sources, roasted the magazines with high snob appeal, and sniffed out the best. Highly recommended are those selections given Nose Awards—Golden, Silver, or Bronze—because when you're a Brat, the nose will know a winner.

The Art of Eating Quarterly Letter

Highly praised, uncompromising, unconventional quarterly offers thorough and authoritative essays on food and wine subjects. For serious amateurs and professionals. (Whatever happened to the art of eating daily? Do not try this at home! *Eating Quarterly* should be approached only by professional refugees and illusionists.)

1 year (4 issues) subscription: $30; sample issue: $7.50

The Art of Eating
P.O. Box 242
Peacham, VT 05862
Tel. (800) 495-3944
Fax (802) 592-3400

California Grapevine

Tasting notes and critical evaluation on new-release, premium California wines and current vintage Bordeaux, plus essays, book reviews, and major competition results. (This publication is well regarded by the wine industry for its wine rankings, based on major competitions. A bit of attitude is thrown in and reviews, which, incidentally do not carry much weight, can be inconsistent—medium well on Snob Factor.)

1 year (6 issues) subscription: $35; sample issue: $6

California Grapevine
P.O. Box 22152
San Diego, CA 92192
Tel. (619) 457-4818
Fax (619) 457-3676

Connoisseurs' Guide to California Wine
Reviews the best of California and other West Coast wines. Highly respected for its coverage of California wines. Uses the star system but most readers refer to it as the "puff" (as in cigar). Easy to read, with some cute symbols to round out the details. A great resource guide to boot—Golden Nose Award.
    1 year (12 issues) subscription: $50

Connoisseurs' Guide
651 Tarryton Isle
P.O. Box V
Alameda, CA 94501
Tel. (510) 865-3150
E-mail: cgcw@ad.com

International Wine Cellar
Covers everything from soup to nuts. Great tasting notes and vintage evaluations, interviews, technical topics, controversial issues, regular coverage of excellent inexpensive wines, and recipes, too. (Formerly *The New York Wine Cellar* [or the artist formerly known as . . .].) Done in an approachable and fun style with a dab of humor here and there. Snobless, nothing to sneeze at—a Nose Award Honorable Mention.
    1 year (6 issues) subscription: $48

Tanzer Business Communications, Inc.
P.O. Box 20021
Cherokee Station
New York, NY 10021
Tel. 1-800-WINE-505

Northwest Palate
Direct from the Pacific Northwest, this publication focuses on the wine, food, and lifestyles of the area. Interesting reading, color photos, wine re-

views, and tasty recipes, too. (This is an unpretentious magazine, and with plenty of great wines to focus on, they don't limit their reviews exclusively to the Pacific Northwest. It's a wine publication with a country, down-home feeling. Golly gee!)

　　1 year (6 issues) subscription: $21; sample issue: $5

Northwest Palate
P.O. Box 10860
Portland, OR 97210
Tel. (800) 398-7842
Fax (503) 222-5312
E-mail: nwpalate@teleport.com

Passport to Savings
Wineries from A to Z that are waiving tasting fees and offer special discounts (5 percent to 30 percent) to card members. Includes information to help plan your next trip to the California Wine Country. Call for a free brochure. (Discounts certainly are a plus if they can help you enjoy more of your favorites.)

　　1 year/2 person booklet: $25
　　($2 postage; CA add 7.25% sales tax)

V.I.T. Wine Tasting Card
Box 689
Napa, CA 94559
Tel. (800) 218-WINE

Quarterly Pocketlist of Top-Rated Wines for $15 or Less
Academic-style grading system based on the ratings of ten major publications. Alternates focus from U.S. wine to imports. More than six hundred wines rated per issue. Pocket-sized. (With the size factor as a bonus, this guide is a good thing. No need to spend an arm and a leg to enjoy good wine—Bronze Nose Award.)

　　1 year/$25.95

Grapevine Associates
P.O. Box 6003
Oxford, OH 45056

Tel. (800) 524-1005
Fax (513) 524-1055
E-mail: bettyhuffman@winepockettlist.com
Internet: www.winepocketlist.com

The Quarterly Review of Wines
Covers a wide range of wine information from all over the globe, from regions, varietals, restaurants, and food pairings to individual and company profiles. (Appeals more to upper than crust, but the information is still worthwhile. What the heck, it's only four times a year.)
 1 year (4 issues) subscription: $14.95

Q.R.W., Inc.
24 Garfield Avenue
Winchester, MA 01890
Tel. (781) 729-7132
Internet: www.qrw.com

Restaurant Wine
Packs a lot into a small package. It includes wine trends, restaurant profiles, special reports, and consistent, international reviews. (Respected by wineries but unpretentious. The magazine is geared toward the obvious—restaurants, but is written in a fun and comprehensive style that will have you reading from cover to cover—Golden Nose Award.)
 1 year (6 issues) subscription: $99

Wine Profits, Inc.
P.O. Box 222
Napa, CA 94559-0222
Tel. (707) 224-4777
Fax (707) 224-6740
Internet: www.restaurantwine.com

Robert M. Parker, Jr.'s, The Wine Advocate
Covers formal tasting information with a precise rating system for reviews that are fair yet sometimes predictable. Highly revered, feared, and respected within the wine industry, a.k.a. "God" on the East Coast, Parker

has been known to make or break a wine. Picking up the pieces can get messy! (Overcooked on Snob but high credibility factor makes for good BRAT glancing—feast with caution.)

1 year (6 issues) subscription: $45

The Wine Advocate, Inc.
P.O. Box 311
Monkton, MD 21111
Tel. (410) 329-6477
Fax (410) 357-4504

Touring and Tasting
Profiles major wine regions around the U.S. Information includes winery profiles, tasting recommendations, maps, and directions. Beware: This publication relies heavily on advertising and may be duly influenced! Restaurant and hotel recommendations are reliable but high on Snob Appeal. (With so much wine and so little time, this publication makes a handy starting point for exploring some great regions.)

1 year (2 issues) subscription: $9

Touring and Tasting
123 W. Padre
Suite B
Santa Barbara, CA 93105
Tel. (805) 563-7585
Fax (805) 563-9985
E-mail: tastingroom@touringandtasting.com
Internet: www.touringandtasting.com

The Underground Wine Journal
Unbiased and comprehensive reviews of world's finest wines in a style that is no-nonsense. It is geared toward "serious wine drinkers," with advice ranging from cellaring recommendations to additions to rarities collections. For those of us who only collect what we can drink in a week, this straightforward publication is still a good read and a great education on how a "serious wine drinker" lives—Bronze Nose Award.

1 year (6 issues) subscription: $48; sample issue: $4

The Underground Wine Journal
1654 Amberwood Dr.
Suite A
So. Pasadena, CA 91030
Tel. (262) 441-6617
Fax (262) 441-6765
E-mail: winejournal@earthlink.net
Internet: www.ugwinejournal.com

Vintage Publications
Offers two colorful, full-size annual guidebooks: *Napa Valley Guide* and *Sonoma County Guide*. Up-to-date maps and guides to wineries, lodging, events, ballooning, golf, parks and campgrounds, historic places, and points of interest. Full restaurant menus and reviews are also included. With too much to do and too little time, it's useful to keep this guide around.
    Send $5.95 for each book plus $3 shipping.

Vintage Publications
2929 Conifer Ct.
Napa, CA 94558
Tel. (800) 651-8953
Internet: www.winecountry.com/guidebooks

Wine Enthusiast
Highly respected, high-gloss monthly journal includes extensive wine ratings from around the world and lists "best buys" from featured regions. Cover stories tend to be geared toward the Rolls-Royce and polo set, but overall, the magazine is packed with enough practical information and enticing images to make anyone a wine enthusiast.
14 monthly issues: $19.95

Wine Enthusiast
P.O. Box 420235
Palm Coast, FL 32142-0235
Tel. (800) 829-5901
Internet: www.wineenthusiast.com

WineMaker

For creating your own great wines. Published annually, *WineMaker* offers articles on bottling, finding the best fruit, and choosing the best kit. The advertisements can be great leads for getting the goods you need.
$4.95
Tel. (530) 758-4596
E-mail: byo@byo.com

Wine Spectator

Articles, restaurant reviews, profiles, and spotlights on varietals and regions with some interesting commentaries in between. Not to mention the infamous "Buyer's Guide" in every issue, which, like Robert Parker, can make or break a wine. This is a highbrow publication that carries a lot of weight in the industry. It can be a great resource if you can get past all of the self-indulgence.

1 year (24 weeks) subscription: $40; 1 year on-line data base subscription: $29.95

Wine Spectator
P.O. Box 37367
Boone, IA 50037-0367
(800) 752-7799
E-mail: winespec@mshanken.com
Internet: www.winespectator.com

Wine & Spirits

In-depth coverage of, you guessed it, Wine & Spirits. Great articles on specific varietals, spirits, and regions, with good reviews and updates on the beverage industry. (Interesting information resources you can draw from, tasteful and straightforward—Silver Nose.)

1 year (8 issues) subscription: $26

Wine & Spirits
2 West 32nd St.
Suite 601
New York, NY 10001
Tel. (212) 695-4660
E-mail: winespir@aol.com

Wine X

What do wine, women, and rock and roll have in common? If anybody knows, it is the creators of *Wine X.* Their magazine breaks all the rules in an attempt to demystify what many people find to be an intimidating beverage. No self-indulgent reports on unpronounceable, let alone affordable, verticals here. This mag is packed cover to cover with a slightly bizarre mix of information from industry events, "X-rated" wines, and irreverent advice from the Surreal Gourmet, to music news and even a horoscope for vino-loving astrologer types — No Snobs Allowed, Golden Nose Award.

1 year (6 issues) subscription: $18; sample issue: $5.00

Wine X
4184 Sonoma Mountain Rd.
Santa Rosa, CA 95404
Tel. (888) 229-4639
E-mail: winex@wco.com
Internet: www.winexwired.com

Wines & Vines

"The Authoritative Voice of the Grape and Wine Industry Since 1919." Includes industry, technical, business, and event listings. Also produces an annual directory listing all North American wineries, which includes winery maps, brand reference index, and roster of industry players. (This handy resource is geared toward the winegrowing and winemaking community and contains access to interesting information. Not really recommended for consumers; however, we must add that the publishers and staff at *Wines & Vines* have been steadfast supporters of the Wine Brats' cause from Day One. My, what visionaries!)

1 year (13 issues) subscription: $32.50; directory: $75; sample issue: $5

Wines & Vines
1800 Lincoln Ave.
San Rafael, CA 94901
Tel. (415) 453-9700
Fax (415) 453-2517
E-mail: geninfo@winesandvines.com

MAKES YOUR MOUTH WANT TO WATER!

Our varietals' guide is yet another collaboration between several members of the coalition. Initially, we wanted to keep this straight-forward and focus on the basic varietals you might encounter in America's wine aisles. Then we went into the world's wine regions earlier in the book and opened the proverbial can of grapes. Yes, there are thousands of varietals. Though we tried to keep it under control, we also felt inspired to inspire you. The key here, which we have stated throughout the book, is that wine is an exploration. We hope that this list is seen as it is meant to be viewed, as opening the door to a world of opportunity.

—j, j & m

Variety Is the Spice of Life, or Our Guide to Most of the Wine Varietals You're Likely to Encounter

by the Wine Brats Coalition

White Varietals

Chardonnay (shar-dun-<u>nay</u>)

A white grape believed to be a variant of the Pinot Blanc grape; also known as Arnoison, Aubaine, Beaunois, Melon Blanc, and Melon d' Arbois. Grown primarily in:

- Australia
- Canada
- France—Burgundy, Alsace, Champagne
- New Zealand
- South Africa
- United States

Best Climate: Cool.

Winemaking: Usually 100 percent varietal. In Australia it's sometimes blended with Semillon and labeled Semillon/Chardonnay. Most Chardonnays spend time in oak, either barrel-fermented and/or aged. Most undergo malolactic fermentation (ML) to soften the acidity of the wine.

Nose: Tropical fruit (pineapple, papaya, mango), apple, pears, citrus, fig, melon, vanilla, butter/butterscotch, oak.

Mouth: Medium to full body, good acidity. Round on the palate when malolactic percentage is high.

*Note: Chardonnay is the most popular wine in the United States. It is preferred even more often than white Zinfandel.

Chenin Blanc (<u>shen</u>-nin <u>blahnk</u>)

A white grape used to make dry to medium-sweet wines.
Grown primarily in:

- France
- South Africa
- United States—California

Climate: Cool to warm.
Winemaking: Chenin Blanc makes fruity, dry to medium-sweet wines made to be drunk young. It usually benefits from little or no oak aging.
Nose: Fruity (peach, apricot, pear, citrus) with light floral (honeysuckle, citrus blossoms) notes.
Mouth: Medium-bodied, fruit-forward with tangy acids.

Gewürztraminer (geh-<u>verts</u>-trah-<u>mee</u>-ner)

A spicier version of the Traminer grape, which it has replaced for the most part.
Grown primarily in:

- Australia
- Austria
- Canada
- France—Alsace
- Germany
- Italy—northern
- Hungary
- United States

Best Climate: Cool.
Winemaking: Like Riesling, this varietal can vary from dry to supersweet. Most wines are fermented and aged in stainless steel. Some see oak.
Nose: Spicy, floral, citrus, peach, nectarine, apricot.
Mouth: Light to medium body, spicy. Full-bodied when made sweet. Medium to strong acids.
*Note: *Gewürz* translated from German means "spice."

Muscadet (muss-ka-<u>day</u>)

Also called Melon de Bourgogne. A white grape used to make dry white wine.

Grown primarily in:

- France
- United States

Climate: Cool to warm.
Winemaking: Muscadet makes dry wine and usually benefits from little or no oak aging.
Nose: Light floral aromas (citrus blossoms, perfume) with citrus (grapefruit, lemon/lime), peach, and melon fruits.
Mouth: Medium body, crisp acids, and fruit-forward.

Pinot Blanc (<u>pee</u>-no <u>blahnk</u>)

A white grape. According to some experts, it's not actually in the Pinot family. According to others, it is.

Grown primarily in:

- Canada
- France—Alsace
- Germany
- United States

Best Climate: Cool.
Winemaking: Pinot Blanc is usually vinified the same way Chardonnay is. Since it's slightly more delicate in body than Chardonnay, ML and oak treatments are generally less.
Nose: Spicy, floral, tropical fruit, citrus, apple.
Mouth: Light to medium body, fruit, spicy. Medium to strong acids.
*Note: Much of the Pinot Blanc planted in the United States is actually Melon de Bourgogne. There are very few vineyards that have the true varietal.

Pinot Grigio (<u>pee</u>-no <u>gree</u>-zjee-oh)

Also called Pinot Gris. A white grape used to make white table wine. Grown primarily in:

- Italy
- France
- Germany
- United States

Climate: Cool to warm.
Winemaking: Pinot Gris can make dry to semisweet wines and usually benefits from moderate to no oak influence.
Nose: Citrus (grapefruit, lemon/lime) and melon fruits with floral (citrus blossoms) elements.
Mouth: Light to medium body, high acids, and usually simple.

Sauvignon Blanc (<u>sah</u>-vin-yon <u>blahnk</u>)

A white grape used to make sweet or dry white wine. Also known as Blanc Fumé in the Loire and Fumé Blanc in California.
Grown primarily in:

- Australia
- France — Bordeaux, Sauternes, Loire
- United States

Best Climate: Warm to hot.
Winemaking: In Bordeaux, Sauvignon Blanc is a blending grape with Semillon. White Bordeaux blends average 80 percent Semillon, 20 percent Sauvignon Blanc. In Sauternes the blends are the same as Bordeaux, but the wines are made sweet. In California, Sauvignon Blanc is usually blended with 5 percent to 15 percent Semillon.

Most Sauvignon Blanc wines are fermented and aged in stainless steel. Some see a little oak aging. Malolactic fermentation is not common, but can be found in some wines.

Nose: Citrus (lemon/lime, grapefruit), gooseberry, floral, grassy, spring flowers.
Mouth: Light to medium body. Crisp acids.
***Note:** Name means "savage" or "wild white."

Riesling (<u>rees</u>-ling)

A white grape, the principal grape of Germany; also important in Alsace and Austria. Late ripening, modest bearer, medium-sized grapes. Also known as Johannisberg Riesling and White Riesling.

Grown primarily in:

- Australia
- Austria
- Canada
- France—Alsace
- Germany
- United States

Best Climate: Cool.
Winemaking: Rieslings can vary from bone-dry (Alsace) to supersweet (icewines). Most are fermented and aged in stainless steel. Some see oak aging.
Nose: Grapefruit, apricot, peach, pear, pineapple, nectarine, floral, dried flowers, honeyed, honeysuckle, perfumed.
Mouth: Light to medium body when dry. Medium to full body, rich and viscous when made as a sweet dessert wine.
***Note:** Riesling crossed with Sylvaner produces Müller-Thurgau (Franken Riesling).

Semillon (sem-ee-<u>yon</u>)

The principal grape of white Bordeaux and Sauternes. Used to make sweet or dry wines. Usually blended with Sauvignon Blanc. Also called Chevrier.

Grown primarily in:

- Australia
- France—Bordeaux, Sauternes, Loire
- New Zealand
- South Africa
- United States

Climate: Warm to hot.
Winemaking: Usually blended with Sauvignon Blanc, sometimes with Chardonnay. Mostly fermented and aged in stainless steel, some wines see oak.
Nose: Figs, citrus, honey, floral, nutty.
Mouth: Light to medium body, medium to strong acids. Full-bodied when made sweet.
***Note:** In Australia this is also known as Hunter Riesling. In South Africa it's called Groensdruift (green grape).

Seyval Blanc (say-voll <u>blahnk</u>)

A white French hybrid grape used to make white table wines. Valued for its winter hardiness.

Grown primarily in:

- Canada
- England
- United States—Eastern and Midwest

Climate: Cool to cold.
Winemaking: Seyval Blanc is usually made in a dry style, producing a simple table wine. It can benefit from barrel aging, but is usually bottled straight from the tank.
Nose: Citrus (grapefruit, lemon/lime, peach) fruits and floral (citrus blossoms, honeysuckle) elements.
Mouth: Light to medium body, high acids, and usually simple.

Vidal Blanc (<u>vee</u>-doll <u>blahnk</u>)

A white French hybrid grape used to make white table wine. Valued for its winter hardiness.

Grown primarily in:

• Canada
• United States—Eastern and Midwest

Climate: Cool to cold.
Winemaking: Vidal can be made in a range of styles of sweetness, from simple table wine to icewine. If dry, it's best consumed right away. If made into icewine, it can age gracefully for ten-plus years.
Nose: Dry—citrus (grapefruit, lemon/lime) fruits and floral (citrus blossoms, honeysuckle) elements.

Icewine—sweet ripe fig, citrus fruits, honey, nuts, and floral essences.
Mouth: Dry—light to medium body, high acids, and usually simple.

Icewine—rich, supersweet, and full-bodied.

Viognier (vee-ohn-<u>yay</u>)

A white grape, whose aroma and flavor are often described as a cross between Chardonnay and Gewürztraminer. One of the "Rhône" varietals. Used in making white Rhône wines and often blended into red Châteauneuf-du-Pape wines.

Grown primarily in:

• Canada
• France—Rhône
• United States

Best Climate: Mild.
Winemaking: Viognier benefits from a bit of oak to balance its abundance of fruit, so most wines see some barrel fermentation and barrel aging.
Nose: Spicy, floral, tropical fruit, citrus, apricot, apple, peach.
Mouth: Medium body, fruity, spicy. Medium to strong acids.

*Note: Viognier is part of the Rhône movement sweeping the U.S. Some wineries, for example Zaca Mesa, are blending Viognier in with their red "Rhône" blends as done in Châteauneuf-du-Pape.

Red Varietals

Alicante Bouschet (all-e-con-tay boo-shay)

A black grape that produces deep red wines.
Grown primarily in:

- Australia
- Corsica
- France
- Italy
- North Africa
- South Africa
- United States

Best Climate: Cool.
Winemaking: In California Alicante Bouschet is grown widely in the Central Valley and usually blended into inexpensive wines. However, a few small wineries in the Golden State produce it as a varietal wine. It is also an authorized variety for the production of Port. Widely grown throughout France and Corsica.
Nose: Dark plum fruit, overripe black grapes.
Mouth: Full body, low tannins, delivers a ruby-Port–like sweetness.

Baco Noir (bah-ko nwar)

A red French hybrid grape known for its winter hardiness. Usually 100 percent (not blended with other grapes).
Grown primarily in:

- Canada
- France
- United States—Eastern and Midwest

Climate: Cool to cold.
Winemaking: Baco Noir can be made in a light, almost nouveau style to a deep, rich red wine. Can benefit from barrel aging.
Nose: Game, red (cherry, berry, plum) fruit with leather, earth, and spice.
Mouth: Light to full body, good acids, black cherry, black plum, spice, and an earthy, gamy finish.

Barbera (bar-<u>bear</u>-uh)

An important red grape grown in the Piedmont region of Italy.
Grown primarily in:

- Italy
- South America
- United States
- Yugoslavia

Climate: Hot.
Winemaking: Varietal.
Nose: Blackberry, cherry, spice, chocolate.
Mouth: Full body, high in both acids and tannins.
*Note: This is a wine that ages for a long period of time and is the most planted grape in Italy.

Cabernet Franc (cab-er-<u>nay</u> frahnk)

A red grape used in the Loire to make red Chinon, and used in Bordeaux generally as a blending grape. Also called Bouchet or Gros-Bouchet in Saint-Emilion and Pomerol, Bouchy in Madiran, and Breton in the Saumur and Touraine (Loire Valley).
Grown primarily in:

- Australia
- Canada
- Chile
- France
- New Zealand

- South Africa
- United States

Climate: Warm.

Winemaking: Generally used as a blending grape in Cabernet Sauvignon and Merlot. On its own it tends to be "hollow," so small amounts of Cabernet Sauvignon and Merlot are added. It benefits from some oak aging and aging in general.

Nose: Floral, red and black fruits, plum, spice, coffee/tea, oak.

Mouth: Medium to full body. Firm but round tannins with a generally slightly softer palate than Cabernet.

*****Note:** Cabernet Franc is known for lending a liveliness to both the color and nose of Cabernet Sauvignon blends.

Cabernet Sauvignon (cab-er-nay so-vin-yon]

A red grape used in making red Bordeaux and varietal wines throughout the world.

Grown primarily in:

- Australia
- Canada
- Chile
- France
- New Zealand
- South Africa
- United States

Climate: Warm to hot.

Winemaking: Cabernet is generally blended with small parts of Merlot, Cabernet Franc, Petit Verdot, and Malbec. It definitely benefits from oak aging (and aging in general).

Nose: Red (cherry, raspberry) and black (blackberry, wild berry) fruits, pepper spice, chocolate, coffee/tea, oak.

Mouth: Medium to full body, tannic (astringent), and usually complex.

*****Note:** Considered to be "King" and most noble of all grapes. Is one of the red grapes permitted to be used in American red Meritage wines.

Gamay (ga-<u>may</u>)

A common grape grown in Burgundy and several other regions, especially used to make Beaujolais wines. It was probably named after the village of Gamay in the Côte du Beaune. Also called Gamay Noir a jus Blanc.

Grown primarily in:

- Austria
- France—Beaujolais

Climate: Cool.
Winemaking: Made generally the same way Pinot Noir is—with a gentle hand. Is usually 100 percent varietal.
Nose: Berry, fresh, sweet fruit.
Mouth: Fruity, light to medium body, medium acids.
***Note:** A very light, fruity style of this wine is Beaujolais Nouveau, which should be consumed within six to eight months after bottling.

Gamay Beaujolais (ga-<u>may</u> <u>boe</u>-joe-lay)

Not the true Gamay grape of France, but rather a clone or strain of Pinot Noir.

Grown primarily in:

- United States

Climate: Cool.
Winemaking: Made generally the same way Pinot Noir is—with a gentle hand. Is usually 100 percent varietal.
Nose: Berry, fresh, sweet fruit.
Mouth: Fruity, light to medium body, medium acids.
***Note:** It is now thought that Gamay Beaujolais (Napa Gamay) is the Valdiguie grape of southern France.

Grignolino (Green-ya-<u>lee</u>-no)

A red grape used to make dry red wine.
Grown primarily in:

- Italy
- California

Climate: Warm.
Winemaking: Grignolino makes dry red wines made to be drunk young. It usually benefits from little or no oak aging.
Nose: Fruity (cranberry, citrus, and pink grapefruit) with light floral notes.
Mouth: Medium body, crisp acids, and tangy fruit.

Malbec (mall-beck)

The small red grape known as Cot, Cahors, or Auxerrois in Cahors; the Cot in the Loire Valley; and the Pressac in Saint-Emilion.

Grown primarily in:

- Argentina
- Australia
- France
- Italy
- United States

Climate: Warm to hot.
Winemaking: Usually used in blends with Cabernet Sauvignon. In the Loire it's blended with Tannat. Produced the same way as Cabernet Sauvignon. Benefits from some oak aging.
Nose: Red and black fruits, earthy, truffles, dark chocolate.
Mouth: Full body, medium tannins, has texture.
***Note:** Known as the "Black Wine" due to its deep color. Accounts for two-thirds of Argentina's red wines.

Marechal Foch (marsh-all foash)

A red French hybrid named after a famous French World War I general. Valued for its winter hardiness.

Grown primarily in:

- Canada
- United States—Eastern and Midwest

Climate: Cool to cold.

Winemaking: Marechal Foch ripens early. It can benefit from barrel aging, but is mostly bottled straight from the tank. It's sometimes produced using carbonic maceration.

Nose: Red (cherry, plum) fruit with light spice, leather, earth, and a hint of game.

Mouth: Light to medium body, good acids, red cherry, black plum, spice, and an earthy finish.

Merlot (mur-low)

The principal red grape from Pomerol and Saint-Emilion in Bordeaux. Grown primarily in:

- Australia
- Canada
- Chile
- France
- New Zealand
- South Africa
- United States

Climate: Warm.

Winemaking: Like Cabernet Sauvignon, Merlot is usually blended with the other "Bordeaux" varietals (Cabernet Sauvignon, Cabernet Franc, Petit Verdot, Malbec). It benefits from oak aging and aging in general.

Nose: Red and black fruits, plum, spice, coffee/tea, oak.

Mouth: Medium to full body. Mild tannins with a generally softer, fleshier palate than Cabernet.

*Note: Merlot is the most widely planted grape in Bordeaux. It is the principal grape used to make the world-famous Chateau Petrus. It is the fastest-growing varietal wine in the United States.

Nebbiolo (neh-bee-oh-low)

An important red grape grown in the Piedmont and Lombardy regions of Italy. The principal grape used to make Barolo and Barbaresco wines.

Grown primarily in:

- Italy
- South America
- United States

Climate: Hot.
Winemaking: Varietal as Barolo and Gratiana Barbaresco, in United States as Nebbiolo.
Nose: Red fruits, nutty, cedar, spicy, mint.
Mouth: Full body, high tannins, and acids.
*****Note:** The three styles in Italy are very different: Barolo, Barbaresco, and Gratiana.

Petit Verdot (peh-<u>teet</u> ver-<u>doe</u>)

A red grape used to blend with Cabernet Sauvignon and Merlot. Grown primarily in:

- Australia
- France
- United States

Climate: Hot (typically last varietal to be harvested).
Winemaking: In France and California, it's often blended with Cabernet Sauvignon and Merlot for color. Small amounts are grown in Australia.
Nose: Distinct, minty, musky, black cherry.
Mouth: Full body, firm tannins, felty, has texture.
*****Note:** One of the rarest and least-planted varietals in California.

Petite Sirah (peh-<u>teet</u> sir-<u>rah</u>)

A red grape grown in California believed to be related to the Durif grape of France. Is not the same grape as Syrah, although both wines are similar in flavor and texture.

Grown primarily in:

- United States

Climate: Warm to hot.

Winemaking: Generally produces a hearty wine that's capable of aging awhile in oak. Sometimes blended with small amounts of Zinfandel and Cabernet Sauvignon.

Nose: Blackberry, currants, spice, herbs.

Mouth: Full body, good tannins, low acids, big red wine with a lingering finish.

*Note: Used in blending for its depth of color and texture. As a varietal it is often confused with Syrah.

Pinot Meunier (<u>pee</u>-no mun-<u>yay</u>)

A red grape used in making champagne and sparkling wines. Sometimes bottled as a varietal.

Grown primarily in:

- France
- Germany
- Switzerland
- United States

Climate: Cool.

Winemaking: Used mostly as a blending grape for rosé and champagne/ sparkling wines. Is generally treated the same as Pinot Noir—with a gentle hand.

Nose: Cherry, berry, melon, fig, pepper spice.

Mouth: Light body, good acids.

*Note: Most widely grown grape of the Champagne region of France. The name Meunier means "miller" in French, and the grape is so named because the underside of the leaves is powdery white, like flour.

Pinot Noir (<u>pee</u>-no <u>nwa</u>)

The famous red grape used to make dry red wine and sparkling wines. Also called Noirien, Savagnin Noir and other names in France, Spatburgunder and Blauer Burgunder in Germany, Rotclevner in Switzerland, and Pinot Nero in Italy.

Grown primarily in:

- Australia
- Canada
- France—Burgundy, Champagne
- Germany
- New Zealand
- United States

Climate: Cool.
Winemaking: Pinot Noir is a very delicate grape, so winemaking has to be gentle. Benefits from oak aging.
Nose: Cherry, berry, pepper spice, earth, herbal, cinnamon, tea/coffee.
Mouth: Light to medium body, good acids, mild tannins, complex.
***Note:** Pinot Noir means "Pine Cone Black." Considered to be the most demanding grape to grow and vinify. There are reported to be at least 150 clones of Pinot Noir.

Sangiovese (san-gea-vesay)

An important red grape grown in the Tuscany region of Italy. It's the principal grape used in making Chianti.

Grown primarily in:

- Italy
- United States

Climate: Warm to hot.
Winemaking: Used as the primary grape in Chianti, it's blended with a variety of other red Italian varietals. In the "Super Tuscans" (and in California wines) it's blended with Cabernet Sauvignon and benefits from some oak aging.

Nose: Medium spice, rich red fruit, milk chocolate.
Mouth: Medium to full body, firm acids, medium tannins.
*Note: Name literally means "Blood of Jove" or "Blood of Christ."

Syrah (sih-<u>rah</u>)

A red grape grown in the Rhône region of France used in making Hermitage, Côte-Rotie, and Châteauneuf-du-Pape wine. Also known as Shiraz in Australia and Hermitage in South Africa. Is not the same as Petite Sirah, although both wines are similar in flavor and texture.

Grown primarily in:

- Australia
- France
- South Africa
- United States

Climate: Warm to hot.
Winemaking: Generally produces a hearty wine that's capable of aging a while in oak. In the United States, it's sometimes blended with small amounts of Zinfandel and Cabernet Sauvignon.
Nose: Blackberry, currants, spice, herbs.
Mouth: Full body, good tannins, low acids, big red wine with a lingering finish.
*Note: This is the grape used for making Penfolds's famous Grange Hermitage wine. It is often confused with Petite Sirah.

Zinfandel (<u>zin</u>-fin-dell)

A red grape grown only in California. Produces both dry and sweet (dessert and Port) wines.

Grown primarily in:

- United States

Climate: Hot.

Winemaking: Usually made 100 percent varietal, but is sometimes blended with other reds, such as Petite Sirah. Benefits from some oak aging.

Nose: Raspberry, cherry, wild berry, briar, pepper spice, coffee/tea, herbs.

Mouth: Medium to full body, spicy, medium tannins.

*Note: It was recently discovered through DNA testing that Zinfandel is related to Primitivo.

Wine Mumbo Jumbo, or Wine Terms and Definitions

Acidity—One of wine's most crucial components. Necessity for aging wines. The combination of tartaric, malic, lactic, and citric acids in the wine give it its zing. Too little of it and the wine's flabby or flat. Too much of it pushes the wine beyond crisp into sour.

Alcohol—Result of yeast fermentation of natural sugars (in this case, grape juice). Largely responsible for the wine's body and mouthfeel. Helps to preserve the wine.

Aerobic—In contact with air.

Anaerobic—Not in contact with air.

Appellation—A geographic area for growing grapes. Examples would be Napa Valley, Beaujolais, Carneros, Sancerre, North Coast, and Vosne-Romanee.

AVA or American Viticultural Area—Like appellation, a geographic area for growing grapes, this title requiring approval by the BATF. Many AVAs have sub-AVAs (or appellations), such as Napa with its Howell Mountain, Carneros, Stags Leap District, etc., and Sonoma with its Russian River, Knights Valley, Alexander Valley, etc.

Aroma—Individual smells in the wine like cherry, vanilla, cinnamon, earthy, and floral.

Astringent/Astringency—Pucker perceived on the tongue, cheeks, and gums, most often from TANNINS in red wines. Severe astringency will cause you to look about the room nonchalantly for a butter knife to pry your tongue from the roof of your mouth. Softens with age, like most things.

Balance—When the fruit, acid, alcohol (and oak if used) are all in harmony. Too much fruit, the wine is cloying. Too much acid, the wine is sour. Too much alcohol, the wine is hot (more like hard liquor). Too much oak, where's the fruit? A great balanced wine is seamless. Where one flavor leaves off, another begins.

Barrels—Most often 59- to 60-gallon white oak cooperage for fermenting/aging wine. The oak source could be French, American, or Hungarian, for example. There are many producers, styles, and types of oak barrels. Every little change in the barrel ultimately changes the way the wine will taste, such as (1) the longer you air-dry the staves of the barrel, the less aggressive the oak becomes in the wine; (2) barrels are burned inside at different levels, from light to medium to heavy, each of which has a significant flavor profile ranging from slightly toasty to caramelly to smoky; and (3) whether the barrel used is new or has been used in previous vintages. New oak imparts stronger flavors and is generally used for top-quality wines, which also increases production costs.

Barrel Thief—A device much like a turkey baster that winemakers use to dip into barrels, allowing them to sample their wines throughout barrel aging.

Body—The mouthfeel/weight of the wine. The classic example is to think of light-bodied wines as nonfat milk, medium-bodied wines as regular milk, and full-bodied wines as half-and-half. The wine's body is a result of sugar, alcohol levels, and/or fermentation techniques (see MALOLACTIC, LEES).

Botrytis—The "noble" rot, this fungus (given the right conditions of cool, moist air, and warm, but not too hot, afternoons) softens the grape's acidity and concentrates its sugars, lending a honeyed aroma/flavor. Sauternes, Barsac, Auslese, Beerenauslese, and Trockenbeerenauslese are the most well known.

Bouquet—The combination of aromas in the wine.

Brix—Brix are a measurement of sugar in the grape juice; roughly, it is a percentage of sugar. At harvest, common levels are 22 to 26 percent. A refractometer is a simple hand-held tool designed to measure the Brix level in the grape juice.

Cellar—A cellar environment constitutes a cool, dark area free of heat, light, or vibration. Fifty-five to sixty degrees is best.

Clones and Cloning—A clone is a variety of vine that has developed different characteristics from other vines of the same varietal by natural selection or biogenetic techniques. A "localized" clone is a vine that evolves through conditions specific to an area by natural order. Biogenetic clones can be developed by research groups such as those at the University of California at Davis to increase yields, resist disease, or to better handle climate conditions in a certain growing region.

Cloying—When the sweetness, fruitiness, or floral flavors oppress your palate. A subjective thing, the taster might feel the wine is unbalanced.

Complex(ity)—When a wine has depth—many aromas, flavors, and nuances.

Corked—When a wine has an odor of wet, rotten wood. The compound responsible for the foul smell comes from tainted corks (hence the term), although studies have shown that it may be generated by tainted BARRELS as well.

Crush—Term for either harvest time or the actual crushing of the grapes.

Cooper/Cooperage—A coopersmith makes barrels. Cooperage is a general term used for wine-storage capacity, often barrels or casks.

Decanting—Pouring the wine out of the bottle into either a decanter (carafe) or glasses to get more air into it, to let it breathe. If a wine is older and throwing sediment, the same would be done, but it would be poured very slowly and gingerly, in an attempt to keep the wine as clear as possible.

Enology—the scientific study of wine.

Fermentation—The process by which yeast converts sugars into alcohol. The formula is "yeast + sugar = alcohol + CO_2." If a wine ferments dry, its alcoholic strength is .55 percent of its BRIX. Fermentation can be stopped (arrested) by either chilling a tank to below freezing or adding alcohol to the fermenting juice, either technique leaving some of the grapes' natural RESIDUAL SUGAR.

Finish—The taste of the wine in your mouth after you swallow/spit. Generally, wines of high quality will have lengthy, balanced finishes. No one component or flavor sticks out at the end like bitterness, heavy oak, or alcohol.

Foil—The "dressing." The decorative material topping the bottle's neck.

Fortified—When a wine's alcoholic strength has been boosted due to the addition of brandy or a neutral spirit such as in Ports, Sherries, and some dessert wines.

Herbal/Herbaceous—Aromas like fresh hay, dill, fennel, and sage are different from VEGETAL aromas.

Hot—The wine is high in alcohol and warms the throat/nose. May cause the wine to be unbalanced, clumsy.

Hybrid—A cross between two different species. They can occur naturally, through cross-pollination, but are mostly produced by man to incorporate certain qualities from each parent for specific reasons, i.e., Seyval Blanc, which ripens early and withstands cold climates.

Labrusca—A species of the vitis genus that's native to North America.

Labruscana—North American term for a native vine variety that has at least one vitis labrusca parent. A Labruscana may be either a hybrid, incorporating genes from other vine species, or a cross between two labrusca parents.

Lees—The dead yeast and bits of skin and pulp that fall to the bottom of the tank/barrel after fermentation. Aging the wine "on the lees" (or French—*sur lie*) after fermentation is said to give a richness/toastiness to the nose. Stirring the lees (*battonage*) is said to give the mouthfeel of the wine more creaminess.

Macro/Meso/Microclimate—Macroclimate is a larger area—say, Napa Valley. Mesoclimate is a more specific area, as an AVA—say, Carneros. Microclimate is the climate immediately surrounding the vines, within a vineyard, for example.

Malolactic Fermentation—The addition of malolactic bacteria to wine converts the malic acids (found in green apples) into lactic acids (found in butter, milk, and cheese), thereby giving the wine a creamier mouthfeel. Most Chardonnays these days undergo complete malolactic fermentation. Many whites will not. Most reds undergo it. It softens the wines acidity.

Must—The juice, skins, and seeds of the grape after crushing but prior to fermentation.

Nose—Akin to BOUQUET. The nose of the wine is its overall collection of smells.

Oak—Many wines are aged or fermented in oak casks.

Oxidized—When the wine has been exposed to oxygen and has taken on a smell similar to sherry. It usually kills any fruit smells.

Phylloxera—The tiny louse that attacks and eventually kills a vine through its root system. It first devastated Europe in the late 1800s, nearly wiping out France's entire wine industry. The pest appeared in California in the 1980s in a mutated form, causing around 95 percent of California's vineyards to have to be replanted at a cost of around $500 million over fifteen years.

Quaff—A dignified way of saying gulp or guzzle. Quaffing wines are those you throw back easily poolside on a hot day, usually with no oak and lower alcohol.

Residual Sugar—The percentage of (natural grape fructose) sugar left in the wine after FERMENTATION. Most people begin to detect RS at levels of about 1 percent. Most "dry" wines fall under those levels. Off-dry wines can go up to 6 or 7 percent, before you enter dessert wine territory, where the wines can go up to 35 percent, or roughly one-third sugar by weight. High residual sugar will help to preserve the wine when combined with ALCOHOL and ACIDITY.

Simple—When a wine lacks depth and complexity, but if balanced, can be very enjoyable. Simple, straightforward, fruity wines are often the ticket.

Sommelier—(pronounced "som-el-yay") A French term for a wine specialist. Usually associated with restaurants. A sommelier's job is to advise patrons on wine selections and to be able to describe certain characteristics of every wine on the establishment's list. Then they should be able to present the wine and serve it properly. Other job responsibilities include buying wines for the establishment and keeping the cellar stocked.

Spicy—Aroma notes like clove, nutmeg, vanilla, cinnamon, and pepper.

Spritz—A slight pin beading of carbonation, barely effervescent.

Structure—Akin to balance, but often relating to the wine's ability to age well. If a wine's got good structure, chances are it has ample acids, tannins, and alcohol.

Tannic/Tannins—Tannins come from the skins, stems, and seeds of the grape, as well as oak barrels. It is perceived as an ASTRINGENCY on the top back part of the tongue. Helps preserve the wine.

Terroir—The combination of soil, topography, and MACRO/MESO/MICROCLIMATE.

Varietal—Wine named after the grape from which it is made, such as Pinot Noir. To name a wine after the grape, it must contain at least 75 percent of that varietal.

Vegetal—Some wines, especially Pinot Noir and Chardonnay, will exhibit these vegetationlike (rather than fruit) bouquets with age.

Vinifera—the European species of vitis; the vine most used for making wine, i.e., Chardonnay, Cabernet Sauvignon.

Vintage Date—If a label is vintage dated, 95 percent of all grapes used to make the wine must have been picked that year.

Viscosity—The thickness, BODY, weight, and mouthfeel of the wine. Usually used when talking about wines with sweetness or high alcohol.

Vitis—the genus of the plant kingdom which includes the vine.